Chinese Macroeconomic Operation

T0359043

Liu Shucheng is a famous Chinese economist who has had a major impact on the study of China's macroeconomics and quantitative economics. Selecting some of Liu's representative studies on Chinese macroeconomy, this book will be a valuable reference for understanding and studying the Chinese economy.

The first five papers appear in the author's collected works for the first time. They mainly study the overall balance of Chinese macroeconomic operation and the relative economic mathematical models. The commodity-currency balance sheet improved the earliest input-output model introduced to China in the 1980s, and the author's frontier research is of great importance for Chinese economic studies. In attempting to solve the problems caused by uncontrollable fixed assets investment, the author examines the periodicity of fixed assets investment in China, including the characteristics, causes, and the impact of investment periodic fluctuation on economic periodic fluctuation. In addition, the author studies Phillips curves in China in a comprehensive and intensive way. These in-depth analyses provide original insights based on the author's extensive research.

Liu Shucheng is the vice-director of the Academic Division of Economics, Chinese Academy of Social Sciences and the chief editor of *Economic Research Journal*. His research interests include macroeconomics and quantitative economics.

China Perspectives series

The *China Perspectives* series focuses on translating and publishing works by leading Chinese scholars, writing about both global topics and China-related themes. It covers Humanities and Social Sciences, Education, Media and Psychology, as well as many interdisciplinary themes.

This is the first time any of these books have been published in English for international readers. The series aims to put forward a Chinese perspective, give insights into cutting-edge academic thinking in China, and inspire researchers globally.

For more information, please visit https://www.routledge.com/series/CPH

Existing titles:

Internet Finance in China
Introduction and Practical Approaches
Ping Xie, Chuanwei Zou, Haier Liu

Regulating China's Shadow Banks
Qingmin Yan, Jianhua Li

Internationalization of the RMB
Establishment and Development of RMB Offshore Markets
International Monetary Institute of the RUC

The Road Leading to the Market
Weiying Zhang

Peer-to-Peer Lending with Chinese Characteristics
Development, Regulation and Outlook
P2P Research Group Shanghai Finance Institute

Chinese Macroeconomic Operation
Liu Shucheng

Forthcoming titles:

Government Foresighted Leading
Theory and Practice of the World's Regional Economic Development
Yunxian Chen, Jianwei Qiu

Free the Land
A Study on China's Land Trust
Jian Pu

Chinese Macroeconomic Operation

Liu Shucheng

Routledge
Taylor & Francis Group

LONDON AND NEW YORK

中国社会科学出版社
CHINA SOCIAL SCIENCES PRESS

First published 2017
by Routledge

2 Park Square, Milton Park, Abingdon, Oxfordshire OX14 4RN
52 Vanderbilt Avenue, New York, NY 10017

Routledge is an imprint of the Taylor & Francis Group, an informa business

First issued in paperback 2020

British Library Cataloguing-in-Publication Data
A catalogue record for this book is available from the British Library

Library of Congress Cataloging-in-Publication Data
Names: Liu, Shucheng, 1945– author.
Title: Chinese macroeconomic operation / Liu Shucheng.
Other titles: Yun xing yu tiao kong. English
Description: Abingdon, Oxon ; New York, NY : Routledge, 2017. |
    Series: China perspectives series | Includes index.
Identifiers: LCCN 2016043228 | ISBN 9781138898677 (hardcover) |
    ISBN 9781315708454 (ebook)
Subjects: LCSH: China—Economic conditions—1949 |
    Macroeconomics—China.
Classification: LCC HC427.9 .L5975213 2017 | DDC 338.951/09044—dc23
LC record available at https://lccn.loc.gov/2016043228

ISBN: 978-1-138-89867-7 (hbk)
ISBN: 978-0-367-59526-5 (pbk)

Typeset in Times New Roman
by Apex CoVantage, LLC

Contents

Figures

Tables

Acknowledgements

This book is a collection of evidence-based studies funded by the Innovation Program of the Chinese Academy of Social Sciences (CASS). It contains my experience regarding both the practices and the theoretical studies of China's economic development.

Here I would like to express my sincere gratitude to Ms. Huang Rui, the translator of this book, for her painstaking efforts devoted to the book; I also thank all of the colleagues at China Social Sciences Press for their professional and energetic support.

My particular thank goes to the CASS Innovation Translation Fund for having the book translated and published.

June, 2016

1 "Commodity-Currency" balance sheet and the mathematical model

The balance between commodity availability and currency purchasing power (hereinafter referred to as "Commodity-Currency" Balance) which is often an issue in the Chinese economy. On the one hand, commodities are in short supply or overstocked due to dull sales; on the other hand, a large number of currencies fall or surge in the market, which goes against the normal operation of social reproduction as well as the improvement of public life. It is really necessary to strike a balance between "commodity-currency" which would be conducive to economic restructuring and the realization of the magnificent target of "Four Modernizations".

This article attempts to conduct a preliminary study on the "Commodity-Currency" balance sheet and its static mathematical model.

I "Commodity-Currency" balance sheet

1. Compilation of "Commodity-Currency" balance sheet

Under socialism, the relationship between commodity production and commodity exchange requires that commodity availability and currency purchasing power should not only be consistent in total amount but also compatible in their structure. Consequently, a comprehensive "Commodity-Currency" balance sheet combining commodity and currency movements organically and reflecting "Commodity-Currency" balance and the situation of social product in a certain period (e.g., one year) directly should be drawn up for China's economic system.

Nowadays in the balance system of the Chinese national economy, the material balance sheet is isolated from the financial balance sheet. A "Commodity-Currency" balance sheet which can combine these two sheets is not available.

An input-output balance sheet (IOBS) put forward by American economist W. Leontief has been applied in China. The IOBS that is currently used in China in the form of currency is divided into four quadrants (see Table 1.1 for its simplified form. Figures are assumed and import goods are only used as the intermediate product). Upper left, upper right, lower left, and lower right of the crisscross dark black line in the table are respectively quadrants I, II, III, and IV. Quadrants I and II are connected horizontally to indicate the physical movement of the social

Table 1.1 Input-output balance sheet in the form of currency

		Material Productive Sector						Renovation and Overhaul of Fixed Assets	Accumulation	Consumption			Subtotal	Export	Total
		Agriculture	Industry	Construction	Transportation	Business	Subtotal			Personal Consumption	Life Service Science Culture Education Health	Administrative Management and National Defense			
Material Productive Sector	Agriculture	42.10	63.40	7.00	6.40	2.40	121.30		4.50	77.20	0.50		82.20	6.50	210.00
	Industry	6.20	78.60	17.10	14.70	27.10	143.70	13.00	43.30	129.20	27.80	19.50	232.80	13.50	390.00
	Construction							2.00	38.00				40.00		40.00
	Transportation	4.20	25.30	2.50			32.00				3.00		3.00		35.00
	Business	5.00	55.00				60.00								60.00
	Subtotal	57.50	222.30	26.60	21.10	29.50	357.00	15.00	85.80	206.40	31.30	19.50	358.00	20.00	735.00
Import		3.50	15.50	1.00	1.30	0.50	20.00				0.20				
Depreciation Fund		2.00	9.80	1.20			14.80				10.90	8.00			
Labor Remuneration		119.70	61.60	6.60	5.70	9.20	202.80				7.60				
Net Social Income		27.30	80.80	4.60	6.90	20.80	140.40				18.70				
Subtotal		149.00	152.20	12.40	13.90	30.50	358.00					8.00			
Total		210.00	390.00	40.00	35.00	60.00	735.00				50.00	27.50			

Unit: Billion Yuan

product. Quadrants I and III are connected vertically to demonstrate the process of its value formation. Quadrant IV shows the reallocation of staff salaries in a non-productive field, the income of government and public organizations, relevant taxation, etc. However, this balance sheet does not tie the movement of the physical and monetary form of the social product closely. In this way it neither reflects how an economic mechanism, involving salary, profit, taxation, state budget, bank credit, and so on, functions nor shows how various capitals eventually form different payable purchasing power. Thus, it fails to disclose the balance situation of "Commodity-Currency". Yet IOBS in the form of currency can provide the basic principles for the compilation of a "Commodity-Currency" balance sheet. We are able to draw a comprehensive "Commodity-Currency" balance sheet through appropriate renovation and extension on IOBS.

The "Commodity-Currency" balance sheet is also divided into four quadrants in which the principle of dividing sectors is the same as the input-output approach, i.e. "pure" division of sectors (see Table 1.2;[1] still assuming import goods only used as an intermediate product). How detailed the items can be set depends on the need and accessibility of data.

2. The main features of a "Commodity-Currency" balance sheet

Comparing it with the IOBS in the form of currency currently in use in China, the "Commodity-Currency" balance sheet has the following prominent features apart from retaining the entire functions of the IOBS.

First, quadrant IV reflects the formation of final income, i.e. the formation of purchasing power of various payable currencies, as the result that the contents in quadrant IV in the original IOBS are moved to the third quadrant. Thus, quadrants I and II are connected horizontally and mainly demonstrate the commodity movement in the "Commodity-Currency" balance sheet. Quadrants I and III are connected vertically, and, meanwhile, quadrants III and IV are connected horizontally. This illustrates the currency movement well. Accordingly, quadrants II and IV now correspond with each other; and this means that final products and final income also correspond with each other, reflecting the balance relation between commodity availability and currency purchasing power.

Second, the horizontal connection of quadrants III and IV in the sheet is able to represent the balance of payment for each currency.

Third, the sheet can not only reflect the balance of commodity and currency movements in material productive departments, but also demonstrate the balance of economic activities of other economic sectors, for instance, the balance between the total labor provided by public service (including material consumption and pure labor) and the currency payment or appropriation, and the balance between activities of the management department (calculated in total cost, including their material consumption and salaries) and appropriation. Hence, the "Commodity-Currency" balance sheet is able to connect different economic sectors and various links of social reproduction (production, distribution, exchange, and consumption) into an overall organic system so as to grasp the "Commodity-Currency" balance on the whole.

Table 1.2 "Commodity-Currency" balance sheet

| | Serial Number | Economic Sectors | | Renovation and Overhaul of Fixed Assets | Accumulation | Consumption | Increase of Bank Credit | Subtotal | Export | Total |
		Agriculture National Defense	Subtotal							
Serial Number		101 113		114	115 129	130 134	135			136
Economic Sectors — Agriculture	1									
National Defense	13									
Subtotal										
Import	14									
Depreciation Fund	15									
Government Budget	20									
Growth of Bank Credit Expenditure	21									
Subtotal										
Total										

3. Indicator system of "Commodity-Currency" balance sheet and basic balance relations

Definition of symbols (refer to Table 1.3) of various indicators are as follows:

x_{eg} ($e = 1, 2, \ldots, 13$; $g = 101, 102, \ldots, 113$) – intermediate product quantity provided by sector e to sector g (where $e = 7, 10, 11, 12, 13$, x_{eg} equals zero); X_e – total intermediate product quantity provided by sector e; X_g – total domestically produced intermediate product quantity consumed by sector g; X – total domestically produced intermediate product quantity; X_e, X_g – where $e = 1, 2, \ldots,$ 9 or $g = 101, 102, \ldots, 109$ is the total output value of various material productive departments, where $e = 10, 11$ or $g = 110, 111$ is the total labor value of various public service departments, where $e = 12,13$ or $g = 112, 113$ is the total cost of activities of management department; X – total amount of X_e or X_g; α_{eg} – direct consumption coefficient, i.e. intermediate product quantity of sector e consumed by sector g per total output value (or total labor value, total cost of activities).

Other symbols include: $u_{14,\,g}$ – import intermediate product quantity used in sector g; U_{14} – total import amount used as intermediate product; $\phi_{14,\,g}$ – import goods consumption coefficient, i.e. import goods quantity consumed by sector g per total output value (or total labor value, total cost of activities).

y_{ej} ($e = 1, 2, \ldots, 13$; $j = 114, 115, \ldots, 134$) – final products (or labor) quantity provided by sector e to sector j or j types of needs; Y_e – subtotal amount of final products (or labor) quantity used in the replacement, renovation, overhaul of fixed assets, accumulation and consumption provided by sector e; Y_j – subtotal amount of final products (or labor) quantity used by sector j or j types of needs; Y – total final products (or labor) quantity used in the replacement, renovation, overhaul of fixed assets, accumulation and consumption; β_{ej} – final products composition coefficient, i.e. the proportion provided by sector e among the subtotal of final products (or labor) quantity of sector j or j types of usages.

$y_{e,136}$ – export product quantity provided by sector e; Y_{136} – total export amount; $\beta_{e,136}$ – export goods composition coefficient.

s_{ig} ($i = 15, 16 \ldots, 20$; $g = 101, 102, \ldots, 113$) – quantity of i types of currencies provided by sector g; S_i – subtotal amount of i types of currencies; S_g – subtotal amount of currencies provided by sector g; S – total amount of depreciation fund and various income; γ_{ig} – currency composition coefficient, i.e. the proportion of i types of currencies among each total output value (or total labor value, total cost of activities) of sector g.

h_{ij} ($i = 15, 16 \ldots, 21$; $j = 114, 115, \ldots, 135$) – expenditure of department of i types of currencies or j types of needs; H_i – subtotal expenditure of i types of currencies; H_j – subtotal expenditure of sector j or j types of needs; H – total currency expenditure; π_{ij} – expenditure composition coefficient, i.e. the proportion of expenditure used in sector j or j types of needs among the total expenditure of i types of currencies.

C_j ($C_j = Y_{\cdot j} - H_{\cdot j}$) – where $j = 114, 115, \ldots, 130$ is the balance difference between final products availability and its currency purchasing power, where

Table 1.3 Indicator system of "Commodity-Currency" balance sheet

	Serial Number	Economic Sectors: Agriculture ... National Defense	Subtotal	Renovation and Overhaul of Fixed Assets	Accumulation	Consumption	Increase of Bank Credit	Subtotal	Export	Total
Serial Number		101.....113		114	115.....129	130.....134	135		136	
Economic Sectors — Agriculture	1 ... 13	$x_{1,101}\cdots x_{1,113}$	$X_{1.}$	$y_{1,114}$	$y_{1,134}$			$Y_{1.}$	$y_{1,136}$	X_1
National Defense		$x_{13,101}\cdots x_{13,113}$	$X_{13.}$	$y_{13,114}$	$y_{13,134}$			$Y_{13.}$	$y_{13,136}$	X_{13}
Subtotal		$x_{.101}\cdots x_{.113}$	$x_{..}$	$Y_{.114}$	$Y_{.134}$			$Y_{.}$	$Y_{.136}$	
Import	14	$u_{14,101}\cdots u_{14,113}$	$U_{14.}$							
Depreciation Fund	15 ... 20	$s_{15,101}\cdots s_{15,113}$	$S_{15.}$	$h_{15,114}$	$h_{15,134}$		$h_{15,135}$	$H_{15.}$		C_{15}
Government Budget		$s_{20,101}\cdots s_{20,113}$	$S_{20.}$	$h_{20,114}$	$h_{20,134}$		$h_{20,135}$	$H_{20.}$		C_{20}
Growth of Bank Credit Expenditure	21			$h_{21,114}$	$h_{21,134}$					$H_{21.}$
Subtotal		$S_{.101}\cdots S_{.113}$	$S_{.}$	$H_{.114}$	$H_{.134}$		$H_{.135}$	$H_{..}$		
Total		$X_{101}\cdots X_{113}$	$X_{.}$	C_{114}	C_{134}				C_{136}	

$j = 131, 132$ is the balance difference between the total labor provided by public service departments and the currency payment or appropriation, where $j = 133, 134$ is the balance difference between the total cost of activities of management department and appropriation; C_{136} ($C_{136} = U_{14} - Y_{.136}$) – balance difference between import and export (import goods can be used as final products apart from being intermediate product. For the sake of simplicity in this article, we assume that the import goods used as final products to be zero; thus, it is not listed in the table); C_i ($C_i = S_i - H_i$) ($i = 15, 16, \ldots, 20$) – balance difference of payment of i types of currencies.

The main balance relationships between the indicators in the "Commodity-Currency" balance sheet are as follows:

First, the total amount of each row connected by quadrants I and II is equal to that of each line connected by quadrants I and III correspondingly, i.e.

$$X_e = X_{e+100} \ (e = 1, 2, \ldots, 13)$$

which can accurately be recorded as :

$$X_e + Y_e + y_{e,136} = X_{e+100} + u_{14,e+100} + S_{e+100}$$

Second, the total amount of each line connected by quadrants II and IV equals to zero under the balance situation, i.e.

$$C_j = Y_j - H_j = 0 \ (j = 114, 115, \ldots, 134)$$

Third, the total amount of each row connected by quadrants III and IV equals to zero under the balance situation, i.e.

$$C_i = S_i - H_i = 0 \ (i = 15, 16, \ldots, 20)$$

Fourth, the total amount in quadrant II (except for import and export), III and IV is equal under the balance situation, i.e.

$$Y = S = H$$

II Static mathematical model of "Commodity-Currency" balance

The mathematical model of "Commodity-Currency" balance is set up with a mathematical formula which establishes the real economic connection between commodity and currency movements in the whole reproduction process according to the "Commodity-Currency" balance method.

Based on the static mathematical model of "Commodity-Currency" balance, we can draw an economic development plan such as that of Residents Welfare Fund,[2] which relies on computer calculation and whose calculating sequence is provided in Figure 1.1. Eight blocks in the figure show the full steps from information input, iterative calculation to the final outcome printing.

Step 1 is to input the information. All the information for the full calculation, including various expenditure increase indicators of the Residents Welfare Fund of planned year Δh_{ij}, ΔH_i, ΔH_j (i = 16, 18, 20; j = 124, 125, 130,

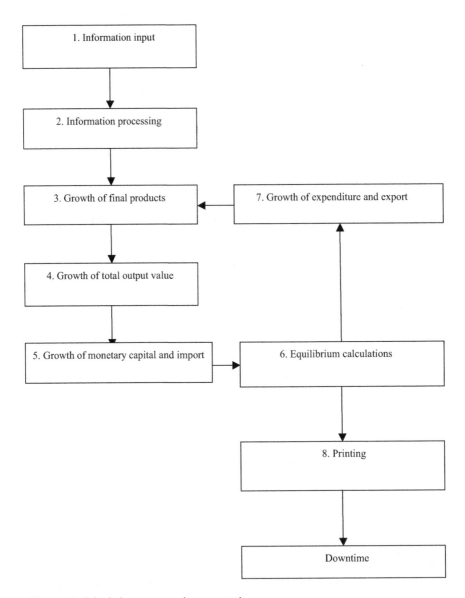

Figure 1.1 Calculation sequence in computation

131, 132, 135), related flux indicator and total and subtotal indicators in the "Commodity-Currency" balance sheet of the reporting year are input.

Step 2 is to process the information. Various coefficients are calculated according to the above indicators of the reporting year; and, if necessary, adjustments and corrections should be made according to the expected variation of the planning year.

Step 3 is the growth of final products. The expenditure growth of the Residents Welfare Fund leads to the growth of final products. Its computing formula is:

$$\Delta Y_{e\cdot} = \sum_j \beta_{ej} \Delta H_{\cdot j}$$

$(e = 1, 2, \ldots, 13; j = 124, 125, 130, 131, 132)$

It is denoted with matrix notation as:

$$\Delta Y = B\Delta H' \tag{1}$$

where ΔY – the column vector of final products growth ($\Delta Ye \cdot$); B – coefficient matrix of final products composition related to the Residents Welfare Fund; $\Delta H'$ – transposing the row vector of expenditure growth ΔH_j ($j = 124, 125, 130, 131, 132$) of Residents Welfare Fund to the column vector.

Step 4 is the growth of total output value. The growth of final products leads to the growth of the total output (or total labor service) of various sectors. Its computing formula is:

$$\Delta X = (E - A)^{-1} \Delta Y \tag{2}$$

where ΔX – the column vector of the growth (ΔX_e) of total output (or total labor service), E – the unit matrix; A – the coefficient matrix of direct consumption.

Step 5 is the growth of monetary capital and import. The growth of total output (or total labor service) of various sectors correspondingly leads to the growth of various monetary capital. Its computing formula is:

$$\Delta S_{i\cdot} = \sum_g \gamma_{ig} \Delta X_g$$

$(i = 15, 16, \ldots, 20; g = 101, 102, \ldots, 113)$

It is denoted with matrix notation as:

$$\Delta S = \Gamma \Delta X \tag{3}$$

where ΔS – the column vector of new growth ($\Delta S_{i.}$) of various monetary capital; Γ – the coefficient matrix of monetary capital composition.

The growth of the total output (or total labor service) of various sectors will also correspondingly lead to import growth. Its computing formula is:

$$\Delta U_{14.} = \sum_g \varphi_{14,g} \Delta X_g$$

$$(g = 101, 102, \dots, 113)$$

It is denoted with matrix form as:

$$\Delta U_{14} = \Phi \Delta X \tag{4}$$

where Φ – the row vector of consumption coefficient of import goods.

Step 6 is equilibrium calculations. Comparing the items of income in $\Delta S_{i.}$ ($\Delta S_{16.}$, $\Delta S_{18.}$, $\Delta S_{20.}$), which relate to the formation of Residents Welfare Fund, with expenditure growth ($\Delta H_{16.}$, $\Delta H_{18.}$, $\Delta H_{20.}$) of Residents Welfare Fund in Step 1, $\Delta S_{16.}$ is less than $\Delta H_{16.}$, and $\Delta S_{18.}$ is less than $\Delta H_{18.}$. Thus, it is necessary to supplement ΔS_{16} and ΔS_{18}. However, ΔS_{20} is greater than ΔH_{20}, and the remaining items will consist of other increased expenditures except for the Residents Welfare Fund. Meanwhile, S_{15}, ΔS_{17}, ΔS_{19} in $\Delta S_{i.}$ will also form various increased expenditures, and import growth ($\Delta U_{14..}$) will be accommodated with export growth. Various increased expenditures and export growth will give rise to the growth of final products, which will bring on further growth of total output and monetary capital income of various sectors. This is an iterative computation process.

Step 7 is the growth of expenditure and export. Excluding the Residents Welfare Fund, the computing formula of various increased expenditures is:

$$\Delta h_{ij} = \pi_{ij} \Delta S_{i.}$$
$$(i = 15, 17, 19, 20; j = 114, 115, \dots, 123, 126, 127, 128, 129, 133, 134, 135)$$

Then, adding all the indicators related to bank credit growth comes to the total growth $\Delta H_{.135}$ of bank credit, namely total growth $\Delta H_{21.}$ of bank credit expenditure; the formula is:

$$\Delta H_{21.} = \Delta H_{.135} = \sum_i \Delta h_{i,135} + \Delta h_{16,135} + \Delta h_{18,135}$$

$$(i = 15, 17, 19, 20)$$

where $\Delta h_{16,135}$ and $\Delta h_{18,135}$ are input in Step 1. Calculating various newly increased credit indicators:

$$H_{21,j} = \pi_{21,j}\Delta H_{21}.$$

$(j = 114, 115, \ldots, 123, 126, 127, 128, 129, 133, 134)$

and adding the above various increased expenditures indicators as per the final usage comes to the subtotal $\Delta H_{.j}$ of various increased expenditures:

$$\Delta H_{.j} = \sum_i \Delta h_{ij}$$

$(i = 15, 17, 19, 20, 21; j = 114, 115, \ldots, 123, 126, 127, 128, 129, 133, 134)$

The above calculation is denoted with matrix notation as:

$$\Delta H_2 = \Delta S_2'\Pi_1 + (\Delta S_2'\Pi_2 + \Delta h_{16,135} + \Delta h_{18,135})\Pi_3 \tag{5}$$

where ΔH_2 – the row vector of increased expenditure ΔH_j ($j = 114, 115, \ldots, 123,$ 126, 127, 128, 129, 133, 134) unrelated to the Residents Welfare Fund; $\Delta S_2'$ – transposing the column vector of monetary capital composed by $\Delta S_{15.}, \Delta S_{17.},$ $\Delta S_{19.}, \Delta S_{20.}$ to the row vector (the column vector of monetary capital composed by $\Delta S_{16.}$ and $\Delta S_{18.}$ is recorded as ΔS_1); Π_1 – coefficient matrix of expenditure composition composed by π_{ij} ($i = 15, 17, 19, 20; j = 114, 115, \ldots, 123, 126, 127,$ 128, 129, 133, 134); Π_2 – the column vector of expenditure composition coefficient composed by $\pi_{i,135}$ ($i = 15, 17, 19, 20$); Π_3 – the row vector of expenditure composition coefficient composed by π_{21j} ($j = 114, 115, \ldots, 123, 126, 127, 128,$ 129, 133, 134).

The ΔH_2 is used as the initial value of the following iterative computation. Formula (5) does not need to add $\Delta h_{16,135}$ and $\Delta h_{18,135}$ after the iterative process starts and can be rewritten as:

$$\Delta H_2 = \Delta S_2'(\Pi_1 + \Pi_2\Pi_3) \tag{6}$$

In addition, for simplicity we assume that total export growth ΔY_{136} equals to total import growth $\Delta U_{14.}$.

Various increased expenditures, except for the Residents Welfare Fund, and export growth lead to the growth of final products, as calculated in Step 3. By now the formula is:

$$\Delta Y = B_2\Delta H_2' + B_3\Delta U_{14.} \tag{7}$$

where B_2 – matrix composed by final products composition coefficient β_{ej} ($e = 1,$ 2, $\ldots$, 13; $j = 114, 115, \ldots, 123, 126, 127, 128, 129, 133, 134$); B_3 – the column vector composed by export composition coefficient $\beta_{e,136}$.

The iterative computation will be carried out in the sequence of Step 7, 3, 4, 5, 6, and the whole iterative process can be recorded as:

$$\Delta S_1^{(K+1)} = \Gamma_1 (E - A)^{-1} (B_2 \Delta H^{(K)\prime} \Delta H_2{}' + B_3 \Delta U_{14.}{}^{(K)}) \tag{8}$$

$$\Delta H_2^{(K+1)} = [\Gamma_2 (E - A)^{-1} (B_2 \Delta H_2^{(K)\prime} + B_3 \Delta U_{14.}{}^{(K)})]'(\Pi_1 + \Pi_2 \Pi_3) \tag{9}$$

$$U_{14.}{}^{(K+1)} = \Phi (E - A)^{-1} (B_2 \Delta H_2^{(K)\prime} + B_3 \Delta U_{14.}{}^{(K)}) \tag{10}$$

where K ($K = 0, 1, 2, \ldots, n$) – the number of iterations; Γ_1 – the matrix composed by composition coefficient of monetary capital γ_{ig} ($i = 16, 18$; $g = 101, 102, \ldots, 113$); Γ_2 – the matrix composed by γ_{ig} ($i = 15, 17, 19, 20$; $g = 101, 102, \ldots, 113$). The iterations will not cease until they satisfy the following conditions:

$$\sum_{K=0}^{n} \Delta S_{16.}{}^{(K)} = \Delta H_{16.}$$

$$\sum_{K=0}^{n} \Delta S_{18.}{}^{(K)} = \Delta H_{18.}$$

Step 8 is to print out various increased indicators and add them to the corresponding indicators of the reporting year. After inputting these indicators, the "Commodity-Currency" balance sheet of the planning year can be appropriately compiled. This model has been tested on the computer with hypothetical data and its sequence has been approved.

China has compiled the IOBS of 61 main products based on 1973 statistics and is compiling nationwide IOBS including more products. Shanxi Province is compiling a region-level IOBS. These exercises indicate the potential of further research and the application of the "Commodity-Currency" balance sheet and its mathematical model.

(Originally published in *Academic Journal of Jinyang*, No.6, 1981)

Note

1 Table 2 is a simplified table in which items of longitudinal columns and their serial numbers represent: agriculture(1), food industry(2), textile industry(3), other light industries(4), machine manufacturing(5), raw material, fuel and power industry(6), construction industry(7), transportation and postal service(8), business, material supply industry(9), life service industry(10), scientific research, culture, education, health(11), administrative management(12), national defense(13), import(14), depreciation fund(15), labor remuneration(16), enterprise development production fund(17),enterprise collective welfare fund(18), bank credit interest (19), state budget(20), bank credit expenditure growth(21).

Items of transverse columns in simplified table and their serial numbers are respectively: agriculture(101), food industry(102), textile industry(103), other light industries(104), machine manufacturing(105), raw material, fuel and power industry(106), construction industry(107), transportation and postal service(108), business, material supply industry(109), life service industry(110), scientific research, culture, education, health(111), administrative management(112), national defense(113), renovation and overhaul of fixed assets(114), agricultural fixed assets(115), food industry fixed assets(116), textile industry fixed assets(117), other light industries fixed assets(118), machine manufacturing fixed assets(119), raw material, fuel and power industry fixed assets(120), construction industry fixed assets(121), transportation and postal service fixed assets(122), business, material supply industry fixed assets(123), life service industry fixed assets(124), scientific research, culture, education, health fixed assets(125), administrative management fixed assets(126), national defense fixed assets(127), current assets growth(128), national reserve growth(129), personal consumption(130), life service(131), scientific research, culture, education, health(132), administrative management(133), national defense(134), bank credit resource growth(135), export(136). For simplicity assumed numeral cases in original table are briefed.

2 Application of the Extended Input-Output Model in social reproduction

I Marxian reproduction formula and the Extended Input-Output Model

The Extended Input-Output (I-O for short) Model is a scientific method studying the important issues of social reproduction, such as the condition of social products, the proportional relationship between the means of production and the means of consumption, the balance between finance, credit and material, the balance between import and export, and employment. By expanding on the I-O model and applying advanced mathematics and computer techniques, we can concretize the Marxian reproduction formula.

In order to illustrate the Extended I-O Model, we examine the Marxian formulation of simple reproduction first. It can be expressed as follows (Marx, 1975):[1]

$$\text{I. } (4000c + 400\Delta c) + (1000v + 100\Delta v + 500\Delta m) = 6000 \tag{1}$$

$$\text{II. } (1500c + 100\Delta c) + (750v + 50\Delta v + 600\Delta m) = 3000 \tag{2}$$

where,[2] c – transferred value of means of production; v – essential labor value; Δc – supplementary means of production in surplus labor value; Δv – supplementary labor remuneration of material production in surplus labor value; Δm – surplus labor value produced in non-production sectors.

The formula demonstrated an important notion that Marx revealed, i.e. social products movement "is not only a replacement of value, but also a replacement in material and is therefore as much bound up with the relative proportions of the value-components of the total social product as with their use-value, their material shape"(Marx, 1885/2001).[3] This is the issue of the conditions of social reproduction. The conditions of enlarged reproduction can be drawn from:

$$1000 \text{ I } v + 100 \text{ I } \Delta v + 500 \text{ I } \Delta m = 1500 \text{ II } c + 100 \text{ II } \Delta c \tag{3}$$

This formula shows the equilibrium conditions of exchanges between two major categories.

$$(4000 \text{ I } c + 400 \text{ I } \Delta c) + (1500 \text{ II } c + 100 \text{ II } \Delta c) = 6000 \tag{4}$$

This formula shows the equilibrium conditions of production and the distribution of the means of production.

$$(1000 \text{ I } v + 100 \text{ I } \Delta v + 500 \text{ I } \Delta m) + (750 \text{ II } v + 50 \text{ II } \Delta v$$
$$+ 600 \text{ II } \Delta m) = 3000 \tag{5}$$

This formula shows the equilibrium conditions of production and the distribution of the means of subsistence.

We can convert Marx's extended reproduction formula into the Extended I-O Model (see Table 2.1).

The balance sheet consists of four quadrants. Upper left, upper right, lower left and lower right of the crisscross in the table are, respectively, quadrants I, II, III and IV. Quadrant I indicates the material consumption of the two major categories – the means of production and means of consumption, as well the distribution of intermediate products of the means of production. Quadrant II illustrates the distribution of final products of both categories. Quadrant III demonstrates the sources and distribution of various incomes. Quadrant IV reflects expenditures, sourced from various incomes, and the purchasing power of various payable currencies. Quadrants I and II are connected horizontally, demonstrating the use-value of social products in their physical shape. Quadrants I and III are connected vertically, together with quadrants III and IV which are connected horizontally, illustrating the value of social products in their monetary form. Quadrants II and IV correspond with each other mirroring the balance between availability and monetary purchasing capacity of final products, and the last row of quadrant IV shows the differences between availability and purchase capacity. In Table 2.1, all these figures are zero, illustrating a balancing relationship between them. Quadrants III and IV correspond with each other as well, reflecting the balance between income and expenditure of monetary capital, and the last column of quadrant IV shows the differences between income and expenditure of currencies. In Table 2.1, all figures are zero, demonstrating a balanced relationship between them. This satisfies the conditions of expanded reproduction.

Making full use of quadrant IV, which displays the formation of final income, can reflect the balance between the availability of products and the purchasing power of currencies and the balance between various currencies. These are the main differences of the expanded I-O balance sheet from the original I-O balance sheet in the form of currency.

Quadrants I and III in Table 2.1 are connected vertically and can be written as:

$$\text{I. } 4000c + 1000v + 400\Delta c + 100\Delta v + 500\Delta m) = 6000 \tag{6}$$

$$\text{II. } 1500c + 750v + 100\Delta c + 50\Delta v + 600\Delta m = 3000 \tag{7}$$

Formulas (6) and (7) are equal to the formulas (1) and (2), respectively.

Table 2.1 Extended I-O balance sheet

Input \ Output		Intermediate Products – First category	Intermediate Products – Second category	Final Products / Means of Production – First category	Final Products / Means of Production – Second category	Means of consumption / Consumption of production – First category	Means of consumption / Consumption of production – Second category	Means of consumption / Consumption of non-production	Total
Material consumption	First category	4000c	1500c	400Δc	100Δc				6000
	Second category					1000v + 100Δv	750v + 50Δv	500 I Δm + 600 II Δm	3000
Labor remuneration		1000v	750v			1000v	750v		0
Net social income	Supplementary means of production	400Δc	100Δc	400Δc	100Δc				0
	Supplementary labor remuneration	100Δv	50Δv			100Δv	50Δv		0
	non-production	500Δm	600Δm					500 I Δm + 600 II Δm	0
Total		6000	3000	0	0	0	0	0	

Quadrants I and II in Table 2.1 are connected horizontally and can be written as:

$$4000 \text{ I c} + 1500 \text{ II c} + 400 \text{ I } \Delta c + 100 \text{ II } \Delta c = 6000 \tag{8}$$

$$1000 \text{ I v} + 100 \text{ I } \Delta v + 750 \text{ II v} + 50 \text{ II } \Delta v + 500 \text{ I } \Delta m$$
$$+ 600 \text{ II } \Delta m = 3000 \tag{9}$$

Formulas (8) and (9) are equal to formulas (4) and (5), respectively.

According to the equilibrium relations shown in the balance sheet, the total amount of each column in quadrants I and III equals that of each row in quadrants I and II. Merging formulas (6) and (8) or (7) and (9) and eliminating the same term on both sides of the equations, we can obtain formula (3).

The principle of the Extended I-O Model is wholly consistent with the Marxian reproduction formula. Without doubt, in reality the value compensation and material compensation of social products is a complicated process. By making use of the Extended I-O Model, we can introduce many factors that Marx has excluded into economic plans and statistical processing according to real economic situations. This will concretize the Marxian reproduction formula.

In Table 2.2 [4] which concretizes the Extended I-O Model, the columns in quadrant I are drawn based on the economic sectors rather than per two categories. These constitute four economic sectors: (1) the sector of material production such as agriculture, food industry, textile, other light industries, machinery manufacturing, raw material, fuel and energy, and construction; (2) the sector of communication and logistics such as transportation, post and telecommunication, retails and trade, and material supply; (3) the sector of public services such as service sector, scientific and cultural research, education, health care, and environmental protection; and (4) the sector of public management and national defense. The longitudinal columns of the quadrant II are identical to those of quadrant I showing various economic sectors. The transverse columns of quadrants II list various usages of final products or labor provided by sectors including renovation and overhaul of fixed assets, accumulation, consumption, export and so on. The transverse columns of quadrant III are identical to those of quadrant I showing various economic sectors. The longitudinal columns list depreciation funds and various monetary incomes including labor remuneration, bonus (or income of household sidelines), reproduction fund of firms, welfare fund of firms, credit interest of banks, government budgetary income and so on. Government budgetary income is composed of the payments of production fund, profit turned over to state and taxation, personal income tax, etc. The longitudinal columns of quadrant IV are identical to those of quadrant III, transforming income to expenditure. The transverse columns are identical to those of quadrant II, reflecting the final use of various incomes. The items of the balance sheet can be set according to the objective and accessibility of data.

The table of the Extended I-O Model is compatible with a set of math equations,[5] which are featured by connecting all the links of the economic sectors and social reproduction (production, distribution, exchange, and consumption) and forming

Table 2.2 Extended I-O balance sheet

Input	Output	Economic sectors Agriculture ...... National defense	Renovation and Overhaul of Fixed Assets	Accumulation	Consumption	Increase of Bank credit	Export	Total
Economic sectors	Agriculture							
	......							
	......							
	National defense							
Import								
Depreciation Fund								
Resident	Labor Remuneration							
	Bonus							
Firm	Production fund							
	Collective welfare fund							
Bank interests for loans								
Government budget	Production fund payment							
	Profits and taxes							
	Individual income tax							
Growth of Bank Credit Expenditure								
Subtotal								
Total								

an overall dynamic system. Through computer-based calculation, a series of inter-related indices in the numerical form can be obtained. Some basic ideas in this process should be noted as follows:

1   Start in quadrant IV to draw up the expenditure plans according to both predicated demand and affordability.
2   Expenditure represents purchasing power of payable currency in which the variation (increase or decrease) will lead to the alteration of final products shown in quadrant II.
3   Alteration of final products will result in variation of total output value. This is calculated from the direct consumption coefficient in quadrant I.
4   The variation of output value of economic sectors will bring about the alteration of various monetary incomes in quadrant III.
5   The alternation of various incomes will transform to the alteration of various expenditures in quadrant IV leading to the changes of final products.

This is a circulatory calculation process in an iteration method, which will not end until a balance between income and expenditure is reached. In this method, various coherent and proportional indexes in the numerical form can be obtained, exhibiting not only the balance between income and expenditure but also the balance between commodity availability and monetary purchasing power. The process of computer-based calculation of the Extended I-O Model is a course of simulating and testing variations existing in actual economic life. On this ground, we are able to analyze in greater detail whether various planned indicators and targets are practicable, what impact they will bring about, how the original plan can be revised, and how various links of reproduction can be coordinated and their coherence can be improved. These are of significance to strengthening economic analysis, carrying out economic projection, improving the comprehensive balance of economic sectors, enhancing the scientific soundness and predictability of plans and statistics, and thereby benefiting the development of a planned economy.

II   Critical issues in using the Extended I-O Model in reproduction

In this section, we turn to look at some important issues in researching reproduction by applying the Extended I-O Model in order to highlight the usability of the model in the planning process.

1.   Balance between finance, credit and material

The balance between finance, credit and material is a constitutional part of the comprehensive balance of China's economy. Let's look at the state budget.

Comrade Mao Zedong once pointed out, "The state budget is a significant issue reflecting economic policies of government because it stipulates the scope and direction of government economic activities" (1949).[6] The issues, such as how the state budget is determined and whether the revenues and expenditures are balanced, have great impacts on the implementation of the Communist Party's policies and successful progression of social reproduction. Monetary capital must be equal to the value of material. If a balance is lacking between revenues and expenditures in the government budget, for instance, expenditures are greater than revenues, it implies an excess of monetary purchasing power over availability of material. Fiscal deficit means material shortages. This will inevitably wreak havoc with conditions of social products and cause turmoil in economic situations. In view of this, it is important to sustain a balance between revenue and expenditure and a slight surplus in each fiscal year.

In order to properly arrange the state budget and sustain a balance between revenue and expenditure, the chain reaction created by budgetary revenue and expenditure in various economic sectors and links of social reproduction must be taken into account. This is a complicated process. By using the Extended I-O Model, we can draw a series of interrelated indicators in the numerical form for various planned budgetary expenditures.

A   The amount of material supplies (including means of production and consumer goods) that can guarantee various budgetary expenditures.

B   The production scale of economic sectors and the speed of economic development that can meet a required quantity of material supplies.

C   The growth rate of the economy that is associated with the development of production and construction of various sectors and, correspondingly, the increase in incomes of residents and enterprises.

D   The additional purchasing power of residents and enterprises that is stimulated by increased income, the types of material and goods that residents and enterprises will purchase, and, correspondingly, the quantity of material supplies to ensure the realization of the additional purchasing power.

E   The quantity of capital that the state should obtain from various sectors for sustaining the balance between revenue and expenditure in order to meet the designated budgetary expenditure originally planned.

Although the calculations are complex, we can obtain full results quickly by applying the iteration method on the computer. It is unimaginable that these calculations are carried out relying on elementary mathematics and simple computing tools. By revising the original program and comparing multiple schemes, we can choose a relatively best-fit solution. It is obvious that errors will occur if merely relying on subjective experiences.

The state budget and expenditure policy may be altered in some circumstances, such as prioritizing the development of some economic sectors and increasing investments in these sectors accordingly, widely raising employees' wages and increasing residents' subsidies in order to substantially increase residents' income, and strengthening national defense. The subsequent changes brought about by these alterations can be calculated speedily by using the model and the results of calculation can be used as evidence for policy-making.

The state budget is expended in economic construction, scientific research, development of culture and education. It is also used in allocating additional credit funds to banks, which helps guarantee the credit balance between revenue and expenditure. As the economic reform goes on, the investment in capital construction through fiscal appropriation has gradually been replaced with bank loans. The circulating capital of firms is nearly all from bank loans. This leads to an increasing percentage of state budgetary expenditures in terms of credit funds. Consequently, the balance of the state budget between revenue and expenditure has a greater impact on the credit balance. In the Extended I-O balance sheet, credit revenue and expenditure are reflected in quadrant IV. By employing the model, issues such as the credit balance between income and expenditure, impact of state finance on credit, and the balance between the purchasing power originated from fiscal loan and availability of corresponding material become clear. The balance between fiscal credit and material availability in this calculation reflects a balance between quantity and structure.

2. *Supply and demand of consumer goods*

The supply and demand of consumer goods is mainly an issue about the balance between the purchasing power of residents and the availability of consumer goods, which is an important component of social reproduction. If the purchasing power of residents is greater than the availability of consumer goods, then it will result in a strained market where supply falls behind demand, leading to a price increase and affecting the stabilization, improvement and enhancement of people's lives. In order to maintain a prosperous market, stabilize price levels, meet the needs of people's lives and fully embody the superiority of socialist system, we must make great efforts in striking a balance between supply and demand of consumer goods and in withdrawing currency from circulation as much as possible. To this end, it is necessary to make use of the Extended I-O Model in finding solutions to a number of issues.

(1) To set the purchasing power of residents and, based on this, to monitor and regulate the growth of purchasing power in economic plans. The purchasing power for consumer goods first depends on the income from salary, workpoints, bonus, sideline, etc. Second, it rests with the proportion of incomes used for consumer goods, service products, cultural and educational attainments, and savings. According to the data provided by the Extended I-O balance sheet in the reporting period and in view of the calculation based on the mathematical model, the purchasing power of residents in a certain period can be predicted. In addition, it is feasible to calculate an acceptable growth rate of purchasing power of residents in a certain period based on production and supply of consumer goods. On the strength of these, the government can adopt proper policies and measures to monitor and regulate income growth and the purchasing power of consumer goods. For example, to stipulate the total sum of salaries and bonuses in a certain period can control growth of purchasing power; and to develop social service, entertainment facilities (such as movies and theaters),

and tourism can absorb the expenditure power of residents. These measures can modify the purchasing power of consumer goods and reduce the pressure on the market.

(2) To identify the demands for various consumer goods once the purchasing power of residents has been established. Demands for consumer goods depend not only on the total quantity of residents' purchasing power, but also on the composition of consumer goods. Variations in occupations and areas of residence (e.g. workers in cities and farmers in rural areas) of people, income level, price level, seasons, and customs and habits have impacts on the demand of consumer goods. For example, when income level is low there is a somewhat larger proportion of income expended on food while expenditures are comparatively smaller on clothes, daily necessities, and housing; and there is a rather larger proportion of expenditure in daily consumer goods while it is fairly smaller in durable goods; and vice versa. In combination with various surveys (e.g. the Family Planning Survey and the Market Survey) and with reference to the data presented by the Extended I-O balance sheet in the reporting period or in previous years, we can project the consumption structure of workers and farmers in a certain period of time. Then, we can calculate the total demand and related purchasing power of residents for consumer goods in this period.

(3) To determine production capacity of various sectors once the demand for consumer goods is identified. The supply for consumer goods is explicitly from the sectors of food industry, textile industry and other light industries and, meanwhile, both implicitly and explicitly from those sectors of raw materials, fuel, power industry and machinery manufacturing. These two aspects are associated with how industrial sectors can properly be organized in terms of economic processes. The reason why China's industrial structure cannot soundly meet the public's needs for food, clothes, dwelling and transportation lays in the disproportion between material production and consumer goods production. By applying the model, we can calculate the production scale and growth of various economic sectors in view of the purchasing power and demands of consumer goods. This will enable us to establish an industrial structure that can comparably develop and fully embody the ultimate objectives of a socialist economy. At present, it is our priority to develop textile and other light industries in order to maximize the production capacity of consumer goods. The question is what should be an appropriate level at which textile and other light industries – household electronic goods (TV, transistor radio, tape recorder, etc.), household electrical appliances (washing machine, refrigerator, etc.), household machineries (bicycle, sewing machine, watch, etc.), food processing, wool spinning, chemical fiber, and clothing and shoes manufacturing – should be advanced. In particular, what should be the growth rate of the six priority fields – the supply of raw materials, fuel and power, technical innovation, capital construction, bank loans, foreign exchange and technology importation, and transportation – which have been designated as the development priority for developing textile and other light industries? The next question is what should be the total sum of production of these prioritized fields. A range of such questions can be answered through a continuous calculation by applying the

model. By this method we are able to provide scientific evidence for compiling economic plans.

3. Investments of capital construction

Capital construction refers to those economic activities of adding fixed assets (machinery, equipment, plant building, etc.) for both simple and expanded reproduction. It is an important physical guarantee for the continuity of social reproduction and is of significance to a long-term balance between supply of production materials and monetary purchasing power. Either oversized or undersized investment will lead to irrationality of economic growth. As denoted above, a series of calculations for balancing finance, credit and material and for supply and demand of consumer goods require adopting the static Extended I-O Model. To estimate investments of capital construction, the Extended Dynamic I-O Model will be used. The main feature of this dynamic model is its introduction of time-lag of capital construction.

What is the most appropriate investment scale of capital construction that will not affect economic life in the same year and, meanwhile, promote production in the following years? To ensure the former, it is required to plan production well and arrange people's lives and then to evaluate how much remains for capital construction. To guarantee the latter, it is necessary to calculate the growing demands of social products for fixed assets in the following years. Then we can set a reliable investment scale of capital construction for balancing the former and the latter.

Investments of capital construction should match the growth of other sectors. It requests, directly, input of the means of production such as building materials, machinery equipment and labors and, directly and indirectly, growing of the sectors such as fuel, electric power and transportation. The development of these sectors leads to an increase in the total income and a rise in the purchasing power of residents. These create further demands for consumer goods. Moreover, to build large-scaled firms, factories and mines adds extra demands for productivity of sectors such as service, education and health care. The issues about appropriately coordinating the development of these sectors can be examined based on the inter-related calculation.

With the aim to meet an increasing demand for material and cultural life, the direction of capital construction investment can also be established through calculation. The direction of capital construction investments refers to the quantity and percentage of capital construction investments in the renovation of old enterprises and building of new firms, in material production, non-material production and logistics, in agriculture and light industry, in heavy industry (among which the quantity and proportion of investments can be divided into agriculture, light industry, and heavy industry itself), in the basic industrial sector and the processing industrial sector. The calculation lays a solid foundation for establishing an appropriate structure of industrial sectors and optimum economic growth.

4.   *Development of service sector and employment of labor force*

Development of the service sector, adjustment of the employment structure of the labor force, and creation of new employment are also important issues in reproduction.

The service sector involves catering, trading, public bath and washing house, hairdressing, repairing, tourism, art and entertainment. It is characterized by service provision for people's daily lives, a small sum of fixed assets allocated to each labor, and labor intensive. What will be the appropriate level to which the service sector expands? On the one hand, this is affected by the residents' income level and depends on the amount of income used in the service products (i.e. purchasing power) in a certain period of time. Generally, when the wage level is low, income used in service goods is relatively small; with an increase in the wage level, the proportion of incomes used in service products will increase accordingly. An optimal scale of developing the service sector can be identified by calculating the growth rate of residents' income and related increase in demands for service products. On the other hand, expansions of the service sector are constrained by the conditions of material production. It requests an input of a quantity of equipment and fixed assets. For example, retail and trade requires building more stores and branches and expanding processing capacity and storage equipment; tourism requires refurbishing sightseeing spots, building hotels and expanding tourist facilities; and entertainment requires building movie theaters and other facilities. How much these constructions will cost? Can funds and material be guaranteed? These questions are concerned with a feasible scale of developing the service sector, and can be answered through calculation as well. Then, a balance between the demand and feasibility can be reached.

In the longitudinal and transverse columns in quadrant I of Extended I-O balance sheet, the subsectors within the service sector are listed one to one, correspondingly. The relations between input and output of these subsectors can be displayed in the balance sheet. The above-mentioned issues can be analyzed by using appropriate mathematical models. This is the additional superiority of the Extended I-O Model over the I-O Model that is currently in use in China.

After identifying the development scale of the service sector, it becomes straightforward to calculate demands for the labor force which can accommodate the expansion of the service sector, so as to make arrangements for labor employment.

(Originally published in *Issues on Socialist Reproduction, Ownership, Commodity Value,* edited by the editorial office of Economic Research Journal, 1982, People's Publishing House of Shandong)

Notes

1   Marx, K. (1975). *Das Kapital.* (Vol. 2, pp.576–577). Beijing: People's Publishing House.
2   Author's annotation: some symbols used in the formula in the original article were relatively complicated and have been changed to simplified ones.

3   Marx, K. (2001). *Capital: A critique of political economy, the process of circulation of capital.* (p.533). S. Moore & E. Aveling (Trans.). London: Electric Book Co. (Original work published 1885).

4   Author's annotation: Table 2 in the original article took up space and was not easy to print. It is hence changed to a simplified table.

5   In order to make the article concise, the mathematical model is not listed here.

6   (1949, December 4). *The People's Daily.*

3 Extended Input-Output Model and its implications

The Extended Input-Output (I-O for short) Model is developed from the I-O Model of social products in the form of currency. It provides a powerful means to assist with creating a comprehensive balance in economic plans and management and establishing a realistic pace and effective approach to economic development, which will truly benefit the Chinese people. This article explores static and dynamic Extended I-O models and their implications for policy-making and implementation.

I Static Extended I-O Model

In comparison with the currently used I-O balance sheet in the form of currency, the major expansion of the static Extended I-O Model includes the following aspects. First, it moves redistribution of non-material production sectors in quadrant IV of the original I-O table to quadrant III. Second, it accordingly lists both material production sectors and non-material production sectors in the longitudinal and transverse columns in quadrant I. Third, it reflects the formation of final incomes (i.e. the formation of purchasing power of currency) by vacating and re-using quadrant IV of the original I-O table. By doing so, quadrants III and IV correspond with each other to reflect the balance between various incomes (such as employees' remuneration, firms' retained profits, state revenue, and bank credit and loan) and expenditures of currency; and quadrants II and IV correspond with each other to demonstrate the balance between final products and final incomes (namely the balance between the availability of commodity and purchasing power of currency), and further to signal the attainment of social products. Obviously, the aforesaid first and second aspects are the alterations to the original I-O table, and the third is its substantial extension. In the subsequent analyses and calculation we divide the whole economy into four sectors: agriculture, industry, culture and education, and administrative management. Meanwhile, we regard import goods as intermediate products and overlook the elements of fixed assets renovation, overhaul and depreciation fund.

In order to grasp precisely the main characteristics of the static model, we shall start with some basic ideas about approaching the issues.

Step 1: to start from quadrant IV. By following the principle of "acting according to one's own capability", we can draw up the currency expenditure plans (various currency expenditures represented by h_{ij}, $H_{i..}$ and $H_{.j}$), including employees' remuneration plan, firms' retained profits plan, state revenue plan and the credit and loan plan of banks. We take employees' remuneration plan for example (see Tables 3.1 and 3.2[1]). Presuming that employees' remuneration in the planning year is all used to purchase consumer goods, the total expenditure is $H_{6.} = H_{.110} = h_{6,110} = 190$ billion yuan.

Step 2: to estimate the supply of final products. The formation of purchasing power of currency brings forward the demand for final products in quadrant II. In this example, it is the residents' expenditure that creates the demand for consumer goods. The calculation is as follows:

$$Y = B_{110} H_{.110} \tag{1}$$

where Y-column vector of final products; B_{110}-column vector of final products composition coefficient ($\beta_{e,110}$) that is applied as consumer goods. In this example, the numerical value is as follows:

$$Y = \begin{bmatrix} 0.368 \\ 0.632 \\ 0 \\ 0 \end{bmatrix} \times 1900 = \begin{bmatrix} 700 \\ 1200 \\ 0 \\ 0 \end{bmatrix}$$

Step 3: to calculate the total output value. In order to guarantee the supply of final products, it is essential to determine the total output value of various sectors, with the aid of the direct material consumption coefficient and the complete material consumption coefficient in quadrant I. This calculation is conducted as done in the original I-O approach. The formula is as follows:

$$X = (E - A)^{-1} Y \tag{2}$$

where X – column vector of total output value; E – unit matrix; A – matrix of direct material consumption coefficient (α_{eg}). Through calculation, the example is as follows:

$$X = \begin{bmatrix} 1150.8 \\ 2107.7 \\ 0 \\ 0 \end{bmatrix}$$

Table 3.1 Calculation example of Extended I-O Model

Input-Output Sectors	Serial No	Sectors				Sub-total	Accumulation — Fixed Assets				Current assets growth	Consumption — Consumer goods	Science Culture Education Health	Administrative Management	Bank Credit Growth	Sub-total	Export	Total
		Agriculture	Industry	Science Culture Education Health	Administrative Management		Agriculture	Industry	Science Culture Education Health	Administrative Management								
Serial No		101	102	103	104		105	106	107	108	109	110	111	112	113		114	
Sectors Agriculture	1	20	50	1		71					5	70				75	6	152
Industry	2	25	120	8	2	155	10	30	2	1	20	120				183	14	352
Science Culture Education Health	3												15			15		15
Administrative Management	4													5		5		5
Subtotal		45	170	9	2	226	10	30	2	1	25	190	15	5		278	20	524
Import	5	4	16			20												0
Employees' remuneration	6	80	102	5	3	190						190				190		0
Firms' retained profits	7	20	10				4	4	1		12		4		5	30		0
National revenue	8	3	54	1		58	2	8	1	1	5		11	5	25	58		0
Growth of bank loan	9						4	18			8					30		30
Subtotal		103	166	6	3	278	10	30	2	1	25	190	15	5	30	278		0
Subtotal of net output value in material productive sector		103	166			269												
Total		152	352	15	5	524	0	0	0	0	0	0	0	0	30	0	0	

Unit: billion yuan

Table 3.2 Examples of the application of the Extended I-O Model (coefficients)

Input-Output	Serial No	Sectors 101 Agriculture	102 Industry	103 Science Culture Education Health	104 Administrative Management	Subtotal 101–104	Accumulation — Fixed Assets 105 Agriculture	106 Industry	107 Science Culture Education Health	108 Administrative Management	109 Current assets growth	Consumption 110 Consumer goods	111 Science Culture Education Health	112 Administrative Management	113 Bank Credit Growth	Subtotal 105–113	114 Export	Total 101–114
Serial No		101	102	103	104	101–104	105	106	107	108	109	110	111	112	113	105–113	114	101–114
Sectors Agriculture	1	0.132	0.142	0.067							0.2	0.368						
Industry	2	0.164	0.341	0.533	0.4						0.8	0.632					0.3	
Science Culture Education Health	3												1.0				0.7	
Administrative Management	4													1.0				
Subtotal 1–4		0.296	0.483	0.6	0.4		1.0	1.0	1.0	1.0	1.0	1.0	1.0	1.0	1.0	1.0	1.0	1.0
Import	5	0.026	0.045															
Employees' remuneration	6	0.526	0.29	0.333	0.6							1.0				1.0		
Firms' retained profits	7	0.132	0.028				0.133	0.133	0.034		0.4		0.133		0.167	1.0		
National revenue	8	0.02	0.154	0.067			0.035	0.138	0.017	0.017	0.086		0.19	0.086	0.431	1.0		
Growth of bank loan	9						0.133	0.6			0.267							
Subtotal 6–9		0.678	0.472	0.4	0.6													
Subtotal of net output value in material productive sector						0												
Total 1–9		1.0	1.0	1.0	1.0													

Step 4: to calculate various currency incomes. The total output value of various sectors deducting material consumption (X_{eg}) forms various currency incomes in quadrant III (represented by S_{ig}, $S_{i.}$ and $S_{.g}$). The calculation includes two parts. Part one is the employees' remuneration income. The formula is as follows:

$$S_{6.} = \Gamma_6 X \tag{3}$$

where S_6 – total amount of employees' remuneration income; Γ_6 – row vector of employees' remuneration income coefficient ($\gamma_{6.g}$). In this example, $S_{6.} = 121.65$ billion yuan.

Part 2 includes other various currency incomes, including firms' retained profits (S_7) and state revenue (S_8) except for employees' remuneration. The formula is as follows:

$$S = \Gamma X \tag{4}$$

where S – column vector composed by S_7 and S_8; Γ – matrix of corresponding currency income coefficient (γ_{ig}) ($i = 7, 8$). The example is as follows:

$$S = \begin{bmatrix} S_{7.} \\ S_{8.} \end{bmatrix} = \begin{bmatrix} 210.9 \\ 347.6 \end{bmatrix}$$

Step 5: to calculate the gap between employees' remuneration income and expenditure. The total amount of employees' remuneration income S_6 calculated from formula (3) is balanced in comparison with the total amount of expenditure H_6, namely:

$$C_6 = S_{6.} - H_{6.} \tag{5}$$

where C_6 – gap between employees' remuneration income and expenditure. In this example, $C_6 = 121.65 - 190 = -68.35$ billion yuan shows that there is a gap of 68.35 billion yuan between their income and expenditure. It is therefore necessary to supplement income as shown in the following iterative calculation.

Step 6: to calculate various new currency expenditures. The firms' retained profit of 21.09 billion yuan and state revenue of 34.76 billion yuan calculated from formula (4) will be transformed to various new currency expenditures in quadrant IV. The calculation formula is as follows:

$$H = S\Pi + S\Pi_{113}\Pi_9 \tag{6}$$

where H – row vector composed by subtotal amount H_j of various currency expenditures as per its final usage; S' – S column vector transposing to row vector;

Π – matrix of expenditure composition coefficient (π_{ij}, $i = 7, 8; j = 105, 106, \ldots, 112$);
Π_{113} – column vector of bank saving or appropriation expenditure composition
coefficient ($\pi_{i,113}$); Π_9 – row vector of bank loan expenditure composition coefficient ($\pi_{9,j}$). In this example,

$$\Pi = \begin{bmatrix} 0.133 & 0.133 & 0.034 & 0 & 0.4 & 0 & 0.133 & 0 \\ 0.035 & 0.138 & 0.017 & 0.017 & 0.086 & 0 & 0.19 & 0.086 \end{bmatrix}$$

$$\Pi_{113} = \begin{bmatrix} 0.167 \\ 0.431 \end{bmatrix}$$

$$\Pi_9 = \begin{bmatrix} 0.133 & 0.6 & 0 & 0 & 0.267 & 0 & 0 & 0 \end{bmatrix}$$

In formula (6), the calculation result of the first term $S\Pi$ is other expenditures
except for bank saving or appropriation; the second term $S\Pi_{113}$ is the expenditure
of bank saving or appropriation, namely the growth of bank credit and loan (calculated in year-end growth compared with that at the beginning of the year); the
second full term $S\Pi_{113}\Pi_9$ is the growth of bank credit and loan contributed by the
growth of savings in banks. Formula (6) can be simplified as:

$$H = S'(\Pi + \Pi_{113}\Pi_9) \tag{7}$$

Through calculation, the value of H in this example is as follows:

$$H = [64.8\ 187\ 13.2\ 5.9\ 163.7\ 0\ 94\ 29.9].$$

Step 7: to calculate increased demand for final products. Various expenditures calculated from formula (7) form the new currency purchasing
power and new demand for final products and labor. The calculation is
as follows:

$$Y = BH \tag{8}$$

where B – matrix of final products composition coefficient (β_{ej}, $e = 1, 2, 3, 4$;
$j = 105, 106, \ldots, 112$)

Step 8: to calculate demand for import and export. Formula (2), which once
calculated the total output value (X) of various sectors, looks into the
demand for import goods (represented by $U_{5,g}$) in production. The calculation is as follows:

$$U_{5.} = \Phi X \tag{9}$$

where U_5 – the total volume of import goods; Φ – row vector of import goods consumption coefficient $(\Phi_{5.g})$. The example is as follows:

$$U_5 = \begin{bmatrix} 0.026 & 0.045 & 0 & 0 \end{bmatrix} \times = \begin{bmatrix} 1150.8 \\ 2107.7 \\ 0 \\ 0 \end{bmatrix} 12.5 \; billion \; yuan$$

It is important to ensure adequate export in order to balance import. It is presumed that foreign exchange required by imports is gained from exports and that imports and exports are balanced as per domestic price. The calculation is as follows:

$$Y = B_{114}U. \tag{10}$$

where B_{114} – column vector of final products composition coefficient $(\beta_{e,114})$ used in exports. Formula (8) and (10) can be combined as follows:

$$Y = BH + B_{114}U_5. \tag{11}$$

Through calculation the numerical value in this example is as follows:

$$Y = \begin{bmatrix} 32.7 \\ 401.9 \\ 94.0 \\ 29.9 \end{bmatrix}$$

Step 9: to apply the iterative calculation. In order to guarantee the supply of final products (or labor) calculated from formula (11), it is necessary to determine the total output value (or total labor) of various sectors. It forms various new currency incomes and then transmits to various expenditures. The whole circulatory iterative calculation can be recorded in the following three formulas:

$$S_6.^{(K+1)} = \Gamma_6 (E - A)^{-1} (BH^{(K)'} + B_{114}U_5.^{(K)}) \tag{12}$$

$$H^{(K+1)} = [\Gamma(E - A)^{-1} (BH^{(K)'} + B_{114}U_5.^{(K)})]'(\Pi + \Pi_{113}\Pi_9) \tag{13}$$

$$U_5.^{(K+1)} = \Phi(E - A)^{-1} (BH^{(K)'} + B_{114}U_5.^{(K)}) \tag{14}$$

where K – times of iteration. The iteration will not cease until satisfying the following conditions:

$$C_6 = \sum_{K=0}^{n} S_6.^{(K)} - H_6 = 0 \tag{15}$$

Namely, the total amount of employees' remuneration income and their total expenditure originally drawn up are balanced. In this example, $K = 8$. The complete calculation results are provided in Table 3.1. We use C_j to represent the gap between various final products and their currency purchasing power, and C_i to represent the gap between various currency incomes and expenditures. From Table 3.1, we can note:

$$C_j = Y_{\cdot j} - H_{\cdot j} = 0,$$

which demonstrates that various final products and their currency purchasing power are all balanced.

$$C_i = S_i - H_{i\cdot} = 0,$$

which illustrates that various currency incomes and expenditures are all balanced as well.

According to a variety of indicators calculated in Table 3.1, we can determine the scale and speed of economic development and the proportion of industrial sectors and draw up the applicable economic plan for the predicted social demands (the demand for consumer goods in this example) based on the comprehensive balance. The scale and speed of economic growth established through a series of calculations are in conformity with the comprehensive balance and able to improve coordination between production sectors. They are thus fairly reliable and tangible.

II   Dynamic Extended I-O Model

The Dynamic Extended I-O Model is characterized by an introduction of the time lag factor of capital construction, which reflects its long-term impact on economic comprehensive balance. Except for some small-scaled projects commenced and completed in the same year, capital construction projects generally stretch over a relatively longer period. Since various construction projects are completed by the end of the year and put into service at the beginning of the following year, the investment in a particular year can only form fixed assets in the following year. In other words, the newly created fixed assets are the result of previous investments. In order to ensure that the economic plans of various years link up with each other, it is necessary to carry through long-term investigation in their comprehensive balance. Thus, we need to analyze expanded reproduction in association with its fixed assets.

The main calculating steps of the Dynamic Extended I-O Model are as follows:

> Step 1: to draw up annual expenditure indicators of residents' purchasing consumer goods in the planning period (e.g. five years or ten years) in light of the plan for the demand and supply of consumer goods, then to

calculate the related total output value and the sum of capital construction investment of production sectors each year through the static Extended I-O Model.

Step 2: to calculate newly increased fixed assets. Although we adhere to the principle of acting according to one's capability and consider the correspondent conditions and possibility in the planning period when drawing up the annual plans for demand and supply of consumer goods, there is still a need to accurately calculate whether the production capacity of newly increased fixed assets can ensure an achievement of the growth indicators of total output value of various sectors per annum. It is important to calculate the total value of newly increased fixed assets of various sectors according to the sum of capital construction investment of material production sectors each year in the planning period through the static Extended I-O Model. The total value of newly increased fixed assets of various sectors is the sum of investment in the previous years (it is assumed that various projects commence at the beginning of the year and complete by the end of the same year). The formula is as follows:

$$V_j^p = \sum_q H_{.j}^{pq} \left(j = 105,106; = p - l_j, \dots, p - 2, p - 1 \right) \tag{1}$$

where p – the year when it goes into operation; q– the investment year; l_j – the project construction cycle of sector j; V_j^p – the total value of newly increased fixed assets possessed by sector j in year p; $H_{.j}^{pq}$ – the project investment sum put into operation in year p used in sector j in previous year q.

Step 3: to calculate the newly increased fixed assets required by sectors. The growth rate of the total output value of various sectors in the planning period requires the appropriate newly increased fixed assets. Its formula is as follows:

$$G_j^p = K_j^p(X_g^p - X_g^{p-1}) \ (g = 101, 102; j = g + 4) \tag{2}$$

where G_j^p – the total value of newly increased fixed assets required by sector j in year p; K_j^p – direct occupancy coefficient of productive fixed assets of sector j in year p. Considering the requirement for maintaining simple reproduction of fixed assets, the volume of annual compensation to fixed assets of various sectors should be added to formula (2).

Step 4: to calculate the gap between the requested and acquired newly increased fixed assets. The demand G_j^p for newly increased fixed assets calculated from formula (2) is balanced in comparison with the acquired newly increased fixed assets V_j^p calculated from formula (1), namely:

$$\Delta G_j^p = G_j^p - V_j^p \ (j = 105, 106) \tag{3}$$

where ΔG_j^p – the gap of newly increased fixed assets. $\Delta G_j^p \neq 0$ shows that there is a gap between the required and actually acquired newly increased fixed assets and that, correspondingly, there is a need to either continuously supplement or reduce investments. By now it is necessary to calculate the variation of capital construction investment each year. It is presumed that $\Delta G_j^p > 0$, namely continuous supplement to investment is required.

Step 5: to calculate an increased sum of capital construction investment. The investment supplement for continuously increased fixed assets (ΔG_j^p) is carried out respectively in each year previously. Its equation is as follows:

$$\Delta H_j^{pq} = \lambda_j^{pq} \Delta G_j^p \ (q = p - l_j, \ldots, p - 2, p - 1) \tag{4}$$

where λ_j^{pq} – investment distribution coefficient of newly increased fixed assets put into operation in year p by sector j in the previous construction period (year q).

Step 6: to calculate growth of final products. Additional investment leads to a growth of final products. The calculation is denoted in matrix as follows:

$$\Delta Y^q = B_1^q \Delta H_1^{q'} \tag{5}$$

where $\Delta H_1^{q'}$ – row vector composed by ΔH_j^{pq} determined from formula (4) transposing to column vector; B_1^q – matrix of final products composition coefficient.

Step 7: to calculate growth of total output value. The final products growth is related to the total output value growth of various sectors. The formula is as follows:

$$\Delta X^q = (E - A^q)^{-1} \Delta Y^q \tag{6}$$

Step 8: to calculate growth of currency income. The total output value growth of various sectors brings about currency income growth. The calculation formula is as follows:

$$\Delta S^q = \Gamma^q \Delta X^q \tag{7}$$

where ΔS^q – column vector composed by ΔS_i^q ($i = 6, 7, 8$); Γ^q – matrix of related currency income coefficient (γ_{ig}^q, $i = 6, 7, 8$).

Step 9: to calculate the growth of various currency expenditures. Various income growths create a currency expenditure growth. The calculation formula is:

$$\Delta H^q = \Delta S^{q'} (\Pi^q + \Pi_{113}^q \Pi_9^q) \tag{8}$$

where Π^q – matrix of expenditure composition coefficient ($\pi_{ij}{}^q$, $i = 6, 7, 8$; $j = 105, 106, \ldots , 112$); $\Pi_{113}{}^q$ – column vector of bank saving or appropriation expenditure composition coefficient ($\pi_{i,113}{}^q$, $i = 6, 7, 8$); $\Pi_9{}^q$ – row vector of bank loan expenditure composition coefficient ($\pi_{9,j}{}^q$).

> Step 10: to calculate gaps of capital construction investment. The row vector ΔH^q verified in formula (8) includes two parts. One is the expenditure related to increased capital construction investment of various material production sectors, namely $\Delta H_1{}^q$. The other is unrelated expenditure which is recorded as $\Delta H_2{}^q$. These numerical numbers show the values prior to iterative calculation which is provided in the following. They are recorded as $\Delta H^{q(0)}$, $\Delta H_1{}^{q(0)}$, $\Delta H_2{}^{q(0)}$. To compare $\Delta H_1{}^{q(0)}$ with growth of capital construction investment established from formula (4):

$$J^q = \Delta H_1{}^{q(0)} - \Delta H_1{}^q \tag{9}$$

where J^q – gaps of capital construction investment. $J^q < 0$ shows that $\Delta H_1{}^{q(0)}$ and $\Delta H_1{}^q$ are unbalanced and needs to proceed with iterative calculation and continuous supplement to capital investment. $\Delta H_1{}^{q(k)}$ does not enter into iterative process. By now it is $\Delta H_2{}^{q(k)}$ that enters into the process denoting other expenditures unrelated to capital construction investment.

> Step 11: to carry out iterative calculation. To add the growth of imports and exports, the whole iterative process can be recorded as:

$$\Delta H^{q\,(K+1)} = [\Gamma^q\,(E - A^q)^{-1}(B_2{}^q\Delta H_2{}^{q\,(K)'} + B_{114}{}^q\Delta U_5{}^{q\,(K)})](\Pi^q + \Pi_{113}{}^q\Pi_9{}^q) \tag{10}$$

$$\Delta U_5{}^{q\,(K+1)} = \Phi^q\,(E - A^q)^{-1}(B_2{}^q\Delta H_2{}^{q\,(K)'} + B_{114}{}^q U_5{}^{q\,(K)}) \tag{11}$$

where $B_2{}^q$ – matrix of final products composition coefficient of expenditure $\Delta H_2{}^q$ that is irrelevant to investment.

The iteration will not cease until it satisfies the following conditions:

$$J^q = \sum_{K=0}^{n} \Delta H_1{}^{q(k)} - \Delta H_1{}^q = 0 \tag{12}$$

We should draw attention to the fact that the total output value of various material production sectors each year varies from that previously calculated from formula (2) on completion of the above calculation. The new growth brings forth the new demand for fixed assets. Consequently, the new equilibrium calculation of fixed assets needs to be processed. In order to avoid such repetitive calculation, we can add a right expedient coefficient ξ_j^p to the requested additional fixed assets G_j^p before calculating formula (3). It can be written as follows:

$$\Delta G_j^p = \xi_j^p G_j^p - V_j^p.$$

Various indicators established through the Dynamic Extended I-O Model can help ensure comprehensive balance within the planning year and between planning years.

III Implications of Extended I-O Model

The Extended I-O Model is developed substantially from the I-O model. It retains all the functions of the original I-O model such as examining the technical and economic links between sectors, investigating economic structure and determining total output values of industrial sectors from the perspective of final products. In addition to these, it can be applied to broader situations.

First, it can be used for a comprehensive investigation of various links of social reproduction and assist in drawing up a more integrated plan. One of the prominent features of the Extended I-O Model is that it can connect all the links of social reproduction, such as production, distribution, exchange and consumption, closely into an organic unity. Let's recall the preceding iterative calculation formula (to make it simple, $B_{114}U_5$ · that is related to imports and exports has been removed). Referring to formula (13) in the static Extended I-O Model and formula (10) in the Dynamic Extended I-O Model:

$$H^{(K+1)} = [\Gamma(E - A)^{-1} BH^{(K)}](\Pi + \Pi_{113}\Pi_9)$$

H is currency expenditure, namely the ultimate usage of currency reflecting the consumption level or currency purchasing power. BH is the demand for final products (Y) demonstrating the exchange between currency purchasing power and final products. $(E - A)^{-1} BH$ is $(E - A)^{-1} Y = X$ showing the production process in satisfying the demand of final products. $\Gamma(E - A)^{-1} BH$ is $\Gamma X = S$, reflecting the distribution and redistribution of currency income. The whole formula illustrates the ultimate usage of various newly formed currency funds. It is clear that regarding the production process as the principal link and being mediated by distribution and exchange, the Extended I-O Model connects all the links of social reproduction dynamically by taking the demand of social consumption (that is originated from the currency purchasing power) as the starting point and destination. By applying the model, we can readily comprehend the interrelations and mutual constraints between the links of social reproduction, carry out simulating tests of various complicated economic programs on the computer for the predicted targets, and finally select a scheme with dependable speed, improved economic advantages and more benefits to people. In this way we can draw up comprehensively balanced economic development plans with clear objectives, suitable proportions, and manageable coordination.

Second, it can assess balance between state revenue and expenditure. In the Extended I-O Model, the formulas indicating state revenue and expenditure are as follows:

$$C_8 = S_8 - H_8. \tag{1}$$

$$S_{8\cdot} = \sum_g S_{8,g} = \sum_g \gamma_{8,g} X_g \tag{2}$$

$$H_{8\cdot} = \sum_j H_{8,j} = \sum_j \pi_{8,j} S_8 . \tag{3}$$

where C_8 is the gap between state revenue and expenditure; S_8 is the total amount of revenue; and H_8 is the total amount of expenditure. The formulas show that we must make efforts in increasing the revenue and cutting expenditures in order to keep a balance between revenue and expenditures.

The state revenue mainly comes from taxation and profits handed over by material production sectors. From formula (2) we note that the level of state revenue is related to the total output value(X_g) of various sectors on the one hand and to the revenue coefficient ($\gamma_{8,g}$) on the other hand. The most fundamental way for boosting state revenues is to strive to increase production and economy – the source of finance and wealth. Meanwhile, the revenue coefficient (the proportion of taxation and profits of each sector delivered to the state by firms in their total output value) is also a critical factor. The formula of revenue coefficient is as follows:

$$\gamma_{8,g} = S_{8,g} / X_g = \left(X_g - \sum_e X_{eg} - S_{6,g} - S_{7,g} \right) / X_g$$

$$= 1 - \left(\sum_e X_{eg} / X_g \right) - \left(S_{6,g} / X_g \right) - \left(S_{7,g} / X_g \right)$$

$$= 1 - \sum_e \alpha_{eg} - \gamma_{6,g} - \gamma_{7,g} \tag{4}$$

It shows that the revenue coefficient moves in the opposite direction from the material consumption coefficient (α_{eg}), employees' remuneration income coefficient ($\gamma_{6,g}$) and firms' retained profit income coefficient ($\gamma_{7,g}$). When the total output value of each sector is fixed, in order to increase state revenue and raise the revenue coefficient, we must reduce costs of raw material and fuel, improve efficiency of machinery and equipment utilization and reduce the material consumption coefficient. Moreover, we need to prevent issuing bonuses excessively and to control the increase in the employees' remuneration income coefficient. Furthermore, we must arrange a reasonable proportion of firms' retained profits so as to guarantee profits and taxation delivered to the state and keep firms' retained profit income coefficient at an appropriate level. Without doubt, with scientific and technical progress and improvement of sound industrial composition, material consumption coefficient, employees' remuneration income coefficient and firms' retained profit income coefficient will increase or decrease to different extents as labor productivity and total output value of each sector increases. When these are happening, it is crucial to ensure an unconditional increase of state revenue. The short formula $S_{8\cdot} = \sum_g \gamma_{8,g} X_g$ reveals the ways of making and accumulating incomes.

The formula (3) otherwise reflects the ways of using incomes. The expenditure of state revenue should adhere to two principles. On the one hand, it is obliged to spend what one earns. The total expenditure is restricted by the total revenue in order to maintain a balance between the total revenue and expenditure. On the other hand, attention should be paid to the ways of spending state revenue, which is reflected in the revenue expenditure composition coefficient ($\pi_{8,j}$). All the issues, such as how much is used in capital construction, how much is used in additional appropriation of current capital, how much is used in scientific, culture, education and health sectors, and how much is used in administrative management and defense, will be considered and judged according to the demand and availability as well as their impacts on the economy. Any significant changes in state revenue expenditure (e.g. a substantial increase or cut-down of the total expenditure or item expenditure and the potential impact of this change on national economy) can be revealed by applying the Extended I-O Model.

Third, it can establish the balance between income and expenditure of credit and loan. With further economic reforms, the bank is playing a more active role in managing economies. The Extended I-O Model, as a further extension of its original form, has introduced a special factor of income and expenditure of credit and loan. We can calculate income and expenditure of credit and loan and their impacts on economic performance. This will benefit increasing, administrating and using credit and loan in a planned way.

Fourth, it can determine the balance between residents' purchasing power and supply of consumer goods, according to growing demands of residents for material and cultural products, and rationalize the economic structure. We have noted from the previous examples that the government can organize production and supply of consumer goods according to residents' purchasing power and ensure balanced production and supply in quantity and with a compatible structure in composition. The whole calculation will reveal the scale in which various sectors shall proceed with production and, correspondingly, the level at which their demands for industrial goods, such as raw materials, fuel, power, machinery and equipment should be. At these scales and levels, industrial sectors will meet the growing purchasing power of residents and the increased supply of consumer goods. In accordance with the calculation, the government can arrange production, construction and livings as a whole, modify development ways of industrial sectors, and gradually build up a rational economic structure.

Fifth, it can disclose the balance between imports and exports. The implementation of an open-door policy and the expansion of international trade have raised the new requirements for imports and exports. The balance between imports and exports is closely tied to China's economic growth. We can investigate this connection and establish a balance between them by employing the Extended I-O Model. In order to analyze imports and exports in great detail, imports and exports can be separately grouped in the Extended I-O table according to product categories and import and export areas, as in the regional I-O table.

Finally, it can investigate the interconnection between material and non-material production sectors and promote the development of services, scientific research, culture, education and health care sectors. In the I-O table we currently use, the sectors of service, scientific research, culture, education and health care are not listed in quadrant I. In reality, however, it is necessary to calculate material consumption of these sectors and incorporate it into the residents' directly purchased consumer goods in quadrant II. This is the grounds for calculating the balance between residents' income and expenditures and the balance between input and output of consumer goods. Thus, it is unclear about the links between the input and output of non-production sectors. In the extended model, material consumption of these sectors is separately listed in quadrant I, net labor income in quadrant III, total labor required by these sectors in quadrant I, and currency payment or appropriation to the activity and capital construction of these sectors in quadrant IV. In this way the interconnection between material and non-material production sectors as well as the activities of non-production sectors is exposed clearly. On this ground, the government can reasonably organize and actively promote the sectors of services, scientific research, culture, education and health care. This will lead to an improvement of people's living standards, in terms of both material goods and cultural life, and realization of the four modernizations.

In reality, economic life is very complicated. We can undertake a range of calculations and analyses of economic phenomena and factors by applying the Extended I-O Model. It is very important to improve the scientific basis and accurate prediction for statistics and planning and to modernize economic plans and management.

We compiled the physical I-O table of 61 products in 1973 and presently are testing the country-level monetary I-O table. Some provinces and cities, such as Shanxi, Henan, Heilongjiang and Beijing, have compiled or are compiling the region-level I-O table, which has created advantages for further research and application of the Extended I-O Model in economic life.

(Originally published in *References of Economic Research*, No.185, Nov.1983)

Note

1 The original table listed various numerical values and the corresponding coefficients in the case in one table, which is very big and not easy to print. Now they are listed in two tables, respectively. Table 2.1 includes various numerical values in the case. Table 2.2 includes the corresponding coefficients.

4 Applied research of the macro-econometric model[1]

Analysis and manipulation of some important parameters

I Application of macro-econometric model

The macro-econometric model is developed from the econometric approach and verified by historical data. It is mainly applied in the four domains.

First, it is used to answer the question of "what the historical track and current situations are", namely to analyze the macroeconomy historically and present-day in a given country or region. Without modifying the original model, it studies interdependence between diverse economic variables (including both exogenous and endogenous variables) in history and at the present time through analyzing a range of parameters.

Second, it is employed to answer the question of "what it will be if it keeps doing as it is", namely to forecast the economic trend in the foreseeable future. What the upcoming trend will be if an economy grows in accordance with the current trend without inputting any new policies and measures. There is no need to manipulate the parameters in the original model to make a prediction, but rather to provide a particular exogenous variable's value in calculating the upcoming endogenous variable's value. For example, presuming that the investment effect coefficient has been constant over 30 years since the founding of the People's Republic of China, a given investment value over the next 20 years can predict the multiple industrial and agricultural output values, represented by the endogenous variable, in the end of the 20th century.

Third, it is applied to answer the question of "what should be done for what it will be", namely to assist planning and demonstrating policies and measures in order to achieve planned development goals. Based on the overall conditions, the Party leaders and government officials at all levels often draw up long-term macroeconomic goals on the basis of investigation and extensive discussion. The policies and measures that convey plans for achievable goals require feasibility studies. For example, the goal is set to quadruple the total industrial and agricultural output value in the end of the 20th century with a certain amount of investment. Accordingly, this requires manipulating the parameters and determining the level of the investment effect coefficient.

Fourth, it is used to answer the question of "what it will be if what is done", namely to simulate, evaluate and opt for the policies and measures in various plans that might generate diverse impacts over the future. Both the exogenous variable's value and parameter require manipulation. An endogenous variable will generate a range of variations, which enable us to choose the best plan from several schemes that can meet our objectives. For example, we can obtain different growths of total industrial and agricultural output values against different volumes of investment and different investment effect coefficients, and then opt for the optimum combined scheme.

The first and second domains are the general application of the macro-econometric model. The third and fourth domains are the goal-directed applications of the macro-econometric model. It is very important to manipulate and analyze the model parameters. In the subsequent section, we turn to the analysis of several important parameters and preliminarily examine the parameter manipulation methods by referring to the compilation and application of the Shanxi econometric model.

II Analysis and manipulation of the production function parameter

The Shanxi econometric model adopts the production function with net output value. Its general form is as follows:

$$N_t^i = b_0^i + b_1^i L_{t-1}^i + b_2^i (K_{t-1}^i / L_{t-1}^i) \tag{1}$$

where i – material production sectors (altogether 19 sectors, namely $i = 1, 2, \ldots, 19$), t – year, N – net output value of each material production sector, L_{t-1} – labor of each material production sector by the end of previous year, K_{t-1} – original value of fixed assets of each material production sector by the end of previous year, (K_{t-1} / L_{t-1}) – tangible fixed assets per regular employee of each material production sector by the end of previous year, b_0 –constant term, b_1 – output coefficient of labor, b_2 – output coefficient of tangible fixed assets per regular employee.

The reason why formula (1) takes on L_{t-1} and K_{t-1} with a one-year time lag is to connect the labor sub-model with the fixed assets sub-model and establish the time difference recursive model system. The reason for choosing (K_{t-1} / L_{t-1}), rather than K_{t-1} alone, as the second explanatory variable is to avoid multicollinearity between K_{t-1} and the first explanatory variable L_{t-1}.

The total output value (X) of each material production sector is as follows:

$$X_t^i = N_t^i / (1 - AT_t^i) \tag{2}$$

where AT – the sum of direct consumption coefficient and fixed assets depreciation coefficient in the input-output model. $1 - AT$ – net output value coefficient.

According to the Shanxi statistical data from 1963 to 1980, the constant term b_0^i, labor-output coefficient b_1^i and output coefficient b_2^i of the tangible fixed assets per regular employee could be determined from formula (1). The results of the regression analysis are ideal through interpolation and extrapolation inspection on historical data of the net output value of various sectors. However, when applying these parameters to predict the trend of the next 20 years with a given workforce and tangible fixed assets per regular employee, the net output value of each sector and the corresponding predicted value of total output value are typically lower than the planned value as part of the strategic objectives of economic development in Shanxi Province. The annual growth rate of net industrial and agricultural output values from 1981 to 2000 is estimated to be merely 4.2% and the annual growth rate of total industrial and agricultural output values to be merely 4.1%. These show that the two parameters ($b_1{}^i$ and $b_2{}^i$) in the net output value production function are generally low according to the analysis of 20-year data, in line with reality. In the past, economic effect indicators such as labor productivity and fixed assets productivity of many sectors rose slowly and even appeared to move downwards for some years, especially due to the impact of the ten-year's turmoil. Shanxi Province and China were in the same situation. Taking the whole labor productivity of public-owned industrial enterprises with independent accounting, for example, their annual growth rate was 8.7% in the five years from 1953 to 1957. It reduced to 4.4% in the eight years from 1958 to 1965 and further reduced to 1.7% in the 13 years from 1966 to1978. It rose slightly in the three years from 1979 to 1981 with a growth rate of 2.1% only. Table 4.1 records the detailed situation of industrial sectors.

Table 4.1 Annual growth rate of labor productivity of publicly-owned industrial enterprises with independent accounting

Year	1953–57	1958–65	1966–78	1979–81
Sector				
Industrial labor productivity	8.7	4.4	1.7	2.1
Including:				
1 Metallurgy	15.8	4.8	−2.0	2.4
2 Electric power	9.3	6.0	3.4	−4.5
3 Coal	8.6	−5.1	0.9	−3.1
4 Oil and petrol	11.8	7.7	5.3	−5.9
5 Chemistry	18.3	10.1	0.8	5.8
6 Machinery	14.8	4.7	2.7	−2.0
7 Building material	11.4	7.8	0.4	1.3
8 Forestry	−0.3	−0.3	−1.4	0.4
9 Food processing	7.2	1.7	−0.2	3.7
10 Textile	2.7	5.1	1.6	4.6
11 Paper-making	11.8	2.3	−2.3	−2.9

Unit: percentage

Note: Calculated according to the data of labor productivity index of publicly-owned industrial enterprises with independent accounting categorized as per industrial sectors. From *China Statistical Yearbook (1981),* by National Bureau of Statistics of China, 1982, Beijing: China Statistics Press.

It would surely underestimate the development pace in the next 20 years if the prediction is based on the previously slow growth rate of labor productivity and fixed assets productivity. In order to achieve the goal of quadrupling the total industrial and agricultural output values, we need to manipulate two production function parameters of net output value with the given labor quantity and tangible fixed assets per regular employee.

One approach is to manipulate output coefficient b_1^i of labor and output coefficient b_2^i of tangible fixed assets per regular employee, respectively. In our earlier calculation it seemed very tricky to do this because of two reasons. First, it was a great workload and difficult to control the process when we manipulated two parameters simultaneously for the production function of the net output value of each sector. There were 19 material production sectors in the Shanxi econometric model. Second, in the above production function, the output coefficient of labor is not equal to labor productivity, and the output coefficient of tangible fixed assets per regular employee is not equal to fixed asset productivity, either. We cannot get an empirical base to manipulate these two parameters to an appropriate extent. In this circumstance, we have to take a rather straightforward approach. That is not to manipulate these two parameters directly but to multiply the formula of the production function of net output value by a new term. Then, formula (1) is altered as shown in the following:

$$N_t^i = [b_0^i + b_1^i L_{t-1}^i + b_2^i (K_{t-1}^i / L_{t-1}^i)](1 + p^i)^t \qquad (3)$$

p^i is the overall efficiency coefficient of each material production sector. It indicates an improvement of output efficiency through the adaption of science and technology, implementation of economic reforms, adjustment of industrial structural and advancement of operation and management. In this approach, only one parameter (p^i), instead of two (b_1^i and b_2^i), is manipulated.

Let's turn to the estimation of the value for overall efficiency coefficient. In 1981, industrial labor productivity in Shanxi Province was only 62.2% of the national level, and its industrial output value per 100 yuan of fixed assets original value was only 58% of the national level. The economic efficiency indicator nationwide will increase continuously in the next 20 years. To reach the national level, Shanxi Province must increase twofold its economic efficiency indicator by the end of the 20th century. This refers to the whole province only. The economic efficiency in each industrial sector could increase differently in Shanxi Province. The overall efficiency coefficient of each material production sector can be grouped into three categories: low, medium and high levels. Low efficiency refers to upholding the historical level and status quo of economic efficiency continually for the next 20 years. High efficiency implies attainment of economic efficiency to the national level by the end of the 20th century. The medium efficiency refers to achieving half of the high economic efficiency. At the same time, we examine potential investment (exogenous variables) received by Shanxi Province from the central government over the next 20 years in the low, medium and high level, too. As a result, there are nine scenarios in our calculation. Having processed the calculations of these scenarios, we could submit at least five sets among them from the calculation results to government departments who are responsible for drawing up the long-term economic plans.

After recalculating the net output value and the corresponding total output value of each sector through formula (3), we divide the total output value of each year by the quantity of workforce and the original value of fixed assets of same year. Then we can obtain economic efficiency indicators, including labor productivity and fixed assets productivity, which should reach the objectives each year as planned.

III   Analysis and manipulation of the parameter of labor demand function

In Shanxi economic model, labor demand function is as follows:

$$L_t^i = d_0^i + d_1^i I_t^i + d_2^i L_{t-1}^i \tag{4}$$

where L_t – the quantity of labor demand of each material production sector in year t, I – fixed assets investment of each material production sector, L_{t-1} – the labor quantity of each material production sector by the end of previous year, d_0 – constant term, d_1 – fixed assets investment coefficient and d_2 – labor coefficient of previous year.

Employment in China, especially in non-agricultural sectors, is uniformly planned and overall arranged. An increase or decrease in employment mainly depends on fixed assets investment in addition to an increase or decrease in the working-age population, number of graduates from universities and mid-schools, number of demobilized and retired servicemen, existing labor force of each sector and structural adjustments of industrial sectors. In considering these factors, formula (4) selects I as the main explanatory variable.

Meanwhile, we proceed to compile the Shanxi population model and calculate the total quantity of available labor until year 2000.

The demand for labor force by each material production sector will considerably exceed the total labor available by the end of the 20th century in the given value of fixed assets investment based on the prediction for the next 20 years through formula (4).

Why is there a high-level demand for labor force, as calculated through formula (4)? How can we manipulate the parameter in the labor demand function?

First of all, let's look at the coefficient d_2 of term L_{t-1}. In formula (4), the relation between the dependent variable of demand quantity for labor L_t and independent variable of the quantity of labor L_{t-1} by the end of previous year is lagged autoregressive. If there is no massive movement of labor force from one sector to another, coefficient d_2 will show the general trend in which the labor force in a certain sector increases (e.g. agriculture) or decreases. This implies that d_2 is relatively stable. The problem is that fixed assets investment coefficient d_1, which is verified based on historical data, is generally high. It illustrates a high level of labor demand set off by fixed asset investment, conforming. with the historical situation. In the past, production expansion mainly relied on the expansion of fixed assets investment and employment due to the low growth rates in labor productivity and fixed assets productivity. If our prediction for the next 20 years is drawn upon this historical trend in combination with the policies of family planning and population control, the demand for labor force will no doubt exceed the supply.

In order to ensure the balance between labor demand and labor supply for the next 20 years, it is necessary to reduce the demand for labor force originating from the expansion of fixed assets investment. At the same time, with the adaption of science and technology and continuous improvement in skills of the labor force, there will be a gradual decline in the demand for labor force brought about by fixed assets investment. In view of this, there is a need to reduce fixed assets investment coefficient d_1 in formula (4).

The manipulation method for coefficient d_1 is to multiply it by a new coefficient q_t which is less than one and greater than zero. This new coefficient can be called the labor adjustment coefficient. Formula (4) is altered as follows:

$$L_t^i = d_0^i + q_t^{\ i} d_1^{\ i} I_t^i + d_2^i L_{t-1}^{\ i} \tag{5}$$

As for setting the value for $q_t^{\ i}$, it can be controlled and determined by collecting the following information: (a) the quantity of total labor available in the next 20 years, which has been verified through the population model; (b) the controllable quantity of labor in sectors, which can be estimated based on availability of total labor and through consultation with relevant departments and experts; (c) the demand for labor force calculated from formula (4) without adding labor adjustment coefficient. This is the basis for manipulation; and (d) the previous variation in the labor demand of each sector requested by ten-thousand RMB investment. Equipped with this information, it becomes relatively easy for us to determine the value of q.

IV   Analysis and manipulation of the parameters in fixed assets function

In the Shanxi econometric model, the fixed assets production function is as follows:

$$K_t^i = \gamma_0^i + \gamma_1^{\ i} K_{t-1}^{\ i} + \gamma_2^i I_t^i + \gamma_3^i I_{t-1}^{\ i} + \ldots + \gamma_\tau^i I_{t-(\tau-2)}^{\ i} \tag{6}$$

where K – the original value of fixed assets of each material production sector, I – investment of fixed assets to each sector, γ_0 – constant term, γ_1 – coefficient of fixed assets original value by the end of previous year, and $\gamma_2, \ldots, \gamma_\tau$ – the fixed assets investment coefficient each year.

We have tried out several fixed assets functions and finally selected formula (6). Under constraint of $\gamma_0 = 0, \gamma_1 = 1$, when calculating various coefficients based on the historical data from 1958 to 1980, the mathematical equations drawn up through interpolation and extrapolation tests show a relatively decent regression result. However, the predicted value of fixed assets in many production sectors for the 20 years derived from formula (6) is generally high with the given fixed asset investment. This causes an unexpected fall in the average annual growth of fixed assets productivity (X / K) in some manufacturing sectors.

The problem lies in the constraint condition $\gamma_1 = 1$. On the one hand, the historical statistical data in reference to the original value of fixed assets K_{t-1} by the end of previous year has already deducted the value of fixed assets scrappage when conducting regression. However, K_{t-1} itself does not deduct any new value of fixed assets disposal because of the assumption $\gamma_1 = 1$ when making the prediction. This implies that the value of fixed assets by the end of previous year are all transferred to the next year, which causes a prediction of incorrect, over-valued fixed assets in the following years. On the other hand, renovation, transformation and upgrading of fixed assets were painfully torpid in the past decades. Accordingly, fixed assets disposal was very stagnant. Although we can replicate the past situation with the constraint $\gamma_1 = 1$, it will inevitably induce a high value of fixed assets when making prediction for the next 20 years with this constraint.

Renovation, transformation and upgrading of fixed assets are bound to accelerate with science and technology progress over the next 20 years. The constraint $\gamma_1 = 1$ is no longer applicable in the fixed assets function in some production sectors in considering that many fixed assets are out-of-date. Alternatively, it is necessary to assign a value less than 1 and greater than zero to coefficient γ_1.

As for the value of γ_1, it can be determined and controlled by the following factors: (1) the aging of fixed assets of each production sector, (2) fixed assets and the related fixed assets productivity, which are calculated from the original equation $\gamma_1 = 1$, as the groundwork of manipulation, (3) rising, rather than descending, fixed assets productivity (X / K) of manufacturing sectors and (4) historical data and experiences of advanced countries (regions), such as the average annual scrappage coefficient indicator of each sector. We do not often attach importance to the statistics of fixed assets scrappage and renovation, and there is a shortage of comprehensive information in this regard. To make up for these weaknesses, we should conduct case studies to obtain the necessary data.

V   Unity of science and "art"

The Shanxi econometric model consists of over 30 sub-models. In addition to the sub-models of net output value, total output value, labor demand and supply and production fixed assets, there are sub-models of local revenue and expenditure, urban and rural residents' income and expenditure, ultimate supply and demand of products, movements of products, and non-material production sector. I will not go into a detailed analysis and manipulation of the parameters in these sub-models[2]

In the process of compiling and applying the Shanxi econometric model, we have profoundly recognized that an all-embracing macro-econometric model is a unity integrating a series of sub-models. Each sub-model has countless mathematical equations. There is a close connection between the mathematical equations and between the sub-models so that a slight move in one part may affect the whole. Given such a fact, a variety of parameters have to be manipulated in an interlocked way when forecasting economic performance, planning economic objectives and testing policies. This is a matter of unity between science and "art". The so-called "art" refers to the need that modelers profoundly comprehend the laws and mechanism of economy in history and at present and consequently are able to make a relatively correct judgment on its trend. They should obtain suffi-cient scientific evidence, rather than making personal assumptions, for each manipulation of parameters. They are meanwhile encouraged to fulfill their poten-tial in using and manipulating the models so as to make the correct judgment on the future trend of economic development.

We usually manipulate the parameter separately in net output value (N) and its corresponding total output value (X) sub-model, labor demand (L) sub-model and fixed assets (K) sub-model. However, with regard to the association between the predicted values of X, L and K, we have detected that the predicted growth rate of labor productivity (X / L) increases year by year in many sectors and the growth rate of tangible fixed assets per regular employee (K / L) also increases year by year, whereas the growth rate of fixed assets productivity (X / K) declines year by year. The growth rate of X / K appears as a series of negatives. On the basis of the formula

$$(X / K) = (X / L) / (K / L)$$

a further analysis indicates that the faster-paced growth rate of fixed assets (K) than that of the total output value (X) inevitably brings about a rise in K / L and a decline in X / K when labor (L) is fixed. This signifies the problems with the parameter in the original fixed assets function. The problems are rooted in inappropriate con-straint $\gamma_1 = 1$ used in forecasting from formula (6). In view of this, we can conclude that only by adjustably applying the macro-econometric model in complicated associations of production sectors with the overall movement of economic factors can we manipulate various parameters appropriately so as to make valid prediction and plans of economic development and design correct policies.

Engels pointed out that:

> anarchy in social production is replaced by conscious organization on a planned basis. The laws of his own social activity, which have hitherto con-fronted him as external, dominating laws of nature, will then be applied by man with complete understanding, and hence will be dominated by man. It is only from this point that the social causes set in motion by men will have, predominantly and in constantly increasing measure, the effects willed by men. It is humanity's leap from the realm of necessity into the realm of freedom.

> (Engels, 1885/2001)[3]

Likewise, there also exists a leap from the realm of necessity to the realm of freedom in the compilation and application of economic models. Economists, econometric theorists and practitioners are especially required to learn from and cooperate with each other all the time. This is a prerequisite for promoting the use of economic models in China.

(Originally published in *The Journal of Quantitative & Technical Economics*, No.4, 1984)

Notes

1 The work was completed under the guidance and attendance of Zhang Shouyi from the Institute of Quantitative & Technical Economics at Chinese Academy of Social Sciences (CASS). I am grateful for the consultation and assistance of Zimin Yan (Institute of Quantitative & Technical Economics, CASS), Guixi Zhang (Department of Economic Mathematics at Beijing College of Economics), Linyun Han and Weiping Niu (Computing station of the Planning Commission of Shanxi Province), Anrong Hu (The Planning Commission of Shanxi Province), and Siqi A (Shanxi Academy of Social Sciences). In this article, we combine the econometric model with input-output model and integrate them into the comprehensive economic model. For the design of the model, see Zhang, Shouyi. (1984). Application of Input-Output Model in Planning. *The Journal of Quantitative & Technical Economics*, No.3.
2 Regarding the revision of the direct consumption coefficient in the input-output model, please refer to the article by Changping Liu from Hubei Institute of Finance and Economics. Liu participated in this project.
3 Engels, F. (2001). *Herr Eugen Dhring's revolution in science (anti-Dhring)*. (p.358). E. Burns (Trans.). London: Electric Book Co. (Original work published 1885).

5 Promotion and application of input-output approach at the regional level

I Necessity and probability of the promotion and application of input-output approach at the regional level

1. A brief introduction to the regional input-output table compilation in China

Recently, the application of the input-output (I-O for short) approach at the regional level (which implies province, municipality, autonomous region, and city) has been promoted heavily in China. The compilation of the earliest regional I-O table can be traced back to 1962 in which researchers from the Department of National Economy Balance of Economic Research Institute at Chinese Academy of Sciences (now known as the Department of National Economy of Economic Research Institute at Chinese Academy of Social Sciences, or CASS) investigated the issues and undertook a trial of compiling the regional I-O table in Shanxi Province. They drew up a report entitled "Survey on the conditions of compiling the inter-sector balance table in Shanxi Province". The survey noted:

> In order to strengthen economic plans and advance comprehensive balance of national economy, we must improve approaches to planning by drawing the previous experiences in addition to adhering to the rules of planned and proportionate development of national economy and appropriately implementing the guidelines, principles and policies of Chinese Communist Party. On the one hand, we need to effectively make use of the balance method and the balance table applied in the past and, on the other hand, further promote the application of inter-sector balance table.

They not only examined the objective conditions (e.g. whether the internal economic structure was all-inclusive and the external economic relationship was unsophisticated) and subjective conditions (e.g. whether there was a supportive base for planning and statistics) for compiling the balance table in Shanxi Province, but also investigated in great detail the gap between the existing planning and statistics systems and the requirements for compiling the inter-sector balance table. They came to the following concluding remarks:

> There are basic conditions to experimentally compile the inter-sector balance table based in Shanxi Province, and there is relatively a large gap between the conditions under which experimental compilation and the actual practice of planning and statistics are concerned. However, as long as we appropriately streamline the inter-sector balance table and lessen the compilation requirements on the one hand and raise the level of planning and statistics as much as possible and make necessary modification in terms of compilation methods on the other hand, this gap can be narrowed at both ends.

The experimental compilation of the regional I-O table was entirely halted due to a number of factors, especially the interference and destruction caused by the ten-year turmoil brought about by the Cultural Revolution. In 1979 with the improved situation which resulted from the policy 'Bringing order out of chaos' made at the Third Plenary Session of the 11th CPC Central Committee, Shanxi Province started again to deliberate on compiling the regional I-O table assisted by the Department of Quantitative Economics, Economy Research Institute (which is now known as Institute of Quantitative &Technical Economics) at CASS and the Department of Planning and Statistics at Renmin University of China.

Shanxi Province pioneered the first regional I-O table in China, specifically carried out by the Statistical Bureau of Shanxi Province. This work commenced with staff training from March 1979 to April 1980. It took two years from actually beginning to compile the table in May 1980 to completing the task in April 1982. The 1979 I-O table of Shanxi Province includes the physical input-output table (PIOT) of 88 products and the monetary input-output table (MIOT) of 56 sectors. Shanxi Province went one step ahead and gathered valuable experience. Soon afterwards, several other provinces and municipalities took similar action one after another.

The Statistical Bureau of Heilongjiang province began a survey in November 1981. It took one year and two months to complete the 1981 province-level PIOT of 115 products and MIOT of 78 sectors in January 1983.

From February to the middle of June 1982, teachers and students from the Department of Economic Mathematics at Beijing College of Economics, supported by Beijing Municipal Bureau of Statistics, took four and a half months to compile Beijing's PIOT of 46 products.

With the help of Tsinghua University, Institute of Quantitative &Technical Economics at CASS, and the Research Institute of Kinetic Energy Economy at Academy of Electric Power Sciences under the Ministry of Water Resource and Electric Power, the Research Unit of Energy affiliated to the Science and Technology Commission of Guangdong Province, a collaborative project between China and the Federal Republic of Germany only took four months from April to July 1982 to complete the1980 provincial PIOT of 153 products and the MIOT of 27 sectors.

The Economy Research Institute under the Planning Commission of Henan Province, in support of the Mathematics Institute and Energy Institute of the

Table 5.1 Compilation of Regional I-O Table in China

Region	Start and end times	Reporting year	Classification of products	Classification of sectors
Shanxi	May 1980 – Apr. 1982	1979	88	56
Heilongjiang	Nov. 1981 – Jan. 1983	1981	115	78
Beijing	Feb. 1982 – Jun.1982	1980	46	
Guangdong	Apr. 1982 – Jul. 1982	1980	153	27
Henan	Apr. 1982 – present	1982	123	78
Shanghai	May 1982 – Dec.1982	1981	197	
Tianjin	May 1983 – present	1982	198	81

Science and Technology Commission of Henan Province, Henan College of Finance and Economics, Department of Mathematics at Zhengzhou University, and the Dispatching Station of Electricity Bureau of Henan Province, started to compile the 1982 province-level PIOT of 123 products and the MIOT of 78 sectors in April 1982. It expected to finish by February 1984.

The Shanghai Bureau of Statistics, in support of the Sectional Economy Research Institute at Shanghai Academy of Social Sciences, Fudan University, Shanghai Jiao Tong University and Shanghai Commercial School, started training staff and undertook a comprehensive investigation beginning in May 1982. It took six months to complete the 1981 municipal PIOT of 197 products in December 1982.

The Planning Commission of Tianjin, in support of the Tianjin Bureau of Statistics, Tianjin Finance Bureau, Tianjin Bureau of Commodity Price, Nankai University, Tianjin University and Tianjin Institute of Finance and Economics, compiled its 1982 PIOT of 198 products and MIOT of 81 sectors. It was well underway in May 1983 and was expected to be completed in early 1984.

The detailed compilation of information in the I-O table in these seven provinces and cities are provided in Table 5.1.

Some provinces, autonomous regions and municipalities are currently preparing for compiling their regional I-O tables. Hebei Province has finished the trial in Handan city. Jilin Province selected several enterprises for trials.

Since the Third Plenary Session of the 11th CPC Central Committee, it was by no means accidental that the application of the I-O approach has been promoted rapidly at the regional level in China. The promotion and application of the I-O approach at the regional level has become both urgently necessary and increasingly feasible in practice.

2. *Necessity of promotion and application of I-O approach at the regional level*

The necessity of promotion and application of the I-O approach at the regional level is mainly drawn from the following factors.

From the perspective of developing productivity, first, there is an imperative need to promote and apply the I-O approach at the regional level in order to give full play to regional advantages and construct socialist modernization.

The Third Plenary Session of the 11th CPC Central Committee made a historically significant decision that the Party and the Chinese government should shift their focus to the construction of socialist modernization. It is crucial for us to stick to the laws of economy in order to accelerate socialist modernization construction and rapidly promote and develop social productivity. This is what Marx pointed out, "economy of time, along with the planned distribution of labor time among the various branches of production, remains the first economic law on the basis of communal production" (1939/1973, p. 173).[1] Marx's view embraces two extended meanings. The so-called time saving refers to using less labor (i.e. the time spent by living labor) and material (i.e. the time spent on materialized labor) to generate more products that can meet the social needs in many areas. The other is to distribute the total labor force between different production sectors through appropriate plans. In order to meet the requirement for saving time, it is essential to investigate which sectors in which regions request more labor force as well as which sectors in which regions request less labor force in China. This is an issue of the distribution of production. Each region has its own distinct sectors originating in different conditions of natural resources, social and historical backgrounds and levels of economic development. The distinct sector is one which uses less labor force and material resources to generate more products that can meet social needs in comparison with sectors in other regions or with the average level of sectors in other regions. By contrast, there are some sectors that rely on input of much more human power and material resources to obtain a certain amount of products. The former represents the advantageous sector of the region and the latter signifies the disadvantageous sector of the region. If every region can effectively, fully and appropriately give play to its own advantages in considering the national interests, it will be possible to accelerate the socialist modernization of China by following the laws of economy. The I-O approach plays a special role in analyzing the consumption structure of input and the distribution structure of output in each sector and in analyzing comparative economic effect in detail so as to determine which are the advantageous sectors and which are the disadvantageous sectors of regions. From this viewpoint, the I-O approach should be promoted and applied extensively at the regional level with the development and construction of socialist modernization and with the promotion of the prominent role of regional advantages.

From the perspective of transformation in production relations and superstructure, second, it is imperative to promote and apply the I-O approach at the regional level in line with the improvement of economic management and the expansion of autonomy of local governments.

The four modernizations is a great revolution. Since its goal is to transform the present backward state of our productive forces, it inevitably entails many changes in the relations of production, the superstructure and the forms of management in industrial and agricultural enterprises. They must be given greater powers of decision in economic planning, finance and foreign trade – always within the framework of a nationwide unity of views, policies, planning, guidance and action (*Selected Works of Deng Xiaoping,* 1984).[2] There are a total of 30 provinces, municipalities and autonomous regions (including Taiwan) in China. A medium-sized province is equivalent to a big country in Europe. Determined by China's geographical conditions, it is necessary to establish a multilayered management system – from the central government to local authorities, from the central government to industrial sectors and from the central government to enterprises – for the planned economy. This system must fit in with the needs of modernized production and distribute labor force in a reasonable and planned way. The government's role in socialist economies is greater than that in capitalist countries. With the greater autonomy, the local government can not only consider how to give play to its own regional advantages, but also cares about the comprehensive balance of regional economy and takes into account regional production, construction and residents' life. Collaboration and communication within and outside regions should also be encouraged. The advantageous sectors of a region can be classified as the first category and some of them may be the second category. In terms of economic sectors, they can also be grouped into heavy industrial, agricultural and light industrial sectors. Local governments should pay attention to local advantages, foster strengths and circumvent weaknesses and be concerned about adjusting the proportional relationship between the material production sector and the consumer goods production sector and between agriculture, light industry and heavy industry in making economic plans and arranging finance. Among these principles, it is particularly important to constantly improve and raise the living standard and cultural engagement of residents on the basis of continuous development of production based on the requirements of socialist economic law. As far as a particular region is concerned, there are special requirements for coordinating the proportional relationship between the material production sector and the consumer goods production sector and between agriculture, light industry and heavy industry. Coordination of the proportional relationship has implications for the distribution of finished products. As to production, it is not necessary to keep self-balance within a region between material production and consumer goods production and between agriculture, light industry and heavy industry. It is not necessary to seek and establish a fully independent economic system within a region by "asking for no help from others". The I-O approach can explain through qualitative study and quantitatively can analyze complicated issues such as how various regions adjust their economic structures in the light of reality, what proportional relationship between production sectors should be created, what type of balance should be established in the distribution structure, and how planned imports and exports and collaboration in special products with other regions should be properly arranged. The application of the I-O approach can reveal these complicated connections, which may have direct or indirect economic and technologic implications, between economic sectors within a region and between regions, and further provide scientific evidence for a comprehensive balance of local economies. There is no doubt that the application of the I-O approach at the regional level will surely be developed swiftly with the further reforms of the economic management system and the expansion of autonomy of local governments.

Finally, with respect to planning and statistics, it is imperative to continuously improve the regional level of economic plans and statistics and to base the medium- and long-term schemes of regional development on scientific evidence.

The 12th National Congress of the CPC has set a grand strategy to quadruple the annual gross output value of industry and agriculture at the end of the 20th century with a continuous improvement of economic effect. Under this country-wide goal, at what level should the annual gross output value of industry and agriculture in a region and in a sector be appropriate? In the course of working towards this objective, local governments should make their best effort on the one hand and act according to their actual capabilities on the other hand. The question is how their "capabilities" can be assessed. To answer this question, we must make an appropriate prediction for future development through scientific methods apart from conducting a proper analysis of local history and making reasonable arrangements according to local situations. This requires us to draw up regional plans and provide accurate statistics on a scientific basis. The I-O approach can play a role in this regard. In particular, it helps to establish the dynamic I-O model for a region, combining the I-O approach with other economic mathematics methods, and setting adjustment and development plans for various sectors by making use of related statistical data with the aid of electronic digital computers. Its results can be consulted by policy-makers. It is bound to promote the application of the I-O approach at the local level with the increasing need for regional plans and statistics.

3. Feasibility of promotion and application of the I-O approach at the regional level

The promotion and application of the I-O approach at the regional level are both urgently necessary and increasingly feasible in practice nowadays.

First of all, the promotion and application of the I-O approach are appreciated and prominently supported by governments at all levels. As advocated by the Central Committee of the CPC, we must learn to manage the economy by economic means. If we ourselves don't know about advanced methods of management, we should learn from those who do, either at home or abroad. Only by learning well can we better guide and proceed with construction of socialist modernization at a high speed and at a high level (*Deng Xiaoping Speeches and Writings*, 1987).[3] Comrade Deng Xiaoping also pointed out, "pending the introduction of a unified national programme of modern management, we can begin with limited spheres, say, a particular region or a given trade, and then spread the methods gradually to others" (1987, p. 71).[4] Deng Xiaoping's instruction points at a right direction under the guidance of Marxism and encourages all parties involved to apply the I-O approach and, where necessary, to make modification and extension during the application. The Party Committee and government of provinces and municipalities, which have already compiled their I-O table, attach great importance and give all-round support in this regard. This is the key way in which the I-O approach can progressively be promoted and applied at the regional level.

Moreover, there are professional personnel for the promotion and application of the I-O approach. In recent years, a vast number of staff workers in planning and statistics in various regions learnt theories of Marxism-Leninism, economics, science and technology, and management skills enthusiastically. Since the I-O approach is closely related to the balance method generally applied to socialist economic plans and statistics, it requires little effort for economists and those in the field to study and apply the I-O approach. Many scientists, researchers and teachers have given lectures and workshops on compiling the I-O balance sheet and learnt precious experiences from practitioners. Such a combination enables the promotion and application of an I-O approach at the regional level to be profoundly based on professional personnel.

Finally, there exists the material condition for the promotion and application of an I-O approach at the regional level. Compilation of the I-O table requires collecting a large quantity of data, processing and calculating the data such as determination of direct consumption coefficient and complete consumption coefficient, and undertaking economic analysis and forecast through economic models. It is inconceivable to handle all these tasks through a simple manual abacus but rather can be accomplished with modern computers. Various regions in China have set up many electronic computer stations or computation centers successively in recent years, which provide a necessary material condition for the promotion and application of the I-O approach at the regional level.

II   Compilation of the I-O table in various regions

Seven provinces have accumulated rich experiences in compiling the I-O table. In establishing objectives, classifying sectors, selecting compilation methods and collecting data, these provinces have also demonstrated different characteristics besides their common experiences.

1.   Establishment of objectives and classification of sectors

To set the objective of compiling the I-O table is to determine the main issues that the regional I-O table is to focus on and attempts to solve. It is both the starting point and end-point of compilation and is directly related to the selection of sectors, classification of products and size of the table. The objective of compiling the regional I-O table is determined by local history, characteristics and trend of economic development. Selection of sectors and classification of products should fit the objective.

The objective of compiling the I-O table established by Shanxi Province was to serve construction of an energy and heavy chemical industries base. It aimed to solve three issues specifically: (1) the appropriate development pace and scale of coal, electric power and heavy chemical industries; (2) cooperation of other sectors and transportation with the development of energy and heavy chemical industries; and (3) improvement of residents' lives in urban and rural areas, culture, education, scientific research and health. Initially the PIOT was designed to contain 61 products and the MIOT to contain 41 sectors. When the above-mentioned objective was defined, the sectors and products relating to coal mining, comprehensive utilization of coal, and people's material and cultural lives were added to both tables. In the end the PIOT was expanded to contain 88 products and the MIOT to contain 56 sectors, which well reflected the objective.

The objective of Heilongjiang Province in compiling the I-O table was mainly to serve as an adjustment of the local economic structure. In classifying sectors, first, they highlighted the sectors with a local advantage such as grain, timber, oil industry and coal mining – the four backbones of the provincial industry. In the PIOT, they separately listed the products with special economic value such as soybeans, sugar, beets and flax. Furthermore, they highlighted the sectors that require further development in the future. For example, nitrogen and phosphate were separately categorized in fertilizer due to the severe phosphorus deficiency in the province. Finally, they highlighted the sectors in which some raw materials and/or products had to be imported from or exported to other provinces. For example, the rubber processing and textile industry were well developed in Heilongjiang, but their raw materials such as rubber and cotton all relied on imports from other provinces. Large machinery equipment and mechanical and electrical products produced in Heilongjiang were mainly exported to other provinces. To expose the import and export of various products between regions is another advantage offered by the I-O table.

The objective set by the Beijing College of Economics was to study the way in which the demand for lives of urban and rural residents can be met through compiling the PIOT. In view of this objective, the supply of pork, eggs, milk, chicken, duck, nuts, candy and pastry among food items was separately categorized in addition to grain, vegetable and cooking oil.

The objective of compiling the Guangdong provincial I-O table was to predict the pace of economic development from 1981 to 2000 and the demand for energy at this speed; it served as a means to draw up and select an optimal energy supply scheme. In compiling the I-O table, the energy industry was subdivided into various types of energy products. In so doing, the overall demand for a variety of energy products is simultaneously predicted with the calculation of the total demand for economic growth in Guangdong Province.

The objective of compiling the Henan provincial I-O table was like the Heilongjiang Province's, that was mainly to deal with the issues of the structural adjustment of the provincial economy. In classifying sectors, first, they highlighted the sectors with local advantage. For example, they subdivided the tobacco industry into flue-cured tobacco production and cigarette production and the textile industry into six subsectors of fiber elementary processing, cotton spinning, wool spinning, hemp, silk spinning and knitting. What is more, they highlighted the sectors that show great promise in future, such as oil drilling, petrochemicals and planting of jute and kenaf fibers. Lastly, they underscored the industries of raw material and fuels. Meanwhile, they subdivided the column of newly created value in the provincial MIOT into seven items of depreciation of fixed assets, labor wages, taxation, profits, fees for overhead capital, interest expenses and other newly created value in order to investigate in-depth the issues like redistribution of national income, financial revenue and expenditure and formation of monetary purchasing power.

Shanghai is the largest industrial city in China with a solid industrial base characterized by comprehensive economic sectors, a combination of large, medium-sized and small enterprises, good conditions for adjustment, and relatively advanced scientific and technological progress. Shanghai's I-O table was compiled mainly to deal with such issues as further adjustment of the economic structure so as to promote overall economic growth in Shanghai, the short supply of energy and raw material, renovation and upgrade of obsolete equipment, traffic congestion, short supply of housing and environmental pollution. In effect, their PIOT was rather complex, which highlighted the products that required small transportation volume, little energy consumption, reduced pollution and less use of land in classifying products. The table also drew attention to promoting both the development of fine processed products and the application of high technology.

The compilation of Tianjin's I-O table was aimed at endorsing Tianjin's macroeconomic model and serving its medium and long-term development plans. To meet this objective, the table was drawn complexly – the largest I-O table among those of provinces and municipalities in China – containing a PIOT of 198 products and a MIOT of 81 sectors. They listed a "scrapped old materials" category since many enterprises in Tianjin used scrap material as raw material in production. A "port operation" was also categorized separately to highlight Tianjin as a port city.

2. *Compilation methods and data collection*

Regarding the compilation methods of the I-O table, two approaches are currently used in compiling the I-O table at the regional level. One is to decompose "pure" sectors directly, called the decomposition approach for short. The other is the UV table approach from which the United Nations Statistical Office derives "pure" sectors indirectly, called the derivation approach. Each of these two approaches has its own advantage and involves different ways of collecting data.

There is a need for a large quantity of statistical data to compile a regional I-O table. The statistical data consist of five categories: (1) the total output value classified according to "pure" sectors; (2) the composition of material consumption of intermediate products; (3) the ratio of products produced within a region to those produced in other regions in material consumption; (4) the composition of final products; and (5) the composition of newly created values in the MIOT. Since the principle of the I-O approach is associated with the statistics, accounting and business calculation systems in China on the one hand and is significantly different from these systems on the other hand, we can neither directly use the extant data nor leave them out completely. We need to conduct a new investigation and collect new data and then process these new materials and data through appropriate disintegration, complementation, estimation and calculation together with the extant data.

Shanxi, Heilongjiang and Henan Provinces adopted the decomposition approach. Shanxi Province conducted three investigations to collect data. The first one was a province-wide investigation involving 2,100 publicly-owned, independent accounting industrial enterprises. The purpose of the investigation was to obtain the controlling data of the total industrial output value of "pure" sectors in the whole of Shanxi Province. The investigation lasted for three months. The second investigation focused on 250 enterprises. It aimed to obtain the most crucial flow data of material consumption between various sectors in quadrant I of the I-O table including material consumption decomposed according to "pure" sectors, decomposition of circulation costs, and decomposition of products from the local area and outside the province in terms of material consumption. The investigation lasted for 11 months. This was one of the most fundamental and crucial steps in the compilation of the I-O table. The third was a special investigation which mainly dealt with the issues on data collection in reference to the use and composition of final products and distribution and redistribution of newly created value. These three investigations were conducted alternately. Similar to Shanxi Province, Heilongjiang and Henan Provinces conducted these three investigations in preparation for the compilation of a province-level I-O table, too.

Guangdong Province and Tianjin municipality adopted the derivation approach by making some improvements to this method. The derivation method was originally applicable only to compile the MIOT. After some degrees of renovation by Guangdong Province, through once-through operation this method could gain monetary I-O coefficient matrix by sectors and physical I-O coefficient matrix by products. Given both different statistical criteria of the value of production output from that of the quantity of production output and different roles of the MIOT from that of PIOT, Tianjin compiled these two tables separately. The mathematical model specifically used in the monetary table was slightly different from that of the United Nations due to the addition of the scrap materials sector. In compiling the physical table, Tianjin redesigned the table based on the United Nations method. There is no scrap materials sector in the physical table, in which table U and table V are square. The derivation approach can make full use of the extant statistical data and hence requires less input of human resources and saves time. Guangdong Province only used 20 members of staff in a month to complete the compilation. Tianjin plans to spend two months to finish the investigation and data collection.

III   Application and issues of the I-O approach at the regional level

1.   *Application of the I-O approach at the regional level in China*

It was gratifying that seven provinces and cities carried through the compilation work, accounting for 24% of 29 provinces, municipalities and autonomous regions (excluding Taiwan) within three years from May 1980 when Shanxi Province started a full investigation for the compilation of the I-O table until May1983 when Tianjin carried out its compilation. Various regions have applied the I-O approach extensively. I shall concentrate on the compilations of Shanxi, Beijing and Guangdong and take them for examples to illustrate the application of the I-O approach at the regional level in China.

The application of the I-O approach in Shanxi Province experienced three stages. At the first stage the Shanxi Statistical Bureau undertook comprehensive economic analyses on several occasions by applying the province-level I-O table. These include: (1) analysis of proportional relationship between two major categories – material production and consumer goods production; (2) analysis of the proportional relationship between industry and agriculture, between agriculture, light industry and heavy industry, and between light industry and heavy industry; (3) analysis of the proportional relationship between accumulation and consumption; (4) analysis of the proportional relationship between accumulation, consumption and two major categories – material production and consumer goods production; (5) analysis of the proportional relationship between economic sectors; (6) analysis of the proportional relationship of social products distribution; (7) analysis of direct and indirect connections between material production sectors; (8) analysis of the economic relations between provinces; and (9) analysis of the macroeconomic effects of Shanxi Province including the consumption effect of materialized labor, consumption effect of living labor, inclusive consumption effect of materialized labor and living labor. At the second stage the Shanxi planning department made economic forecasts by applying the I-O approach and examined the Sixth Five-year Plan of Shanxi Province. These provided evidence for drawing up the province-level Seventh Five-year Plan and long-term program at the end of the 20th century and served in developing Shanxi Province into the national base of energy and heavy chemical industries. By applying the physical I-O Model, dynamic I-O Model, comprehensive economic model that combined the I-O model and Econometric Model, and the Optimization Model in I-O analysis, they calculated several programs on the scale of coal mining development, the corresponding development of various sectors and the lives of urban and rural residents. These programs were used to be mutually verified and complemented for decision-making and, as an outcome, to lead the planning of Shanxi Province to a new level. At the last stage various professional units, departments and commissions of Shanxi Province acted to guarantee the application of the above-mentioned models and to consolidate and expand it through holding a range of seminars on quantitative economics, including the I-O approach, and training professionals extensively. This laid a solid foundation for further promoting and applying scientific methods in economic management.

Through applying the 1980 Beijing PIOT, the Beijing College of Economics concentrated on the lives of urban and rural residents, and examined the current economic situation and predicted its future trend in three aspects: (1) food – as regards the Beijing's agricultural structure in 1980, cereal crops accounted for 83.5%, while vegetables made up 7.8% and cash crops 5% only in the crop sowing area of rural Beijing. This planting structure was extremely unsuitable for the capital city of China with an urban population of millions. It was an urgent task to develop a diversified agricultural economy and build the rural area of Beijing into the base of farm and sideline products; (2) clothes – so far as production and markets of pure cotton cloth and chemical fabric, Beijing imported a large quantity of cotton from other parts of China every year as planned and, at the same time, exported chemical fiber raw material to other regions as planned, which aggravated the transportation congestion. Obviously, Beijing should make full use of the advantage with abundant chemical fiber raw materials by increasing production of chemical fabric, improving quality, reducing costs, enriching designs and specifications, and expanding domestic and international sales. Beijing should reduce the planned import of cotton and production of pure cotton cloth simultaneously. In combining the linear programming method, researchers calculated the optimal production program of three products – pure cotton cloth, pure chemical fabric and woolen cloth – in 1984. Based on the calculation, they drew the conclusion that pure chemical fabric production needed to increase two times, pure cotton cloth production to reduce by 27%, and woolen cloth production to remain unchanged. This conclusion matched the preceding analysis; (3) energy – turning to crude coal production and usage, anthracite is the principal category of coal used in daily life of Beijing residents. Coal used in industry mainly relies on planned imports from other parts of China. According to the prediction of households' coal consumption, it is far from sufficient to merely increase crude coal output by Beijing itself in line with the estimated demand for crude coal in 1985. The most important measure is, in addition to an increase in planned imports properly, to reduce coal consumption; especially, there is great potential in reducing coal consumption of industrial sectors. Researchers pointed out that a large quantity of coal consumption by heavy industry in Beijing not only aggravated the short supply in coal, but also brought severe pollution to Beijing and affected everyday life of residents. It was absolutely right that the central government tended to control a further development of heavy industry in Beijing.

Guangdong Province combined the I-O approach with regression analysis and the conventional planning method and made a prediction for its macroeconomic development and demand for energy for the next 20 years. They took six steps to complete this task. In the first step, they applied the 1980 provincial I-O table to analyze technical and economic relations between various sectors and between various products and to determine matrix A of the direct consumption coefficient of input and output. In the second step, they adopted the regression analysis to investigate the economic situations from 1970 to 1980 in Guangdong Province and extrapolate final demand vector Y_1 of various stages from 1981 to 2000. In the third step, they adopted the conventional planning method to calculate final demand vector Y_2 in each period according to the initially planned economic development level in 2000.In the fourth step, they compared final demand vector Y_1 with final demand vector Y_2 and made a mutual correction to determine final demand vector Y. In the fifth step, they applied the I-O Model to predict total demand vector X $[X = Y(I-A)-{}^1Y]$ including the total demand for various energy products. In the sixth step, they took the energy demand as an exogenous variable and input it into the Markal Energy Supply Model to calculate various schemes of energy supply.

These exercises illustrate that the I-O approach has become a powerful means of improving the level of modernizing economic management, planning, forecasting and decision-making at the regional level of China.

2.   Challenges to the promotion and application of the I-O approach at the regional level

First of all, the regions that have not yet compiled the I-O table should actively create conditions and carry out its compilation as soon as possible. The compilation of a region-level I-O table is the prerequisite of compiling the national I-O table. It will be a less arduous task to compile and improve the national I-O table if all the provinces, municipalities and autonomous regions have completed their own regional tables. In the past provinces and cities lacked ready-made experience and had to learn a great deal in compiling the I-O table. Now some provinces and cities have accumulated valuable experience carrying out this work. Other provinces and cities can learn from them and avoid problems in carrying out their compilation and to achieve improved effects.

Moreover, the regions that have already compiled the I-O table should make full use of the table and carry out extensive empirical research in application of the table. At present the compilation of the I-O table focuses on the structure of material production sectors, which is related to the very features of the I-O table. It is a drawback that the original I-O table is unable to examine important issues like the distribution and redistribution of national income, comprehensive finance, balance between input and output in non-material production sectors and balance between purchasing power and availability of commodity. We need to renovate the table and expand its functions. Some regions have already attempted this and some are preparing for this accordingly. There is much to do in combining the I-O approach with other quantitative analyses of economics such as econometric analysis, systematic analysis and optimization analysis.

Furthermore, there are many issues in regards to standardization and institutionalization of compilation, combination between the physical table and monetary table, and diversification of compilation methods based on local characteristics and realities in China.

Last but not least, we need to gain insight into specific issues in compiling the I-O table. For example, various regions have collaborated extensively since implementing the policy of revitalizing the economy. How should the output value and production yield be recorded if one region invests or dispatches labor force to another region? The sectors such as railway, highway, and post and telecommunications operate nationally as a unified network while the compilation of the region-level I-O table takes the administrative region as the boundary. In this case, how should labor income therein be calculated? There are some more issues concerned with data collection, processing, and conversion that require further research.

(Originally published in *Application of Input-Output Approach in China*, People's Publishing House of Shanxi, 1984)

Notes

1 Marx, K. (1973). *Grundrisse: Foundations of the critique of political economy (rough draft)*. (p.173). M. Nicolaus (Trans.). London: Penguin Books. (Original work published 1939).
2 *Selected works of Deng Xiaoping*. (1984). (1st ed., Vol. 2, pp.146, 157, 164) Beijing: Foreign Languages Press. The Bureau for the Compilation and Translation of Works of Mars, Engels, Lenin and Stalin Under the Central Committee of the Communist Party of China (Trans.). Beijing: Foreign Languages Press.
3 *Deng Xiaoping speeches and writings*. (1987). (2nd ed., p.71). Oxford, England: Pergamon Press.
4 *Deng Xiaoping speeches and writings*. (1987). (2nd ed., p.71). Oxford, England: Pergamon Press.

6 Preliminary study of the periodicity of fixed assets investment in China

The scale of fixed assets investment has been frequently beyond control over the past 30 years in China. Although the extents and rationales are different from time to time, it is harmful to economic stability and adjustment.Under an in-depth economic reform with a focus on cities at present, it is extremely important to understand and respect the regularity of fixed assets investment and effectively control its scale so as to maintain sound economic development, to carry out the reforms smoothly and to promote the economic development and construction with mutual benefit.

Does fixed assets investment in China have periodicity? If it does, what characteristics are there? What are the causes for periodicity? How can we identify periodicity in order to control the scale of investment and development of the national economy? These issues have not been fully investigated in the cycle of economic studies in China. This article attempts to preliminarily explore these issues.

I Periodicity and characteristics of fixed assets investment in China

The statistics of the total fixed assets investment (within the economic organization with public ownership)[1] and its growth rates from 1952 to 1984 in China are provided in Table 6.1. The growth rates are also displayed through the growth curve of fixed assets investment fluctuation in Figure 6.1. It is revealed from the column of growth rate in Table 6.1 and the growth curve in Figure 6.1 that the fixed assets investment grew every three or four years (positive sign) and then fell for one or two years (negative sign) over the past 32 years in China. This exhibits an obvious periodicity.

The periodicity of fixed assets investment shows some interesting features.

First, the duration of each cycle generally lasts for 4 to 5 years. One cycle commences with an increase of total fixed assets investment from the previous year's and ends with a decrease of total fixed assets investment from the previous year's. The investment growth rate is upward in the former case and downward in the latter case. The fixed assets investment in China has gone through seven cycles over the past 32 years.

Table 6.1 Total fixed assets investment and growth in China

Year	Total investment (billion yuan)	Growth rate (%)	Serial Number of Cycle
1952	4.356	+85.68	
1953	9.159	+110.26	
1954	10.268	+12.11	
1955	10.524	+2.49	1
1956	16.084	+52.83	
1957	15.123	−5.97	
1958	27.906	+84.53	
1959	36.802	+31.88	
1960	41.658	+13.19	2
1961	15.606	−62.54	
1962	8.728	−44.07	
1963	11.666	+33.66	
1964	16.589	+42.20	
1965	21.69	+30.75	3
1966	25.48	+17.47	
1967	18.772	−26.33	
1968	15.157	−19.26	
1969	24.692	+62.91	
1970	36.808	+49.07	4
1971	41.731	+13.37	
1972	41.281	−1.08	
1973	43.812	+6.13	
1974	46.319	+5.72	5
1975	54.494	+17.65	
1976	52.394	−3.85	
1977	54.83	+4.65	
1978	66.872	+21.96	
1979	69.936	+4.58	6
1980	74.59	+6.65	
1981	66.751	−10.51	
1982	84.531	+26.64	
1983	95.196	+12.62	7
1984	116.00	+21.85	

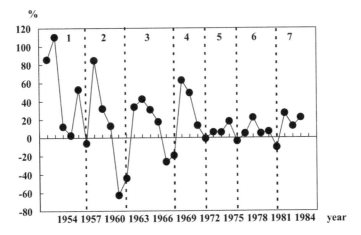

Figure 6.1 Growth curve of fixed assets investment fluctuation in China

The first cycle: from 1953 to 1957, lasting for 5 years;
The second cycle: from 1958 to 1962, lasting for 5 years;
The third cycle: from 1963 to 1968, lasting for 6 years;
The fourth cycle: from 1969 to 1972, lasting for 4 years;
The fifth cycle: from 1973 to 1976, lasting for 4 years;
The sixth cycle: from 1977 to 1981, lasting for 5 years;
The seventh cycle: from 1982 to present (1984), an ongoing cycle already
  lasting for 3 years.

All the complete cycles, except for the third which lasted for six years, extended
for 4–5 years.

Second, the vibration amplitude of fixed assets investment growth in each cycle
gradually tends to be moderate. The vibration amplitude refers to the gap between
the peak point and trough point of each cycle of fixed assets investment. It presents
in the six cycles as follows:

The first cycle: 116.23 (110.26 + 5.97);
The second cycle: 147.07 (84.53 + 62.54);
The third cycle: 68.53 (42.20 + 26.33);
The fourth cycle: 63.99 (62 .91 + 1.08);
The fifth cycle: 21. 50 (17.65 + 3.85);
The sixth cycle: 32.47 (21.96 + 10.51).

Extreme ups and downs in investment have a significant impact on the national
economy. The vibration amplitude of fixed assets investment growth in China
gradually became reduced, which demonstrated that the China's economy has
gradually been on the right track by learning lessons from the past.

Third, those troughs of fixed assets investment growth, which is a negative growth, gradually move upward in each Five-year Plan.Their positions are as follows:

The fifth year (1957) during the First Five-year Plan;
The fourth and fifth years (1961, 1962) during the Second Five-year Plan;
The second and third years (1967, 1968) during the Third Five-year Plan;
The second year (1972) during the Fourth Five-year Plan;
The first year (1976) during the Fifth Five-year Plan;
The first year (1981) during the Sixth Five-year Plan.

This illustrated that in the First Five-year Plan and Second Five-year Plan, massive investment was made in the first few years and the trough came in the end of the period. Contrarily, the trough was at the outset of the Fifth Five-year Plan and Sixth Five-year Plan resulting in difficulties in making an adjustment.

II   Causes for periodicity

After all, we need to explain what has caused the periodicity of fixed assets investment in China. Is it purely a subjective error or objective phenomenon, or is it a bit of both? How is it different from the fixed capital investment cycle and the cyclic economic crisis under a capitalist system?

Under the capitalist system, the cyclic economic crisis leads to periodicity of massive renovation and investment of fixed capital. The latter lays the material foundation of the former. Marx pointed out: "The cycle of interconnected turnovers embracing a number of years, (in which capital is held fast by its fixed constituent part) furnishes a material basis for the periodic crises. During this cycle business undergoes successive periods of depression, medium activity, precipitancy and crisis. True, periods in which capital is invested differ greatly and far from coincide in time. But a crisis always forms the starting-point of large new investments" (1885/2001, pp. 248–249).[2] The periodicity of economic crisis and fixed capital investment is rooted in the contradiction inherent in the capitalist production mode itself, i.e. the contradiction between highly socialized production and private possession of the means of production under capitalism. It is based on the grounds of the relative surplus of capitalist commodity production.

Everything on the earth moves and evolves in a wave-like or imbalanced manner. It is not surprising that fixed assets investment in China rises and falls from the viewpoint of philosophy. Nevertheless, the periodic fluctuation of fixed assets investment in China is different from that under capitalism.

First, China is a socialist country with publicly-owned means of production and, correspondingly, dominance of a planned economy and management. We can control and regulate the scale of fixed assets investment through planned management and various means and measures. The periodicity of fixed assets investment in China is not rooted in the socialist economic system itself.

What is more, China is a developing socialist country. There is no relative surplus of commodity production but rather relative insufficiency in material supply. The main challenge is the contradiction between the increasing demand for material and cultural products and lagging productivity. In fixed assets investment this has been shown as the contradiction between the great demand for massive construction initiatives and insufficient material supply. Massive economic construction is restricted by several sets of proportional relationships. One of the proportional relationships is between agriculture, light industry and heavy industry. Fixed assets investment must be guaranteed by the supply of the means of production mainly through heavy industry. Massive investment requires a rapid expansion of heavy industry. On the other hand, if this expansion is proved to be so rushed that it exceeds China's economic capacity, it has to squeeze the growth of agriculture and light industry and leads to a disproportional relationship between these sectors. Another proportional relationship is between accumulation and consumption. Most fixed assets investment comes from available shares of national income savings. The total national income is fixed in a certain period of time. A massive amount of accumulation in national income often leads to low-level consumption including both individual consumption and social consumption. When investment is oversized, the accumulation rate is overrated and reduction in consumption is excessive, causing an imbalance between accumulation and consumption. The last proportional relationship is between construction and production. Fixed assets investment in economic construction ties up labor force, material resources and finance in a relatively long period of time and consequently affects effective supplies for production. If construction consumes material resources excessively, it will affect the routine and scale of production, intensify the existing short supply in energy, transportation and raw materials, and lead to disproportional relationship between construction and production. Since the founding of the PRC, it has been inevitable to engage in massive economic construction in order to build China into a wealthy and powerful nation from a fragile economy. With each expansion of investment, however, the insufficient material supply has become increasingly noticeable and gradually caused a severe imbalance between the major sectors of the national economy and brought tension and chaos to socio-economic well-being. For this reason we need to make a range of adjustments, through which the major proportional relationships of the national economy become more appropriate. It is more frequent than rare that a new round of massive investment starts and consequently a new contradiction between construction and production follows. From this perspective, the periodicity of fixed assets investment in China is beyond our control to a certain extent.

Finally, China is a developing socialist country and the socialist system itself still moves forward with improvement without adequate experience in economic management. We should keep a clear mind, avoid a premature growth, effectively control the macroeconomy and avoid having the economy going up and down when engaging massive investment. In the past we did not do well in this regards.

The unnecessary violation in the periodic fixed assets investment in China can to some extent be attributed to subjective errors.

III   Getting control of the periodicity of fixed assets investment

China is now in the process of economic reforms with a focus on urban areas. This will surely bring changes to the economy and further affect the periodicity of fixed assets investment. Facing changed situations, we need to continuously study and explore its characteristics and patterns in order to improve our understanding of the changes of investment periodicity.

On the whole, the preceding periodicity of fixed assets investment with one cycle lasting for four or five years in China will not change at a stroke and may continue for a while. This is because we have to continue massive investment in order to achieve the magnificent development objective of the national economy by the end of the 20th century. Although we have gone through several Five-year Plans, massive investment is still restricted by the major proportional relationships of the national economy as insufficient supply for material cannot be solved at one go. There is still a long way to go to give play to various economic means and leverages and to implement effective adjustment and restructuring of the national economy during the economic reforms with a focus on urban areas.

Provided that there are no major changes in the next few years, the trough year of fixed assets investment will predictably emerge in 1986 and 1991 or so in view of the previous patterns. This is just a sketchy forecast. As long as we understand and get control of the periodicity of fixed assets investment, we could reduce errors in the investment periodicity, enhance consciousness and initiative so as to control and make use of the periodicity to serve our aims. In particular, we should draw attention to the following aspects: (1) when the investment growth rate rises from the previous year, we should not increase the rate too hastily so as to miss opportunities of sustainable growth; (2) during the rise of investment growth each time, we should leave plenty of leeway and tend not to encourage the peak of investment too steep so as to reduce vibration amplitude and extend the duration of the investment cycle; (3) when the investment growth rate becomes negative marked by the trough year or reduction of investment from the previous year, we should reduce the scale of investment in time and deliberately let investment decline; (4) in the trough year, it is crucial to effectively control and adjust investment without a hasty reduction in investment at one go. It is also important to prevent an excessive descent of the trough and to cut the adjustment period as short as possible; and (5) we should promote reforms of the economic system and management, improve the scientific level of economic planning, management, prediction and decision-making, give full play to various means and economic leverages, and realize effective regulation and control over the macroeconomy.

(Originally published in *Economic Research Journal*, No.2,1986.)

Notes

1 The data from 1952 to 1983 are taken from *China Statistical Yearbook, 1984* (*China statistical yearbook, 1984*. (1984). (p.301). Beijing: China Statistics Press.). The 1984 data are extracted from *1984 Bulletin of Statistics for National Economic and Social Development of the State Statistical Bureau of People's Republic of China* (1985, Mar.10. *The People's Daily*). All are calculated according to current-year prices.
2 Marx, K. (2001). *Capital: A critique of political economy, the process of circulation of capital.* (Vol. 2, pp.248–249). S. Moore & E. Aveling (Trans.). London: Electric Book Co. (Original work published 1885).

7   Re-study on the periodicity of fixed assets investment in China

An analysis of its stages

It is vital to understand and seize the regular pattern of fixed assets investment in order to carry out the economic reforms further. In the article "Preliminary Study on Periodicity of Fixed Assets Investment in China", (1986)[1] I have preliminarily investigated the periodicity of fixed assets investment in China and its main characteristics and triggers. This article intends to analyze various stages within a cycle of fixed assets investment in order to understand the characteristics and causes of periodicity in detail. This will enable us to take the initiative in control of the scale of investment so as to promote economic reforms and develop China's economy.

I   The stages of the investment cycle

China has gone through seven investment cycles altogether during the 33 years from 1953 to 1985 (see Figure 7.1)[2] in view of the changes favorable or unfavorable to the growth of total fixed assets investment in all economic organizations of public ownership each year. Each cycle generally includes four stages: recovery, peak, continual growth with a reduced pace and trough. In detail, four patterns can be extracted from these seven cycles.

Pattern I (see Figure 7.2 a): the recovery stage of investment goes first, and then the peak stage is followed by continual growth. Although investment continuously increases at the third stage, the growth rate has declined. At last it is at trough stage. The two cycles, respectively from 1963 to 1968 and from 1977 to 1981, fell into this pattern.

Pattern II (see Figure 7.2 b): investment goes from the trough stage directly into the peak stage and the recovery and peak unite into one stage. The two cycles, from 1958 to 1962 and from 1962 to 1972, fell into this pattern.

Pattern III (see Figure 7.2 c): the recovery stage of investment lasts slightly longer. Investment goes from the peak stage directly into the trough stage. There is no continual growth stage after the peak stage. The cycle from 1973 to 1976 fell into this pattern.

Pattern IV (see Figure 7.2 d): there are twin peaks within the cycle. The two cycles, from 1953 to 1957 and from 1982 to 1985 (that has yet completed), fell into this pattern.

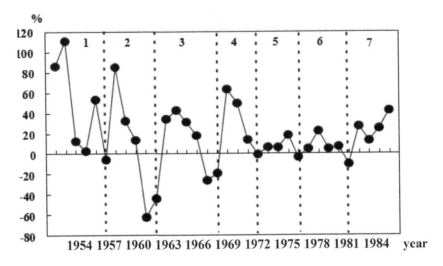

Figure 7.1 Fluctuation curve of fixed assets investment growth in China

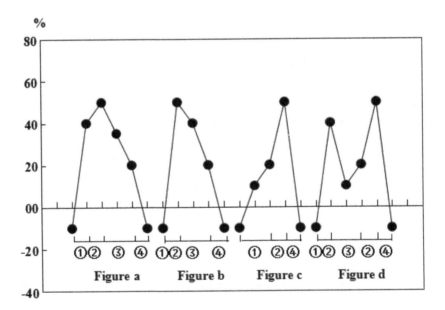

Figure 7.2 Sample curves of fixed assets investment in each stage within a cycle

It is evident that these four patterns display different characteristics from one another under different backgrounds. However, it is also clear that these patterns have some similarities. In the subsequent analysis we shall focus on pattern I and consider its implications for the other three patterns accordingly.

1. The recovery stage

At the recovery stage various influences begin to emerge altogether.

From the perspective of interaction between investment and production, investment begins to increase driving production to grow. At this point, the idle production capacity and the production potential begin to bring into being and develop at the trough stage, and investment gradually drives production to expand from industrial goods (e.g. raw materials and machinery) to consumer goods. Expansion of production in turn promotes investment by inputting an increasing amount of investment into the sectors and firms without idle production capacity or without effective transformation of production capacity, leading to a greater growth in investment. This situation, sculptured by the interaction between investment and production, is often described as "the excellent situation which becomes better and better".

From the perspective of policy-makers at all levels, all are optimistic for gradually improved situations. Decision makers of macroeconomic policies satisfy with the proportional relationship between the major sectors of national economy and economic capacities to expand investment and production. They thus feel much more confident to approve investment projects. Decision makers of economic organizations regard it as the "golden opportunity" to complete construction projects and increase investment. This behavior stems from the "soft financial constraint" under the old system which is characterized by the 'egalitarian practice of everyone taking food from the same big pot' in financial management and lack of political, economic and legal responsibilities for the use of investment. Some canceled and suspended projects at the trough stage are suddenly reinstated. Consequently, investment gets increasingly expanded. This is the cause for pattern II of investment cycle (Figure 7.2 b) where investment goes from the trough stage directly into the peak stage and the recovery and peak unite into one stage.

2. The peak stage

At the peak stage various influences rise to push investment growth to the peak.

From the perspective of interaction between investment and production, the idle production capacity and production potential are made full use of and brought into full play when impelling investment from the recovery stage to the peak stage. Production speedily develops and reaches the upper limit of production capacity. For example, the growth rate of heavy industry (according to comparable price) was as high as 36.9% in 1953, 39.7% in 1956, 78.8% in 1958, 21% in 1964, 43.9% in 1969, 16.8% in 1975, 15.6% in 1978, 9.9% in 1982 and 17.9% in 1985, respectively, among the nine peak years. Except for 1982, the remaining eight years were also the peak years in which heavy industry developed rapidly. As various idle production capacity and production potential are made full use of and brought into full play, investment in expanding production accordingly slows down. Meanwhile, promoting investment through production expansion drives investment to the peak, exceeding the upper limit of production capacity and corresponding supply of material.

From the perspective of policy-makers at all levels, all are filled with exultation and regard it as the best time to push investment to the peak. Decision makers of macroeconomic policies are most likely to emphasize the pace of investment growth as it can indeed surge at this stage. This in turn increases the pace of investment growth. Decision makers of economic organizations regard it as the best time in which they can fully display their talents and effortlessly achieve expected outcomes. They thus arrange production at full capacity and carry out economic initiatives ambitiously, involving expansion in investment, production and employees' welfare. A great number of unplanned projects squeeze in. All these factors press the scale of investment to the peak.

3.   The continual growth stage

At the continual growth stage, various influences begin to drag down the pace of investment growth.

From the perspective of interaction between investment and production, the investment growth begins to slow down and is constrained by the material base since investment at the peak stage has exceeded the upper limit of production capacity and the subsequent material supply. The slowdown of investment growth curbs the expansion of production. The demands for industrial products such as raw materials, machinery and equipment start to decline successively. Production growth slows down accordingly. A slowdown in production development holds back the function of production expansion in promoting investment, leading to a greater decline in investment. For example, the investment growth declined from 84.53% in the peak in 1958 to 31.88% in 1959 and 13.19% in 1960, both of which were years of continual growth. The investment growth declined from 42.20% in the peak in 1964 to 30.75% in 1965 and 17.47% in 1966, all of which were years of continual growth. The investment growth rate declined from 62.91% in the peak in 1969 to 49.07% in 1970 and 13.37% in 1971, all of which were years of continual growth. The investment growth declined from 21.96% in 1978 and 26.64% in 1982, the two peak years, to 4.58% in 1979 and 12.62% in 1983, the two continual growth years, respectively.

From the perspective of policy-makers at all levels, all remain reasonably optimistic because investment still rises though its growth pace has slowed down. Policy-makers of central and local governments continue to emphasize the growth rate in favor of maintaining a high-speed or over-speed growth than that of the previous year. If this proves impossible, they are moderately happy as long as investment remains growing. They may be aware of over-scaled investment and the need for its cutting-down. But they will hesitate to cut down investment, being afraid of the impact on the growth rate of production and financial revenue. Decision makers of economic organizations still make every effort to push for investment, despite of some difficulties, since the planned expansion of production have been put into operation and towards completion in their last stage. For example, they continue to compete for investment and loans tenaciously and divert circulating funds and renovation and transformation funds into construction projects, or "eat the food stored up for the next year", drawing on indispensable funding and material reserved for future. With an intensified shortage in investment, on the other hand, they may store up some materials that are unnecessarily required for the time being for all contingencies.

4. The trough stage

First, we take a look at the major proportional relationship in the beginning of a trough stage. In order to ensure a rapid development of investment and production, the growth of the means of production usually exceeds that of consumption goods during the period from the recovery stage to the peak stage and then to the continual growth stage. Under the conditions that there are a fragile economic base, low efficiency and long-term shortage in resources in China, the sectors of the means of production often compress the production of consumption goods in a short-term, particularly in the consumption of energy, transportation and raw materials. This has often resulted in a disproportional relationship between these two major sectors, representing an imbalance between agriculture, light and heavy industries. At the same time, the accumulation rate will continuously remain at a relatively high level at the first three stages in order to guarantee an investment growth. This gradually leads to a disproportion between accumulation and consumption. The contradiction between construction and production caused by contesting for resources has become prominent when the production capacity and the corresponding capacity of material supply stretch to the upper limit. Materials tend to be in short supply progressively, which aggravates the unfilled shortage. Now the demand for investment is increasingly greater than the supply of investment and the total social demand exceeds the total supply, causing a prolonged construction period, price rise and financial straits. The socio-economic life is filled with chaos. It has become inevitable to make an appropriate adjustment of the national economy.

If there emerges a pushing force at the continual growth stage after the peak stage, such as indispensable adjustments in the major proportional relationship of the national economy and a policy-driven incentive to production potential, the investment growth may recover. This is the source for the emergence of dual peaks as denoted in pattern IV of the investment cycle (see Figure 7.2 d). However, the investment growth will still enter into the trough stage as it moves when these effects fade away. If the economic development becomes less sustainable after reaching the peak, there will appear no continual growth stage as denoted in pattern III of the investment cycle (see Figure 7.2 c) and investment will go from the peak stage directly to the trough stage.

At the trough stage, various influences move downward to the lowest point. From the perspective of interaction between investment and production, the two forces – investment in promoting production and production in promoting investment – move to mutually trim down. Decrease in production causes greater decline in investment, which makes investment fall to the bottom and exceeds the level of production decline. For example, investment dropped −5.97% in 1957, −62.54% in 1961, −44.07% in 1962, −26.33% in 1967, −19.26% in 1968, −1.08% in 1972, −3.85% in 1976 and −10.51% in 1981, respectively, (at the current-year price) in the eight trough years. The growth rates of heavy industry (according to comparable price) in these eight years were, respectively, 18.4% (that was lower by 21. 3% comparing with 39.7% of the previous year), −46.5%, −22.6%, −20.0%, −5.1%, 7% (which was lower by 14.4% comparing with 21.4% of previous year), and 0.5% (which was lower by16.3% comparing with 16.8% of previous year), and −4.7%.

From the perspective of decision makers at all levels, all are under pressure in this circumstance. The central and local governments oversee the complete picture of the national economy. They have to cut down and adjust the economic plans through various measures, such as tightening finance and credit and strengthening control over the supply of urgently demanded goods. More often than not it is more difficult for decision makers of economic organizations to accept the austerity and rigid measures. They endeavor to complete some construction projects earlier and are reluctant to cut off other projects that require more time to be completed. Although adjustment measures encounter some degree of resistance at the firm level, they are finally put into action under the stress of the economic situation.

Adjustment can stop worsening and gradually improve various proportional relationships at the trough stage. The severe contradiction between the total demand and supply become less intense. Investment growth gradually makes progress entering into the recovery stage. A new round of the investment cycle begins.

II   The investment cycle and economic reforms

China is presently carrying out all-around reforms of its economic system and structure. Can the reforms eliminate the investment periodicity?

In view of the experience of Hungary and Yugoslavia, investment periodicity continues after the economic transformation. By analyzing the data on hand, the investment growth in socialist Hungary experienced three cycles during the 12 years from 1966 to 1977. Each cycle lasted for 3–4 years in general (see Table 7.1). The total fixed investment growth in Yugoslavia presented three cycles during the 22 years from 1959 to1980. Each cycle lasted for 7–8 years (see Table 7.1).

It is clear that there is an inner connection between periodically moving investment and the development of a commodity economy. As pointed out by Marx, the intrinsic unity of commodity use-value and value had obtained their modes of motion of external antithesis of development in circulation (antithesis of commodity and currency, antithesis of supply of physical goods and payable demand, antithesis of sale and purchase). Marx further stated "these modes imply the possibility of crisis".

To say that these two independent and antithetical acts have an intrinsic unity is the same as to say that this intrinsic oneness expresses itself in

an external antithesis. If the interval in time between the two complementary phases of the complete metamorphosis of a commodity become too
great, the intimate connection between them, their oneness, asserts itself
by producing – a crisis.

(Marx, 1867/2001, p. 164)[3]

Marx's illustration implies that with the expansion of commodity economy there
are a split-up of the use-value from the monetary value of commodities and separa-
tion of the use-value of investment (such as material, machinery and equipment)
from the monetary value (capital) of investment as to time and place. This discordance triggers a periodic "crisis" of the capitalist economy. Marx also pointed out
that this "is merely possibility. The conversion of this mere possibility into a reality
is the result of a long series of relations that, from our present standpoint of simple
circulation, have as yet no existence" (p. 164).[4] What Marx called "a long series

Table 7.1 Investment periodicity in Hungary and Yugoslavia

Year	Hungary		Yugoslavia	
	Investment growth rate of socialist economic sector (%)	Duration (year)	Total fixed investment growth rate (%)	Duration (year)
1959			+14.5	
1960			+19.5	7
1961			+11.2	
1962			+6.4	
1963			+8.6	
1964			+15.0	
1965			−9.1	
1966	+10		+4.1	
1967	+22	3	+3.3	
1968	0		+5.6	
1969	+10		+10.7	7
1970	+17	4	+17.0	
1971	+11		+4.6	
1972	−2		+1.8	
1973	+3		+4.2	
1974	+10	4	+9.1	8
1975	+15		+9.7	
1976	0		+8.2	
1977	+13		+11.2	
1978		4	+11.1	8
1979			+9.2	
1980			−2.0	

of relations" refers principally to the production relation of capitalism at that time. Under the condition of socialized production, the interrelation between investment and production should be part of "the long series of relations" due to the massive scale of both investment and production. This inclusion can clearly display the role of investment in expanding production and the role of production in promoting investment as well as the investment periodicity as a genuine existence in the real world. These functions exist in a socialist economy, too. On the other hand, poor planning and human errors will intensify the amplitude of periodic fluctuation under the socialist system.

The economic reform of socialist countries is intended to further advance the planned commodity economy. This has an effect on investment periodicity in two dimensions. On the one hand, it is beneficial to improve the economic management system, give play to the adjustment of economic leverages, raise the scientific level of economic plans, management, prediction and decision-making, and control investment periodicity through the economic reform. On the other hand, the Chinese government has gradually shifted from direct control of enterprises to indirect management with the evolution of a commodity economy. In this circumstance, we need to pay attention particularly to macroeconomic adjustment and control in order to avoid intense investment periodicity.

It is important to mention that investment periodicity provides various conditions for implementing economic reform measures. We should correctly assess different conditions and take their advantages where possible. For example, when the economic situation is improved and the bearing capability in all aspects is rather strong at the recovery and peak stages, we should take this opportunity to implement significant reform measures that require solid support of finance and material. We should consolidate, modify and add new ones to these measures at the continual growth and trough stages. Other reform measures that don't require considerable provision in finance and resources can be carried out at the continual growth and trough stages and give play to their roles at the recovery and peak stages. This will benefit a smooth implementation of economic reforms with minor resistance and greater outcomes.

(Originally published in *Economic Research Journal*. No. 6, 1986)

Notes

1 Preliminary Study on Periodicity of Fixed Assets Investment in China. (1986). *Economic Research Journal*, 2.
2 The annual growth rate is calculated based on the data of the total fixed assets investment using that given year prices. In two aspects the investment growth rate curve drawn up in this article is different from that examined in my article "Preliminary Study on Periodicity of Fixed Assets Investment in China". First, in the investment growth rate curve of this article, I supplement with the 1985 data taken from 1985 *Bulletin of Statistics for National Economic and Social Development of the State Statistical Bureau of People's Republic of China.* (see 1986, March.1, *The People's Daily*). Second, I revise the 1984 data taken from *China Statistical Yearbook, 1985* (*China statistical yearbook, 1985.* (1985). (p.416). Beijing: China Statistics Press).

3 Marx, K. (2001). *Capital: A critique of political economy, the process of production of capital.* (Vol. 1, p.164). S. Moore & E. Aveling (Trans.). London: Electric Book Co. (Original work published 1867).
4 Marx, K. (2001). *Capital: A critique of political economy, the process of production of capital.* (Vol. 1, p.164). S. Moore & E. Aveling (Trans.). London: Electric Book Co. (Original work published 1867).

8 The third study on the periodicity of fixed assets investment in China

A historical analysis of each cycle

Following *Preliminary Study on Periodicity of Fixed Assets Investment in China* (1986)[1] and *Re-study on Periodicity of Fixed Assets Investment in China: Analysis of its Stages* (1986),[2] this article intends to analyze each of the seven cycles one by one during the past 33 years from 1953 to 1985. Through this analysis, we will be able to understand the backgrounds and characteristics of these seven cycles, uncover their common patterns and further comprehend the periodicity of fixed assets investment.

I The first cycle (1953–57)

There were two peaks in the first cycle from 1953 to 1957. The first peak was in 1953 with an increase of the total fixed assets investment of publicly-owned enterprises (same hereinafter) from 4.356 billion yuan in 1952 to 9.159 billion yuan in 1953, a growth rate of 110.26% (calculated based on the current-year prices, same hereinafter). The years 1954 and 1955 were characterized by sustainable growth – a continuous increase of total fixed assets investments, 10.268 billion yuan and 10.524 billion yuan, respectively. But the growth rates dropped down to 12.11% and 2.49%, respectively. The second peak was in 1956 with an increase of total fixed assets investment of 16.084 billion yuan and the growth rate of 52.83%. 1957 was the trough of the cycle with a reduction of total fixed assets investment to 15.123 billion yuan and with a negative growth rate of 5.97%. This cycle lasted for 5 years (see Figure 8.1).

The investment growth with dual peaks in this cycle was first related to construction projects of the first five-year plan. The Chinese government started socialist construction as presented in the economic plans in 1953. A total of 141 Soviet Union-sponsored projects were initiated successively in 1953, and the total number of such projects reached 156 in 1954 when 15 new projects were added in. By 1956 many key projects entered a construction peak. This explained why there were two times of investment upsurges during the cycle.

Moreover, the harvest conditions of crops had a direct impact on the investment fluctuation, which usually lagged behind for one year. There was a good harvest in 1952 with an increase of the total value of agricultural production of 15.2%, a grain yield growth of 14.1% and a cotton growth of 26.5%. Following the harvest,

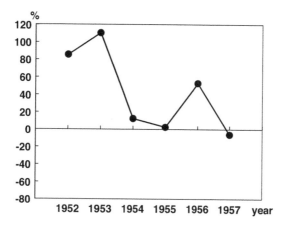

Figure 8.1 The first cycle

investment increased substantially in 1953.There were severe natural disasters, a poor harvest and a surge of town population, 10.86 million, in 1953 and 1954. Consumer goods, especially grains, became short in supply. This caused a slow growth of investment in 1954 and 1955. There was a good harvest in 1955 with a growth of the total value of agricultural production of 7.6%, a grain yield growth of 8.5% and a cotton growth of 42.5%. The amount of investment increased again in 1956. There was a bad year of farming in 1956. Contrary to the slow growth in grain and the reduction in cotton, there was a surge of town population, 9 million, within one year. Consumer goods, like grain, once again became short in supply, and subsequently investment fell in 1957.

Furthermore, the interactions between industrial production and investment had an impact on the investment fluctuation. Investment increased 110.26% in 1953, driving the gross industrial product to grow by 30.3%, in which heavy industry increased 36.9% and light industry increased 26.7% (see Table 8.1). The investment growth rate was calculated according to current-year prices, and the growth rate of the value of industrial output was calculated according to comparable prices. Although both growth rates were not fully comparable, we can perceive some trends without affecting the analysis. In Table 8.1, the growth rate of total value of agricultural production was calculated according to comparable prices as well (same hereinafter). Since investment increased too dramatically and had exceeded the upper limit of the growing capacity of industrial production at that time, the supply of industrial goods and consumption goods tended to be deficient. Subsequently, the investment growth slowed down in 1954 and 1955. The industrial growth also slowed down accordingly. Although the industrial growth rate slowed down, it still exceeded the growth of investment, and there were surplus both in the government revenue and material

Table 8.1 Growth of total fixed assets investment and gross output value of industry and agriculture

Year	Growth of total fixed assets investment	Growth of value of industrial output			Growth of total value of agricultural production
		Gross product	Heavy industry	Light industry	
1952	85.68				
1953	110.26	30.3	36.9	26.7	3.1
1954	12.11	16.3	19.8	14.3	3.4
1955	2.49	5.6	14.5	0.0	7.6
1956	52.83	28.1	39.7	19.7	5.0
1957	−5.97	11.5	18.4	5.7	3.6

Unit: percentage

supply in 1954 and 1955. These laid the material and financial bases for the second investment peak in 1956. Investment increased 52.83% in 1956, driving the total industrial output value to grow by 28.1%, in which heavy industry increased 39.7% and light industry19.7%. But since the growth of investment exceeded the upper limit of industrial capacity, industrial goods became severely in short supply, and the demand in excess of the supply in the light industrial sector was aggravated. There were a financial deficit of 1.83 billion yuan and an imbalance of receipt and payment of credit funds in 1956. The government had to input its financial surplus from the past years excessively and issue an additional amount of currency notes. The national economy was in turmoil, resulting in an extreme shrinkage in the scale of investment in 1957. At the trough of investment fluctuation in 1957, the investment growth was negative. But industrial growth was still positive though its rate was lower than the previous year. This laid the base for the recovering economy in the next cycle.

What is more, the political situation and economic plans had an impact on the investment fluctuation. By the end of 1952, the national economy recovered smoothly with the implementation of a range of economic policies and measures over the three years after the founding of new China. The socialist system had been consolidated and the whole country was stabilized and unified. The victory of the Korean War had created a relatively peaceful international environment for China's development. All these brought about sound conditions domestically and internationally for the emergence of the first investment peak in 1953. There appeared a nationwide upsurge of the Socialist Transformation in agriculture, handicraft production and capitalist industry and commerce at the end of 1955 and in 1956, which vigorously pulled investment to the second peak in 1956. But we were not cautious enough under the favorable conditions – unrealistically setting high targets and acting urgently. In order to speed up and invest more construction projects in 1953, we drew on the financial surplus of the previous year. This brought about immediate difficulties. Especially with the continually supplemented capital construction projects and the fast expansion in the scale of investment in 1956, the output of economic sectors was imbalanced in some regions. The overheated economy and premature policy measures aggravated the fluctuation amplitude of investment growth. Generally speaking, we still lacked experience in the first cycle of fixed assets investment. But we were able to identify the issues timely and deal with them decisively so as to ensure that the first five-year plan completed successfully in various aspects.

II   The second cycle (1958–62)

The fluctuation amplitude in the second cycle of fixed assets investment was the largest. The year 1958 was characterized by both recovery from the first cycle and the peak of the second cycle. The total fixed asset investment shot up from 15.123 billion yuan in 1957 to 27.906 billion yuan in 1958, with an increase of 12.783 billion yuan within one year and a growth rate of 84.53%. The years 1959 and 1960 showed sustaining growth with the total investment of 36.802 billion yuan and 41.658 billion yuan and the growth rates of 31.88% and 13.19%, respectively. Subsequently, the investment of fixed assets in 1961 and 1962 fell into the trough with a total investment of 15.606 billion yuan and 8.728 billion yuan, respectively, and the growth rates of −62.54% and −44.07%, respectively. This cycle also lasted for five years (see Figure 8.2).

The most aggravated fluctuation amplitude of investment growth in this cycle was related to the investment peak in 1958.

First of all, 1958 should be a recovery stage in terms of the rule of investment cycle. After the trough in 1957, the imbalanced and disproportional economic

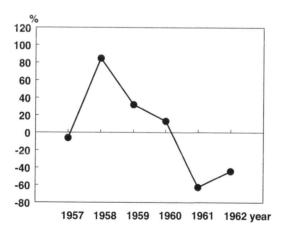

Figure 8.2 The second cycle

relations had been improved through a range of measures. By the end of 1957, 68 key construction projects (out of 135 that were sponsored by the Soviet Union) had been completed or partly completed. Some of them had been put into operation. The Soviet Union totally sponsored 156 key construction projects. Twenty-seven construction projects (out of 64 that were sponsored by the Eastern European socialist countries) had been completed and put into operation. The Eastern European socialist countries totally sponsored 68 construction projects. In addition, some self-funded construction projects had been completed and put into operation. These modern industrial backbone enterprises and overall achievements of the first five-year plan created solid material and technical bases for the second five-year plan starting from 1958. Logically, 1958 was a recovery year for investments and the economic situation should be fairly stable even without the implementation of the Great Leap Forward.

However, seeking short-term benefits by policy-makers, which was oriented by the political situation and economic plans, theatrically provoked the expansion and intensified the fluctuation amplitude of investment. Following the Anti-Rightist Campaign in 1957, the central government initiated the Great Leap Forward and the People's Commune movement in 1958. Being self-complacent to what had been achieved rapidly provoked the rise and spread of the "leftist views", represented by undue haste and premature growth in economic development. This resulted in a high-speed expansion of investment. The planned investment was supplemented several times. At the firm level, enterprises endeavored to raise funds, take up circulating capital, add costs as will, or draw on surplus. All these anthropogenic factors suddenly dragged investment from a routine recovery to a sharp rise, which got away from the common element of investment expansion. In addition, the Anti-Rightist Campaign and Great Leap Forward continued in 1959 and 1960. Suffering from chaos and disturbance for three consecutive years, the overall national economy became disproportional and imbalanced, and investment fell into the trough in 1961 and 1962.

In this cycle the interaction between industrial production and investment and the impact of agriculture on investment were also evident. Investment increased 84.53% in 1958. This caused the total industrial output value to grow by 54.8%, in which heavy industry increased 78.8% and light industry increased 33.7%. The surge of investment exceeded the upper limit of production capacity, rendering a slow growth of investment, and a slow growth of industrial production accordingly, in 1959 and 1960. The overloaded growth for three consecutive years from 1958 to 1960 sapped the vitality of the national economy. The decline of agricultural production from 1959 and the decrease of light industrial production from 1960 intensified the situation, causing an absolute decline in the total investment as well in industrial production in 1961 and 1962. However, since the decline of industrial production was less than that of investment, the adjustment of the proportional relationship between the economic sectors provided the probability that the growth of investment would be recovered in the next cycle (see Table 8.2)

Table 8.2 Growth of total fixed assets investment and gross output value of industry and agriculture

| Year | Growth of total fixed assets investment | Growth of value of industrial output | | | Growth of total value of agricultural production |
		Gross product	Heavy industry	Light industry	
1957	−5.97				
1958	84.53	54.8	78.8	33.7	2.4
1959	31.88	36.1	48.1	22.0	−13.6
1960	13.19	11.2	25.9	−9.8	−12.6
1961	−62.54	−38.2	−46.5	−21.6	−2.4
1962	−44.07	−16.6	−22.6	−8.4	6.2

Unit: percentage

III   The third cycle (1963–68)

The first half of the third cycle was characterized by the recovery of investment and the development of the national economy. The second half of the cycle inversely suffered from economic destruction and a decline of investment, caused by the political situation. The year 1963 was the recovery stage with a total fixed assets investment of 11.666 billion yuan, an increase of 33.66% comparing with the previous year. The peak of the cycle was in 1964 with a total investment of 16.589 billion yuan, increasing by 42.2%. The years 1965 and 1966 prolonged the growth with the total investment of 21.69 billion yuan and 25.48 billion yuan, respectively, and growth rates of 30.75% and 17.47%, respectively. The years 1967 and 1968 marked the trough where the total investments were 18.772 billion yuan and 15.157 billion yuan, respectively, and growth rates were −26.33% and −19.26%, respectively. This cycle lasted for six years (see Figure 8.3).

Let us look into the movement of investment. In the trough of the previous cycle, under the principle "Adjustment, Consolidation, Supplementation and Improvement", investment began to reduce to the scale to which agricultural production and the national economy could afford. The principle was implemented continually from 1963 to 1965. Investment grew steadily after the recovery, peak and sustaining stages. The overall economic situation was all-around improved. During the eight years from 1958 to 1965, China had established an industrial system with considerable production capacity and technical progress for the first time despite unsteady growth. The material and technical foundations for China's modernization, which we now depend on for a further growth, were mostly built up at this time. Realistically speaking, the national economy should have entered into a new development phase and investment should have reached a new peak from 1966 onwards, as happened with the dual peaks in the first cycle.

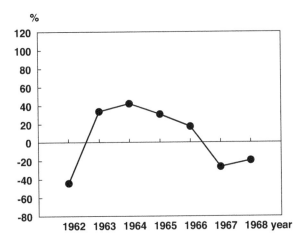

Figure 8.3 The third cycle

However, the political movement disrupted the pace of economic development. Instead of reaching a new peak, investment fell into the trough of the cycle in 1966. The Cultural Revolution was launched in May and June 1966. Until 1968, the whole country was in turmoil caused by the 'Overthrowing all' and 'Unleashing civil war in an all-around way'. The overall economy failed to operate properly, and the economic situation deteriorated sharply. These factors inevitably resulted in a definite decline in the scale of investment. In comparison with 1958 when we intensified the peak by taking the economic advantage, the fall of the investment scale in the trough in 1967 and 1968 was the consequence of going against the economic laws.

The interaction between industrial production and investment and the impact of agriculture on investment also demonstrated the above phenomenon within the cycle. The scale of investment recovered with an increase of 33.66% in 1963. This drove a growth of total industrial output value by 8.5%, in which heavy industry increased 13.8% and light industry increased 2.3%. There appeared a peak in the investment growth in 1964 with a growth rate of 42.20%. It further drove the total industrial output value to grow by 19.6%, in which heavy industry increased 21.0% and light industry increased 17.8%. In 1965 the investment growth came down slightly with a growth rate of 30.75%, while the growth rate of total industrial output value continued to rise up to 26.4%, especially the growth rate of light industry by 47.7%, exceeding that in heavy industry, which was 10.2%. Meanwhile, agriculture performed exceptionally well with a consecutive increase in its gross value. These factors provided remarkable conditions for a further expansion of investment and construction. Going with this trend, the investment growth in 1966 should have appeared as the second peak. Nevertheless, suffering from the

Table 8.3 Growth of total fixed assets investment and gross output value of industry and agriculture

Year	Growth of total fixed assets investment	Growth of value of industrial output			Growth of total value of agricultural production
		Gross product	Heavy industry	Light industry	
1962	−44.07				
1963	33.66	8.5	13.8	2.3	11.6
1964	42.20	19.6	21.0	17.8	13.5
1965	30.75	26.4	10.2	47.7	8.3
1966	17.47	20.9	27.5	14.5	8.6
1967	−26.33	−13.8	−20.0	−7.1	1.6
1968	−19.26	−5.0	−5.1	−4.9	−2.5

Unit: percentage

Cultural Revolution, the scale of investment and total industrial output value did not go beyond those of the previous year. Both investment and industrial production fell continuously and agricultural production deteriorated as well in the two consecutive years of 1967 and 1968 when investment was trapped in the trough of this cycle (see Table 8.3).

IV   The fourth cycle (1969–72)

The growth of fixed asset investment in the fourth cycle gained recovery shortly and then went all the way down. The year 1969 was marked by convergence of the recovery and peak of this cycle with a total investment of 24.692 billion yuan, an increase of 62.91% in comparison with the previous year. The years 1970 and 1971 sustained the growth with the total investment of 36.808 billion yuan and 41.731 billion yuan, respectively, and the growth rates of 49.07% and 13.77%, respectively. The trough of this cycle was 1972 with a reduction of total investment to 41.281billion yuan and a growth rate of −1.08%. This cycle lasted for four years (see Figure 8.4).

In this cycle, the interaction between industrial production and investment intertwined with the impact of political situations and economic plans on the investment. The extent to which industrial production decreased was less than that of investment in the trough lasting for two years in the third cycle, and the pace at which industrial production decreased slowed down in 1968. These factors came along with the relatively stable political situation in 1969, and the investment cycle entered into the recovery phase. Because of the small scale of investment in 1968 (15.157 billion yuan, which was less than 15.606 billion yuan in 1961 and equivalent to 15.123 billion yuan in 1957), the scale of investment recovered moderately in 1969, the peak of the cycle, with a growth rate of 62.91%. Recovery of investment growth drove industrial production to recover and grow with an increase of total industrial output value by 34.3% in 1969, in which heavy industry increased 43.9% and light industry increased 25.2%. In 1970 an abundance of construction

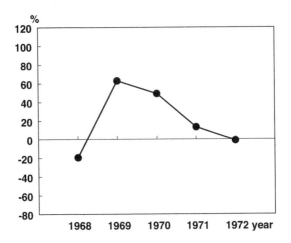

Figure 8.4 The fourth cycle

Table 8.4 Growth of total fixed assets investment and gross output value of industry and agriculture

Year	Growth of total fixed assets investment	Growth of value of industrial output			Growth of total value of agricultural production
		Gross product	Heavy industry	Light industry	
1968	−19.26				
1969	62.91	34.3	43.9	25.2	1.1
1970	49.07	30.7	42.3	18.1	11.5
1971	13.37	14.9	21.4	6.5	3.1
1972	−1.08	6.6	7.0	6.2	−0.2

Unit: percentage

projects imprudently went ahead in inland China with the principle 'All be prepared against war'. The counter-revolutionary clique headed by Lin Biao intervened in the national economy and put even more construction projects in operation, causing a rapid expansion of investment – an increase in investment of 12.116 billion yuan within 12 months. The year of 1970 became another year, after 1958, in which the scale of investment exceeded 10 billion yuan. The investment continued to rise in 1971, leading to "the three breakthroughs" – the number of employees went over 50 million, the spending on wages went beyond 30 billion yuan, and the grain and crops sales beat 40 billion kilograms. The scale of investment exceeded the bearing capability of industrial and agricultural production. The expansion of investment gradually slowed down in 1970 and 1971. The investment cycle reached its trough in 1972 (see Table 8.4).

V   The fifth cycle (1973–76)

The recovery of investment remained longer in this cycle. There was no sustaining growth after the peak of the cycle. The years 1973 and 1974 were the recovery stages with total fixed assets investment of 43.812 billion yuan and 46.319 billion yuan, respectively, and the growth rates of 6.13% and 5.72%, respectively. The year 1975 was the peak with a total investment of 54.494 billion yuan and a growth rate of 17.65%. The following year of 1976 fell into the trough with a total investment of 52.394 billion yuan and a growth rate of −3.85%. This cycle lasted for four years (see Figure 8.5).

The preceding characters of the fourth cycle were related to the continuous political unrest originating with the Cultural Revolution. Disturbed by the Cultural Revolution, "the three breakthroughs" which occurred in the trough of the previous cycle became more severe in this cycle. This dragged on the recovery of investment in 1973. "The three breakthroughs" were not effectively controlled until 1973. In 1974, the scale of investment should have gained an impressive expansion though it did not reach the peak. The "Gang of Four" launched the 'Criticize Lin Biao and Confucius Campaign'. After crushing Lin Biao's counter-revolutionary clique in September 1971, the moderately stable political situation turned to unrest and was chaotic again, resulting in a slow growth of investment in 1974, which was even lower than the year before. This caused the recovery to last for two years, during which heavy industry appeared as a negative growth in this cycle. In 1975, comrade Deng Xiaoping took over policy-making and implementation of economic affairs. He began to adjust the economic structure with the effect that the economic chaos discontinued, and that there appeared a peak of investment and the revival and rapid growth of industrial production. Going with this trend, the investment increased in 1976. Nonetheless, the subsequent campaign 'Anti-right Deviationist Wind' dragged the national economy, which

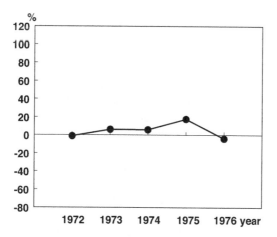

Figure 8.5 The fifth cycle

Table 8.5 Growth of total fixed assets investment and gross output value of industry and agriculture

Year	Growth of total fixed assets investment	Growth of value of industrial output			Growth of total value of agricultural production
		Gross product	Heavy industry	Light industry	
1972	−1.08				
1973	6.13	9.5	8.7	10.6	8.4
1974	5.72	0.3	−1.6	2.7	4.2
1975	17.65	15.1	16.8	13.0	4.6
1976	−3.85	1.3	0.5	2.4	2.5

Unit: percentage

struggled to remain in development over ten years in turmoil, to the edge of breakdown. The investment declined unquestionably and industrial and agricultural production growth rates fell (see Table 8.5). The crushing of the "Gang of Four" in October 1976 ended the ten-year turmoil of the Cultural Revolution. China entered a new era.

VI   The sixth cycle (1977–81)

After crushing the "Gang of Four", there appeared a stable political situation in China and the national economy soon recovered and began to grow. But there were hidden risks. The year 1977 was the recovery phase with a total fixed assets investment of 54.83 billion yuan and a growth rate of 4.65%. The year 1978 reached the peak of the investment cycle with a total investment of 66.872 billion yuan and a growth rate of 21.96%. The years of 1979 and 1980 sustained growth with total investments of 69.936 billion yuan and 74.59 billion yuan, respectively, and growth rates of 4.58% and 6.65%, respectively. The year 1981 fell into the trough with a decline of total investment to 66.751 billion yuan and a negative growth rate of 10.51%. This cycle lasted for five years (see Figure 8.6).

The hidden risks in the economic prospect were associated with the long-standing influence of Leftism on the planning and policy-making processes. As the national economy recovered and developed rapidly, the fixed assets investment grew in 1977 and reached the peak in 1978. The total industrial output value increased successively 14.3% in 1977 and 13.5% in 1978, respectively. Since the national economy recovered just from the political turmoil and the relationship of various sectors was still disproportional, the foremost task should be to adjust economic structures side by side with healing and developing industrial and agricultural production. By contrast, the fast-paced growth and unrealistic targets of China's economy emerged again as a result of over-anxiousness for quick effects, which was influenced by the widespread, durable Leftism that

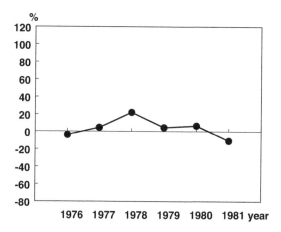

Figure 8.6 The sixth cycle

had not been attentively cleared out. The scale of investment increased 12.042 billion yuan in 1978, which became the third year, in addition to 1958 and 1970, in which the total investment growth exceeded 10 billion yuan. The accumulation rate surged to 36.5% in 1978, a third year in which the accumulation rate reached up above 35% in addition to 1959 (43.8%) and 1960 (39.6%). The fragile economy which had survived in the ten-year turmoil could not withstand this sharp rise, and the long-lasting disproportional relationship of the national economy inevitably became aggravated. The Third Plenary Session of the 11th Central Committee of CPC in December 1978 was the great turning point with a lasting impact on China's modern history since 1949. The CPC shifted its focus to construction of socialist modernization. Soon after 1978, the Central Committee of CPC put forward the Eight-character principle 'Adjustment, Reform, Rectification, and Improvement'. The Eight-character principle, however, was not successfully executed in 1979 and 1980, the sustaining growth stages of investment cycle, due to unawareness of the severity of the setbacks brought about by the ten-year turmoil and premature progression in the subsequent years and a lack of in-depth understanding of the necessity of adjustment. These dimensions posed hidden risks to the national economy. In 1979 and 1980, there were the largest fiscal deficits (17.06 billion yuan and 12.75 billion yuan, respectively) since the founding of new China. With an excessive money supply and an escalation of prices, the serious problem with a disproportional national economy did not change fundamentally. In this circumstance, the further adjustment of the economic structure was undertaken in 1981. The scale of investment was cut down, 10.51% lower than the previous year. The value of heavy industrial output declined 4.7% accordingly (see Table 8.6).

Table 8.6 Growth of total fixed assets investment and gross output value of industry and
agriculture

Year	Growth of total fixed assets investment	Growth of value of industrial output			Growth of total value of agricultural production
		Gross product	Heavy industry	Light industry	
1976	−3.85				
1977	4.65	14.3	14.3	14.3	1.7
1978	21.96	13.5	15.6	10.8	9.0
1979	4.58	8.5	7.7	9.6	8.6
1980	6.65	8.7	1.4	18.4	3.9
1981	−10.51	4.1	−4.7	14.1	6.6

Unit: percentage

VII   The seventh cycle (1982–85, not completed yet)

Up to now this ongoing cycle has lasted for four years. In view of the situation in
this period, the scale of fixed assets investment each year was enormous, and the
annual growth of investment was over10 billion yuan consecutively for four years,
which was exclusive since the founding of the PRC (see Table 8.7). The growth of
fixed assets investment presented a fluctuation with dual peaks. The year 1982 was
characterized by both the recovery and the first peak of this cycle with a total fixed
assets investment of 84.531 billion yuan and a growth rate of 26.64%. The years
1983 and 1984 were sustaining growth with the total investment of 95.196 billion
yuan and 118.518 billion yuan, respectively, and the growth rates of 12.62% and
24.50%, respectively. 1985 was the second peak (by estimate, the investment
expansion would slow down in 1986, and we thus regard 1985 as the second peak)
with a total investment of 165.2 billion yuan and a growth rate of 39.39% (see
Figure 8.7).

In this cycle, the fixed assets investment continuously maintained at a large scale
and its growth appeared as another peak. These were affected by the following
factors.

First, the consecutive growth and coordinating development of agriculture, light
industry and heavy industry created a profound material base for continuous and
massive investment. Due to the impact of Leftism on rural policy, the growth of
agricultural production bitterly slowed and was unstable in the past decades. In the
recent years, remarkable achievements have been made through a series of reform
measures, especially the implementation of the Household Contractual Responsibility System, in the countryside. Agricultural production has increased substantially and uninterruptedly in several years, which was rare in the modern history
of China. The total value of agricultural production increased 11.1%, 9.6%, 17.1%
and 13%, respectively, from 1982 to 1985. At the same time, with the policy of
revitalizing the domestic economy and opening up to the outside world, industrial

Table 8.7 The annual investment growth over 10 billion yuan by years

No.	Year	The cycle	Total fixed assets investment (billion yuan)	Annual growth (billion yuan)
1	1958	The 2nd cycle	27.906	12.783
2	1970	The 4th cycle	36.808	12.116
3	1978	The 6th cycle	66.872	12.042
4	1982	The 7th cycle	84.531	17.780
5	1983	The 7th cycle	95.196	10.665
6	1984	The 7th cycle	118.518	23.322
7	1985	The 7th cycle	165.200	46.682

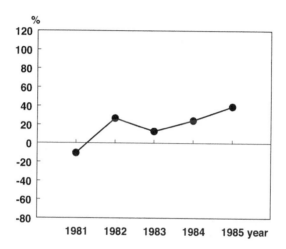

Figure 8.7 The seventh cycle

production was also booming and increased continuously. The total industrial output value increased 7.7%, 10.5%, 14% and 18%, respectively, from 1982 to 1985 (see Table 8.8). Agricultural development promoted a growth of light industry and an expansion of heavy industry. Industrial development and the growth of investment mutually promoted one another. The Chinese economy has been strengthened remarkably.

Second, the relationship between accumulation and consumption was proportionally coordinated. Their mutual benefits were conducive to the investment growth. The accumulation rate reached 31.5% to 36.5% successively each year in the fifth and sixth cycle except for the trough phase. The accumulation rates were 28.8%, 29.7% and 31.2%, respectively, from 1982 to 1984. Meanwhile, the consumption of urban and rural residents rose year by year. It only increased 2.2% in

Table 8.8 Growth of total fixed assets investment and gross output value of industry and agriculture

Year	Growth of total fixed assets investment	Growth of value of industrial output			Growth of total value of agricultural production
		Gross product	Heavy industry	Light industry	
1981	−10.51				
1982	26.64	7.7	9.8	5.7	11.1
1983	12.62	10.5	12.4	8.7	9.6
1984	24.50	14.0	14.2	13.9	17.1
1985	39.39	18.0	17.9	18.1	13.0

Unit: percentage

the 26 years from 1953 to 1978. But it increased 5.3%, 7.6% and 10.9%, respectively, on the basis of its rather high-level growth in previous years, from 1982 to 1984. It was evident that the massive construction was upheld over the years along with the continuous improvement of people's living standards.

Lastly, the investment structure changed. With regard to the sources of investment, self-raised and other funds than state-revenue input increased rapidly in the total fixed assets investment. It was 41.361 billion yuan in 1983 and rose to 51.492 billion yuan in 1984, an increase of 10.131 billion yuan within 12 months and a growth rate of 24. 5%. Domestic loans and foreign currency loans also increased quickly, a rise of 34.5% and 60.3%, respectively, in 1984 compared with that of 1983. As far as the usage of investment is concerned, non-productive construction investment, especially residential investment, held a relatively large proportion in the total fixed assets investment. In the three years from 1982 to 1984, the proportions of non-productive construction investments were 45.5%, 41.7% and 40.3%, respectively, among which the proportions of residential investments were as high as 25.1%, 21.1% and 18.1%, respectively. In so far as the usage of investments in economic sectors, the investment in energy industry, transportation, and post and telecommunications increased quickly. In 1983 and 1984, the investment in energy industry increased 26.3% and 27.6%, respectively, and in transportation and post and telecommunications increased 28.7% and 37.1%, respectively, all exceeding the growth rate of total fixed assets investment in those two years.

It is crucial to keep calm and pay attention at any time to the issues such as losing control of the investment scale and coordinating the proportional relationship in all aspects in spite of the smooth growth of investment and the transition of the national economy. At present, Chinese policy-makers face issues and challenges. For example, the social demand overdoes the social supply, the purchasing power is over availability of commodities, energy, transportation and raw materials are in short supply, and there is a high rate of inflation. According to the features and trends of the six previous cycles and the situation of the first four years in the seventh cycle, the pace and scale of investment should remain stationary in 1986.

VIII Summary

The analysis of the seven cycles reveals some common characteristics as well as distinct features of each cycle. The factors that affect the periodicity of fixed assets investment in China consist of two types: the internal-material dimension and external-non-material dimension. These two types of factors interlace with each other – the former underpins the investment cycles and the latter conditions the investment cycles.

The internal-material dimension mainly involves the three interrelated factors.

1   Management of investment, such as arrangements of starting up a number of key construction projects, reaching the peak, and changes in the investment structure.

2   Impact of agriculture. Agriculture impacts investment through supplying grain, vegetables and meat. It affects light industrial production through supplying raw materials, like grain, cotton and various cash crops. It further impacts investment through supplying consumer goods and capital accumulation. Agriculture also impacts investment through labor supply. Agriculture as the foundation of the national economy plays a decisive role in investment variations in China. Bumper harvests often bring a boom of investment or sustained growth in the subsequent year.

3   Influence of industry. The most direct impact comes from heavy industry since it provides raw materials, such as machinery, equipment, steel, cement and energy, for investment projects. Heavy industry and investment interact with each other generating either a positive or negative impact on each other. The growth of heavy industry and investment often reach the peak and come to the trough simultaneously. Looking into each of the investment cycles, we can detect some interesting traits of growing investment, heavy industry and light industry. First, at the peak stage the pace of investment growth was faster than that of heavy industry, and the pace of heavy industry growth was faster than that of light industry. There were nine peak years for 33 years, eight of which fell into this pattern. The exception was 1985 when the investment growth was faster than that of heavy industry, but the heavy industry growth was slightly lower than that of light industry. Since the investment growth exceeded the capacity of heavy industry and since the investment and heavy industry growth exceeded the capacity of light industry, the investment growth declined after its peak. Second, at the trough stage, the growth of light industry was faster than that of heavy industry, the growth of heavy industry was faster than that of investment; or the decrease of light industry was less than that of heavy industry, and the decrease of heavy industry was less than that of investment. There were eight troughs over 33 years, six of which fell into this pattern. The years 1957 and 1972 were the

exceptions. The growth of light industry was slower than that of heavy industry, but the growth of heavy industry was faster than that of investment. This could explain why investment growth rose again after it fell into the trough: light industry laid the basis for heavy industrial development and both light industry and heavy industry laid the basis for investment growth. The paces of investment, heavy industry and light industry growth were different at the stages of investment recovery and sustained growing.

The mutual impacts between the material factors and investment are reflected through a range of proportional relationships, such as between agriculture, light industry and heavy industry, between accumulation and consumption, between current-year production and long-term development, and between supply and demand. It is worth noting that the adjustment of the structures of agriculture, light and heavy industries and other major proportional relationships of national economy is not once and for all. In fact, it is a process involving distinguished measures determined by the different movements of the interrelationship between investment, heavy industry and light industry at the peak and trough stages. It is vital to make adjustments every few years, as there is usually a peak every few years, as long as we endeavor to avoid any intensified amplitude. In view of this position, we are obligated to make adjustments consciously, actively and timely when there is a need in reality. It would have serious consequences if we remained inactive when facing challenges.

The external-non-material dimension mainly includes three interrelated factors.

1   The impact of the political situation. China is a country with public owner-ship of the means of production and correspondingly the prevailing planned economy. Government officials and most managers at all levels are publicly appointed. The functions of the market mechanism and various economic leverages such as price, interest rate, taxes and wages are imperfect and inadequate. Under this circumstance, investment and the entire economic activities are exceedingly affected by political situations, both domestic and international ones. They have a positive or negative role in investment growth. Positively, they promote investment growth at the recovery, peak and sustained stages and ensure effective adjustment at the trough stage. Negatively, they intensify the peak of investment cycle excessively or make it fall into the trough prematurely and severely.

2   The impact of plans and policies. The planning process and policy-making are subjective behaviors. When they are drawn up and implemented accord-ing to economic rules, they might prevent investment shock and promote routine operation of the economy. Conversely, when they deviate from economic rules or are implemented inappropriately, they might intensify investment amplitude and cause disorder in the economic performance. China had a vulnerable economic foundation and short supply in material for a long period. Under the planned economy, it was dominated by Leftism in

decision-making and became over-anxious for success. As a consequence of "trying to run before one can walk", the country suffered haste making waste. It is worth noting that we have accumulated numerous experiences and lessons, positively or negatively, in making investment over 30 years since the founding of the new China. These experiences and lessons can be summarized into such principles as: doing our best while acting according to our capability, prioritizing agriculture production and consumer goods market over industrial production and capital construction investment within the same year, focusing on economic performance of the current year and meanwhile foreseeing its future trend, assuring the short-term balance while leaving room for long-term growth and retreating adequately when making an adjustment. These principles should be firmly remembered and carried forward.

3 The impact of the economic management system. The reason why the political situations and planned economy have a significant impact on investment is associated with the economic management system. The excessively centralized management and rigid administrative system creates investment and economic activities with inflexibility and low vitality. The Big Rice Bowl system makes the financial management lose its responsibility and lack efficiency. The economic reform, market mechanism and various economic leverages, all of which are gradually brought into full play in China's economy, will be beneficial to weakening any harmful interference of political situations in investment and overcoming adverse impacts of economic plans. These will enhance the rationality and accountability of investment, improve economic efficiency of investment and ensure investment based on economic rules.

(Originally published in *The Journal of Quantitative & Technical Economics*, No.9, 1986)

Notes

1 Preliminary Study on Periodicity of Fixed Assets Investment in China. (1986). *Economic Research Journal*, 2.
2 Re-Study on Periodicity of Fixed Assets Investment in China: Analysis of Its Stages. (1986). *Economic Research Journal*, 6.

9 Impact of investment periodical fluctuation on economic periodical fluctuation

A further study on the periodicity of fixed assets investment in China

Periodical fluctuation of fixed assets investment, as the dominant factor, directly and physically influences the economic periodical fluctuation. This article intends to further explore the impact of investment periodical fluctuation on economic periodical fluctuation on the basis of my three previously published articles (Liu Shucheng, 1986)[1] on investment periodicity in China. Economic periodical fluctuation is represented by indicators such as national income, total output value, gross output value of industry and agriculture. We will recognize through the following analysis that it is very important to control investment periodical fluctuation so as to guarantee a steady growth of the national economy in the long-term.

I Classification criterion of economic cycle

Before examining the impact of investment periodical fluctuation on economic periodical fluctuation, we first look at the economic fluctuation in China. For the issue as to whether there was certain regularity or periodicity in economic fluctuation in China over the past 30 years, some commentators believed that the fluctuation was quite irregular. The lengths of fluctuation varied from 2, 3, 4, and 6 to 7 years ("Analysis of Features", 1987).[2] Other scholars argued that the fluctuation was relatively regular and there is a certain periodicity ("Periodicity of Fixed Assets Investment", 1986).[3] Regarding the average length of the economic cycle, some thought that it was approximately more than four years where others thought that it was about eight years.

The reason for different understandings lies in the classification or categorization of the cycle of economic fluctuation. Different classifications or categorizations lead to different understandings.

There are mainly two different classifications as follows:

The first is to classify the cycle according to its impact on economic development and its length. As per this criterion, there are four categories of cycles.

1 Minor Cycle with an average length of approximately four years. Proposed by American economist Joseph Kitchin in 1923, the minor cycle is termed the "Kitchin Cycle", which has a comparatively minor impact on economic

development with a shorter period and is therefore called as the "Minor Cycle". The United States experienced a total of 37 minor cycles during the past 130 years from 1807 to 1937 with an average length of 3.51 years.

2   Intermediate Cycle with an average length of approximately eight years. Proposed by French economist Clement Juglar in 1860, the intermediate cycle is termed the "Juglar Cycle", which has a comparatively significant impact on economic development and is therefore called the "Major Cycle". One Juglar intermediate cycle consists of about two Kitchin cycles. The United States experienced a total of 17 intermediate cycles during the past 142 years from 1795 to 1937 with an average length of 8.35 years.

3   The Mid-long Cycle with an average length of approximately 20 years. Put forward by American economist Simon Kuznets in 1930, the medium-long cycle is termed as "Kuznets Cycle", which generally occurs in housing construction industry and is therefore also called the "Building Cycle". One Kuznets cycle consists of about two or three Juglar cycles. The medium-long cycle often coincides with one of the two intermediate cycles and greatly influences economic development.

4   The Long Cycle with an average length of approximately 50 years. Proposed by Soviet economist Nikolai Kondratieff in 1925, the long cycle is termed the "Kondratieff Cycle", which has a long duration and is therefore called a "Long-term Fluctuation" or "Long Wave Fluctuation". One Kondratieff cycle consists of about six Juglar cycles.

The second is to classify the cycle according to the nature of economic fluctuation. As per this criterion, there are two categories of cycles: (1) Classical Cycle, where the economy declines in the absolute amount at the trough of economic fluctuation and there is negative growth in economic development; and (2) Growth Cycle, where the economy does not decline in the absolute amount, but the growth rate is getting slow at the trough of economic fluctuation. There is positive growth in economic development.

Regardless which criterion is applied to classify the cycle of economic fluctuation, there is no strict limit for the length of the cycle since economic fluctuation in nature is unlike seasonal changes which have a fixed pattern. Generally, the economy fluctuates in a relatively less regular way. When analyzing the lifetime of fixed capital of a capitalist society and the length of economic crisis, Marx held that "the lifetime of industry and of industrial capital lengthens in each particular field of investment to a period of many years, say of ten years on an average" (1885/2001, p. 248).[4] Marx specifically examined the fluctuation of the British cotton textile industry in nearly 50 years from 1815 to 1863 and recorded it in five cycles with an average length of approximately10 years, where the small fluctuation within each cycle was not recorded as crisis (1975).[5] When investigating and analyzing the British economic crisis during this period, Engels divided it into two stages. The first stage was "from 1815 to 1847. It can be shown that a crisis occurred about every five years". The second stage was "from 1847–1867. The cycle is decidedly decennial" (Marx, 1894/2001).[6] In addition, Engels divided this period into two phases from 1825 to 1842 and from 1842 to 1868. He wrote that

> the recurring period of the great industrial crisis is stated in the text as five years. This was the period apparently indicated by the course of events from 1825 to 1842. But the industrial history from 1842 to 1868 has shown that the real period is one of ten years; that the intermediate revulsions were secondary.
>
> (1965, p. 373)[7]

We realize that Engels once divided the cycle into the minor cycle and major cycle. Regarding the length of a cycle, as Marx pointed out "it is merely a question of different periods of time" (1885/2001, p. 245);[8] it is a question that we should, through the analysis, understand and get to grips with the regularity of economic fluctuation, which is inherent though it is relative and less obvious.

II   Economic periodical fluctuation in China

According to the criterion of classification, we examine the economic fluctuation situation in China from the fluctuation of annual national income growth rate at comparable price in the following three cases:

In the first case, we investigate each fluctuation of the annual national income growth rate regardless of its degree and length. There were nine fluctuations (see Table 9.1 and column 3 in Figure 9.1[9]) in 34 years from 1953 to 1986, in which three were classical fluctuations and six were growing fluctuations. The lengths of fluctuations were 2, 3, 4, 5 and 6 years, respectively. It is obvious that this type of fluctuation is very irregular.

In the second case, we examine the two tiny adjacent fluctuations with the length of 2 and 3 years and regard it as the minor cycle. There seven minor cycles (see column 4 in Table 9.1) during the past 34 years, in which three of them were classical fluctuations and four were growing fluctuations. The lengths of fluctuation

Table 9.1 Fluctuation of annual national income growth rate

Year	Growth rate (%)	Type and length		
		All fluctuations	*Minor cycle*	*Intermediate cycle*
1953	14.0	2 years		
1954	5.8	(growing fluctuation)	5 years	
1955	6.4		(growing fluctuation)	
1956	14.1	3 years		

Year	Growth rate (%)	Type and length		
		All fluctuations	Minor cycle	Intermediate cycle
1957	4.5	(growing fluctuation)		10 years
1958	22.0			(classical fluctuation)
1959	8.2	5 years	5 years	
1960	−1.4	(classical fluctuation)	(classical fluctuation)	
1961	−29.7			
1962	−6.5			
1963	10.7			
1964	16.5			
1965	17.0	6 years	6 years	6 years
1966	17.0	(classical fluctuation)	(classical fluctuation)	(classical fluctuation)
1967	−7.2			
1968	−6.5			
1969	19.3			
1970	23.3	4 years	4 years	
1971	7.0	(growing fluctuation)	(growing fluctuation)	
1972	2.9			8 years
1973	8.3	2 years		(classical fluctuation)
1974	1.1	(growing fluctuation)	4 years	
1975	8.3	2 years	(classical fluctuation)	
1976	−2.7	(classical fluctuation)		
1977	7.8			
1978	12.3	5 years	5 years	
1979	7.0	(growing fluctuation)	(growing fluctuation)	
1980	6.4			
1981	4.9			10 years
1982	8.3			(growing fluctuation)
1983	9.8	5 years	5 years	
1984	13.5	(growing fluctuation)	(growing fluctuation)	
1985	12.3			
1986	7.4			

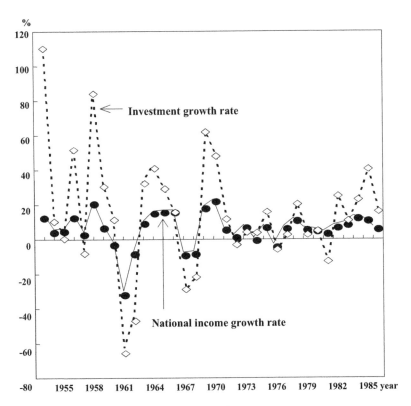

Figure 9.1 Fluctuation of national income growth rate

were 5 years four times, 4 years two times and 6 years once with an average length of 4.9 years. Obviously, this type of fluctuation is very regular.

In the third case, we regard the two minor adjacent cycles with the length of less than 5 years as one intermediate cycle and examine it accordingly. There were four intermediate cycles (see column 5 in Table 9.1) during the past 34 years, in which the first three were classical fluctuations and the last one was a growing fluctuation. The lengths of fluctuation were 6, 8 and 10 years, respectively, with an average length of 8.5 years. Apparently, this type of fluctuation is more regular than that under the first case and less regular than that under the second case.

We are able to investigate each economic fluctuation in China in the first case (all fluctuations) and carefully analyze the tangible influence factors, which is important and valuable for drawing up annual plans. The examination under the second case (the minor cycle) reveals several mid-term stages of economic development in China, which is beneficial for the mid-term analysis. This is vital for arranging the five-year plan and social and economic influential activities (such as unveiling the timing of various economic reform measures and their influences). The investigation under the third case (the intermediate cycle) has great value in designing long-term economic plans (e.g. 10 years) in China. This kind of intermediate cycle indicates several large stages of economic development in China, which reflects the impact and outcome of important political and economic activities. For example, the first intermediate cycle (1953–62) demonstrated the tortuous course from the planned and massive construction projects in China since 1953 to the successful completion of the first Five-year Plan and then to The Great Leap Forward and its severe consequence. The second intermediate cycle (1963–68) displayed the achievements of Three-year Adjustment and the devastating consequences brought by the subsequent outbreak of the Cultural Revolution. The third intermediate cycle (1969–76) just met the middle and late stages of the Cultural Revolution and illustrated the rough development of the economy in China. The above three intermediate cycles were classical, each of which ended up in the decline in absolute national income. The fourth intermediate cycle (1977–86) was a growing fluctuation;, namely, there was no negative growth in national income during the 10 years. This indicated that China's economy entered into a new development cycle after the Third Plenary Session of the 11th Central Committee of CPC.

The fluctuations of annual growth rate (according to comparable price) of total output value, which are approximately the same as that of national income, are listed in Table 9.2. The main difference is that, in the 1976 fluctuation at the trough stage, the national income fluctuation is a classical fluctuation whereas the fluctuation of total output value is a growing fluctuation. The fluctuation of total industrial and agricultural output value is the same as that of the total output value, thus there is no need to amplify it.

This approach is termed as "link relative method" which examines fluctuation through the annual growth rate of various aggregate economic indicators. The

Table 9.2 Fluctuation of annual growth rate of total output value

Starting and Ending Year	Type and length		
	All fluctuations	Minor cycle	Intermediate cycle
1953–55	3 years (growing fluctuation)		
1956–57	2 years (growing fluctuation)	5 years (growing fluctuation)	10 years (classical fluctuation)
1958–62	5 years (classical fluctuation)	5 years (classical fluctuation)	
1963–68	6 years (classical fluctuation)	6 years (classical fluctuation)	6 years (classical fluctuation)
1969–72	4 years (growing fluctuation)	4 years (growing fluctuation)	
1973–74	2 years (growing fluctuation)		8 years (growing fluctuation)
1975–76	2 years (growing fluctuation)	4 years (growing fluctuation)	
1977–81	5 years (growing fluctuation)	5 years (growing fluctuation)	
1982–86	5 years (growing fluctuation)	5 years (growing fluctuation)	10 years (growing fluctuation)

advantage of this approach lies in easily examining the relative fluctuation of economic growth rate between years. On the other hand, its disadvantage rests with being unable to display the fluctuation of absolute economic indicators that moves round the long-term historical trend. To make up for it, we apply the "trend percentage method" to investigate the national income fluctuation discussed subsequently.

We define Y to represent the actual value (calculated according to comparable price and indicated in index, taking 1952 as 100) of the absolute national income each year and T to stand for the serial number of years (taking 1953 as 1). From 1953 to 1986, the formula of historical trend of absolute national income is (by applying the least square method to estimate parameter with the correlation coefficient r = 0.97) as follows:

$$\log Y = 2.00402 + 0.02535T \tag{1}$$

formula(1) can be recorded as:

$$Y = 100.92994 \times (1 + 0.0601)^T \tag{2}$$

Formula (2) demonstrates that national income increased 6.01% annually on average from 1953 to 1986 from the perspective of the long-term development trend. We can verify the historical trend value (represented by $\hat{Y}$) of the absolute national income each year from formula (1) or (2), list them in column 3 of Table 9.3 and draw them in Figure 9.2. We can then figure out the percentage (represented by y) of the actual value (Y) of absolute national income each year to its historical trend value (represented by $\hat{Y}$). The calculation formula is as follows:

$$y = (Y - 1) \times 100\% \tag{3}$$

The trend percentage (y) calculated from formula (3) is listed in column 4 of Table 9.3 and drawn in Figure 9.3. This signifies the deviation degree of the actual value of absolute national income amount each year from its historical trend value. From Table 9.3, Figure 9.2 and Figure 9.3, we can comprehend not only the situation of the four intermediate cycles, but also the variation of absolute national income level moving round the historical trend line throughout the 34 years. From 1953 to 1960, the absolute national income level had been always above the historical trend line showing that the national income had been increasing. National income entered into the trough in 1961 and reached the bottom in 1962, thus completing the first intermediate cycle. It started to recover from 1963 and returned to be above the historical trend line until 1966. It took five years from 1961 to 1965 to remove the impact of The Great Leap Forward for the three years from 1958 to 1960. Subsequently, the Cultural Revolution broke out and the national income entered into the trough and reached the bottom in 1968, thus completing the second intermediate cycle. National income recovered from the bottom in 1969 and increased slightly from 1970 to 1973. Soon afterwards it entered into the trough again and reached the bottom in 1976, thus completing the third intermediate

Table 9.3 Fluctuation of absolute national income moving around the historical trend

Year	Actual value Y (index)	Trend value $\hat{Y}$ (index)	Percentage y (%)	Intermediate cycle (number of years)
1953	114.0	106.1	7.4	
1954	120.6	112.6	7.1	
1955	128.3	119.4	7.5	
1956	146.4	126.6	15.6	
1957	153.0	134.3	13.9	10
1958	186.7	142.4	31.1	
1959	202.1	151.0	33.8	
1960	199.2	160.1	24.1	
1961	140.0	169.8	−17.6	
1962	130.9	180.1	−27.3	
1963	144.9	191.0	−24.1	
1964	168.8	202.5	−16.6	
1965	197.5	214.8	−8.1	6
1966	231.0	227.8	1.4	
1967	214.3	241.6	−11.3	
1968	200.4	256.2	−21.8	
1969	239.1	271.7	−12.0	
1970	294.7	288.1	2.3	
1971	315.3	305.5	3.2	
1972	324.5	324.0	0.2	8
1973	351.4	343.6	2.3	
1974	355.2	364.4	−2.5	
1975	384.7	386.5	−0.5	
1976	374.4	409.8	−8.6	
1977	403.6	434.6	−7.1	
1978	453.2	460.9	−1.7	
1979	484.9	488.8	−0.8	
1980	515.9	518.4	−0.5	
1981	541.2	549.7	−1.5	10
1982	586.1	583.0	0.5	
1983	643.5	618.3	4.1	
1984	730.4	655.7	11.4	
1985	820.2	695.3	18.0	
1986	880.9	737.4	19.5	

cycle. The economy had been sluggish during the ten-year turmoil from 1967 to 1976, which dragged the national economy to the edge of breakdown. Consequently, it took another five years from 1977 to 1981 to pull the absolute national income level back above the historical trend line until 1982 after crushing the Gang of Four. The national economy had been in depression for 21 years from 1961 to

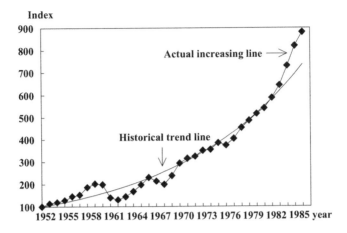

Figure 9.2 Actual increasing line and historical trend line of absolute national income

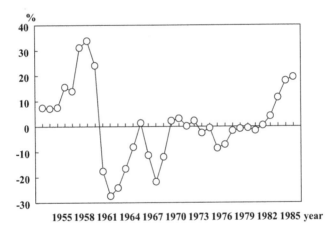

Figure 9.3 Fluctuation of absolute national income moving around the historical trend

1981 as a consequence brought about by the three-year Great Leap Forward and ten-year turmoil. The absolute national income level had always been above the historical trend line from 1982 to 1986. National income grew greatly in 1985 and 1986, but there still existed development momentum.

III   Impact of investment periodical fluctuation

Investment periodical fluctuation and economic periodical fluctuation as material factors interplay with each other directly. Various non-material factors such as the political situation, plan-making and economic management affect these two fluctuations simultaneously. On the one hand, the non-material factors directly act on both fluctuations and, on the other hand, they greatly act on one fluctuation through the other. In terms of the fluctuation function, investment periodical fluctuation affects economy through investment demand and supply of production capacity dominantly and is decisive in economic fluctuations. Economic periodical fluctuation restricts and controls the magnitude and length of investment fluctuation from the material aspect. On the whole these two fluctuations synchronize in time with the same direction as shown in the previous Figure 9.1,[10] but the investment fluctuates greater than the economy. Here we shall focus on the impact of investment periodical fluctuation on economic periodical fluctuation.

1. Impact of current-year investment on current-year economic fluctuation

The influence of current-year investment on current-year economic fluctuation is both demand-oriented and supply-oriented. In terms of demand orientation, the increase and decrease in direct and indirect demand generated by current-year investment will lead to economic fluctuations. In terms of supply orientation, the total current-year investment includes three parts. The first part is used for small projects that are put into operation in the current year. The second part is used for projects that started previously and are put into operation in the current year. The third part is used for new and unfinished projects. The first two parts form the newly increased fixed assets in the current year, of which its increase and decrease will bring about economic fluctuations. The annual increase or decrease of newly increased fixed assets has fluctuated synchronously with that of total investment over 30 years.

It can be illustrated through econometric analysis how the current-year investment influences the current-year economic fluctuation.

1 Fluctuation of growth rate. We take Y' to represent the annual growth rate (calculated according to comparable price) of national income and I' to represent the annual growth rate (calculated according to current-year price) of total fixed assets investment of public ownership. According to the data from 1953 to 1986, the quantitative relation between Y' and I' calculated by applying the least square method (same hereinafter) is as follows:

$$Y' = 2.93 + 0.25I' \qquad\qquad (4)$$
$$r = 0.83$$

The above formulas indicate that the correlation degree between the annual growth rate of national income and investment is 83%. Influenced by other factors, national income increases 2.93% per year. On this basis, as investment increases or decreases every 1%, national income will increase or decrease 0.25%.

It is not identical to the impact that current-year investment on current-year economic fluctuation displays in light industry and heavy industry. We define H'

to represent the annual growth rate (calculated according to comparable price) of total heavy industrial output value and use L' to represent the annual growth rate (according to the comparable price) of total light industrial output value. The implication of I' is the same as above. According to the data from 1953 to 1986, it is calculated as follows:

$$H' = 6.63 + 0.56I' \tag{5}$$
$$r = 0.86$$
$$L' = 5.71 + 0.30I' \tag{6}$$
$$r = 0.75$$

As shown in the above formulas, the correlation degrees between the annual growth rates of total heavy industrial output value and investment and between the annual growth rates of the total light industrial output value and investment are 86% and 75%, respectively. Impacted by other factors, the total heavy and light industrial output values increase 6.63% and 5.71%, respectively, per year. On this basis, as investment increases or decreases every 1%, total heavy and light industrial output values will increase or decrease 0.56% and 0.30%, respectively, because the demand of investment mainly comes from heavy industry.

2   Fluctuation of absolute amount. We take Y to represent national income (calculated according to current-year price) and I to represent total fixed assets investment of public ownership (calculated according to current-year price). According to the data (unit: 100 million yuan) from 1953 to 1986, the quantitative relation between Y and I is as follows:

$$Y = 453.52 + 4.00 \, I \tag{7}$$
$$r = 0.98$$

As displayed in the above formulas, the correlation degree between absolute national income amount and total investment is 98%. The cause for this high correlation degree is that the correlation between national income and investment in the long-term trend is implied. Eliminating the long-term trend, the correlation degree will be reduced as demonstrated below. The above formula illustrates that, influenced by other factors, national income increases 45.352 billion yuan per year. On this basis, as total investment increases or decreases every 10 billion yuan, national income will increase or decrease 40 billion yuan.

3   Fluctuation of absolute amount moving around the historical trend. We still define y to stand for the percentage of actual value (Y calculated according to comparable price) of absolute national income amount to its historical trend value (Y) (see formula (3)) and i to represent the percentage of actual value (I is calculated according to current-year price) of absolute total fixed assets investment amount of public ownership to its historical trend value (I). According to the data from 1953 to 1986, the quantitative relation between y and i is as follows:

$$y = -1.03 + 0.28 \; i \tag{8}$$
$$r = 0.88$$

in which

$$i = (I - 1) \times 100\% \tag{9}$$
$$\log I = 1.95861 + 0.03293 \; T \tag{10}$$
$$r = 0.90$$

formula (10) can be recorded as:

$$I = 90.90965 \times (1 + 0.0788 \,)^{T} \tag{11}$$

As described in formula (8), the correlation degree between the percentage of actual value of absolute national income amount to its historical trend and the percentage of total investment to its historical trend value is 88%. Influenced by other factors, the percentage of national income to its historical trend drops 1.03% per year. On this basis, as the percentage of total investment to its historical trend increases or decreases every 1%, the percentage of national income to its historical trend will increase or decrease 0.28%.

2. Influence of previous-year investment on current-year economic fluctuation

Due to time lag, the previous investment forms newly increased fixed assets of current year and affects current-year economic fluctuation. This originates from supply-side.

We take Y to represent national income, t to represent current year, K_{t-1} to represent the original fixed assets of previous year, $\dot{K}_t$ to be the current-year scrappage of the original fixed assets, α to represent the effect coefficient of output of the original fixed assets, ΔK_t to represent the newly increased fixed assets of current year, β to represent the effect coefficient of output of newly increased fixed assets. The production of national income in the current year is as follows:

$$Y_t = \alpha_t \times (K_{t-1} - \dot{K}_t) + \beta_t \times \Delta K_t \tag{12}$$

In formula (12), the newly increased fixed assets (ΔK_t) of current year is accumulated by previous investment. We define $I_{t,\tau}$ to represent previous investment, $\xi_{t,\tau}$ to represent rate of previous investment transferred and in use in year t. The newly increased fixed assets of the current year are as follows:

$$\Delta K_t = \sum_{\tau} \xi_{t,\tau} \cdot I_{t,\tau} \tag{13}$$
$$(\tau = 1, 2, \ldots, n)$$

Substitute formula (13) into formula (12):

$$Y_t = \alpha_t \cdot (K_{t-1} - \dot{K}_t) + \beta_t \cdot (\sum_{\tau} \xi_{t,\tau} \cdot I'_{t,\tau})$$

(14)

As depicted in formula (14), previous investment affects current-year economic fluctuation in three aspects: the amount $(I_{t,\tau})$ of previous investment, the rate of previous investment transferred and in use $(\xi_{t,\tau})$ and the effect coefficient (β_t) of the output of newly increased fixed assets formed by previous investment. I omitted the calculation of formula (14) here as it is relatively complicated.

The above qualitative and quantitative analyses illustrate that investment periodic fluctuation as the dominant factor directly influences economic cyclical fluctuation. It is important to control investment periodic fluctuation and to prevent investment from drastic ups and downs in the development of the national economy in the long-term.

(Originally published in *The Journal of Quantitative & Technical Economics*. No.10, 1987)

Notes

1   Shucheng, Liu. (1986). Preliminary Study on Periodicity of Fixed Assets Investment in China. *Economic Research Journal*, 2; Shucheng, Liu. (1986). Re-Study on Periodicity of Fixed Assets Investment in China: Analysis of Its Stages. *Economic Research Journal*, 6; Shucheng, Liu. (1986). The Third Study on Periodicity of Fixed Assets Investment in China: Historical Analysis of Its Cycles. *The Journal of Quantitative & Technical Economics*, 9.

2   Jian, Lu. (1987). Analysis of Features, Causes and Mechanism of Economic Cycle in China. *Economic Research Journal*, 4.

3   Ye, Lin. (1986). Periodicity of Fixed Assets Investment and Economic Development in China. *Journal of Tianjin Normal University*, 6.

4   Marx, K. (2001). *Capital: A critique of political economy, the process of circulation of capital*. (Vol. 2, p.248). S. Moore & E. Aveling (Trans.). London: Electric Book Co. (Original work published 1885).

5   Marx, K. (1975). *Das Kapital*. (Vol. 1, pp.498–499). Beijing: People's Publishing House.

6   Marx, K. (2001). *Capital: A critique of political economy, the process of capitalist production as a whole*. (Vol. 3, Pt. 5, Chap. 30, Note 100). S. Moore & E. Aveling (Trans.). London: Electric Book Co. (Original work published 1894).

7   Engels, F. (1965). Preface of 'British Working Class' German, 2nd, 1892. *The complete works of Marx and Engels*. (Vol. 22, p.373). Beijing: People's Publishing House.

8   Marx, K. (2001). *Capital: A critique of political economy, the process of circulation of capital*. (Vol. 2, p.245). S. Moore & E. Aveling (Trans.). London: Electric Book Co. (Original work published 1885).

9   The original data from 1953 to 1985 in each table of this article are all taken from *China Statistical Yearbook, 1986*, (*China statistical yearbook, 1986*. (1986). Beijing: China Statistics Press); The 1986 data are extracted from *1986 Bulletin of Statistics for National Economic and Social Development of the State Statistical Bureau of People's Republic of China* (1987, Feb. 21. *The People's Daily*).

10 Investment curve in Figure 9.1 is the annual growth rate (according to current-year price) curve of total fixed assets investment in the scope of public ownership.

10 Applied research of the industrial and agricultural production function in China

I Application of the production function in China

The production function primarily refers to the Cobb-Douglas production function set up through the econometric method. The application of the production function in China is characterized as follows.

First, the applied research of the production function in China began in the early 1980s,[1] whereas the research and application of input-output analysis began in the early 1960s,[2] a delay of 20 years. Input-output analysis is directly related to the economic theory and balance method employed in economic planning in China. With the development of China's socialist modernization construction and science in recent years, the application and research of the production function has just started, but it is still immature.

Second, although the applied research of the production function is immature, it develops quickly. According to incomplete statistics, there were more than 60 articles published on the production function in China in just two years from January 1983 to April 1985. These articles could be divided into three categories. The first category mainly studied the theoretical production function from the perspective of plutonomy. The second category primarily explored the methodology of the production function in terms of econometrics such as the study of the production function of multiple factors with more than three input elements, the study of the production function of Constant Elasticity of Substitution (CES), the study of refinement and decomposition of fixed assets and the study of labor refinement and decomposition. But due to the lack of requisite data, these studies generally have not been put into application for the time being. The third category chiefly investigated the Cobb-Douglas production function. Most articles were in this category.

Third, the research of the production function is widely applied. In terms of participants, in addition to the institutions, colleges and universities that are involved, the research and application of the production function are carried out in government sectors such as the State Planning Commission, the National Economic Council, the State Scientific and Technological Commission, National Bureau of Statistics, the State Administration for Commodity Prices, Research Center of Technology and Economy of the State Council and government sectors of some provinces, municipalities and autonomous regions. In terms of content, application involves the subsequent aspects. It quantitatively analyzes the role of various factors that affect economic growth and their interrelations, forecasts the scale and speed of production development and takes the production function as an important element of the macroeconomic model in studying the balance between the supply and demand of the means of production, labor resources and product and the related major proportional relationship of the national economy. In terms of the scope of application, there are production functions of single product and individual enterprise, production functions of industry and sector, production functions of provinces, municipalities and autonomous regions and a national aggregate production function.

II   Study of the industrial aggregate production function in China[3]

1.   *The industrial aggregate production function in China*

(1)   Function form

In *China Statistical Yearbook* (1984),[4] there is a lack of complete aggregate temporal data, mainly capital data for the whole industry in China. But the aggregate temporal data is relatively complete for publicly-owned industrial enterprises with independent accounting. Thus according to the data drawn from *China Statistical Yearbook*, we mainly explore the aggregate production function of publicly-owned industrial enterprises with independent accounting in China. Since *China Statistical Yearbook* only provides the gross data of fixed assets, circulating fund and labor force for publicly-owned industrial enterprises with independent accounting and does not include further elaborated data of the composition of fixed assets and constitution of the labor force, we are unable to adopt a complicated form of production function and will primarily investigate the simple Cobb-Douglas production function.

First we choose the production function:

$$Y = A K^{\alpha} L^{\beta} e^{\lambda t} u$$

wherein: Y – index of total industrial output value of public ownership, taking 1952 as 100 and calculated at comparable prices. Since there is no net industrial output value of public ownership in the above yearbook, the calculation is based on the total output value; K – capital of publicly-owned enterprises with independent accounting (100 million yuan) calculated according to current-year price, K takes K_1, K_2, K_3, K_4, respectively; K_1 – the total amount of fixed assets original value and normed current fund; K_2 – the total amount of fixed assets net value and normed current fund; K_3 – fixed assets original value; K_4 – fixed assets net value; L – the number of staff and workers (10,000) of publicly-owned industrial enterprises by the end of year; t – year; and u – error term. The function is specified as:

$$Y = A K_1{}^\alpha L^\beta e^{\lambda t} u$$
$$Y = A K_2{}^\alpha L^\beta e^{\lambda t} u$$
$$Y = A K_3{}^\alpha L^\beta e^{\lambda t} u$$
$$Y = A K_4{}^\alpha L^\beta e^{\lambda t} u$$

(2)   Data processing

The sample period was from 1952 to1982. In Figure 10.1 there are variation curves (all are converted to index in the figure) of Y, K_4, L of 31 years. Variation curves of K_1, K_2 and K_3 almost conform with that of K_4 and will not be drawn.

As shown in Figure 10.1, Y, K_4, L are abnormal data during the 5 years from 1958 to 1962. If we remove the data of these five years and connect the curves of Y, K_4, L from 1952 to 1957 and from 1963 to 1982, respectively, namely assuming no abnormal fluctuation occurred, these three curves of Y, K_4 and L are perfect and in conformity with the time developing trend (see Figure 10.2). When we adopt the data from 1952 to 1982, we should first smooth the data from 1958 to 1962 through the interpolation method.

In Figure 10.3 there is a substitution curve between labor force L and fixed assets net value K_4 from 1952 to 1982. The data from 1958 to 1962 is exceptional as shown in Figure 10.3 and needs to be smoothed. If we connect the two

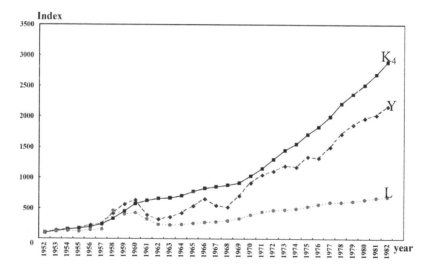

Figure 10.1 Variation curves of Y, K_4, L

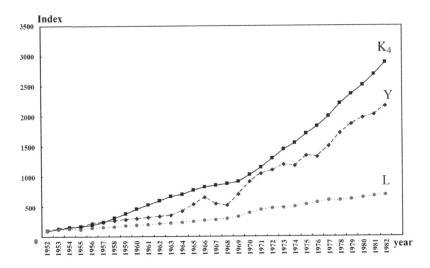

Figure 10.2 Variation curves of Y, K_4, L (data from 1958 to 1962 is smoothed)

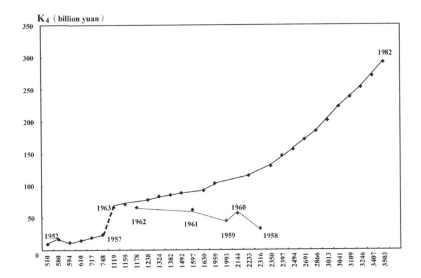

Figure 10.3 Curve between L and K_4

lines from 1952 to 1957 and from 1963 to 1982 and assume no abnormal fluctuations occurred, the resulting curve demonstrates the normal relationship between L and K_4.

(3)   Parameter estimation

By employing the smoothed data, we adopt the ordinary least square method (OLS) to estimate the above production function.[5] The results are as follows (the digit in the parentheses below each parameter of the function is the standard deviation of the parameter estimate value, same hereinafter):

$$\ln Y = -1.735 + 0.17\ln K_1 + 0.90\ln L + 0.020t \tag{1}$$
$$(2.593)\ (0.014)\ (0.071)\ (0.0004)$$

$$\ln Y = -1.493 + 0.14\ln K_2 + 0.89\ln L + 0.024t \tag{2}$$
$$(2.571)\ (0.011)\ (0.073)\ (0.0003)$$

$$\ln Y = -2.000 + 0.18\ln K_3 + 0.94\ln L + 0.017t \tag{3}$$
$$(2.596)\ (0.012)\ (0.065)\ (0.0004)$$

$$\ln Y = -1.710 + 0.15\ln K_4 + 0.93\ln L + 0.021t \tag{4}$$
$$(2.517)\ (0.008)\ (0.066)\ (0.0003)$$

formula (1): $R^2 = 0.99$ SE $= 0.097$ F $= 1399.41$ DW $= 0.95$
formula (2): $R^2 = 0.99$ SE $= 0.097$ F $= 1394.07$ DW $= 0.95$
formula (3): $R^2 = 0.99$ SE $= 0.096$ F $= 1435.19$ DW $= 0.95$
formula (4): $R^2 = 0.99$ SE $= 0.096$ F $= 1435.37$ DW $= 0.96$

(4)   Result analysis

R^2: The total correlation coefficient R^2 in this group of four production functions is 0.99, respectively, which is very high. This illustrates that the goodness-of-fit of the regression curve of the production function derived from K, L, t as explanatory variables to the observed value of sample of Y is satisfactory. Figure 10.4 is the

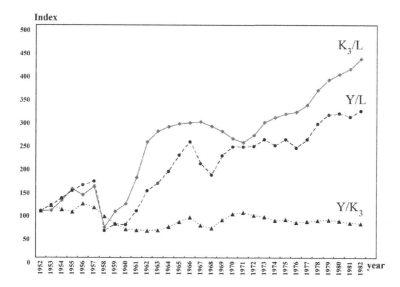

Figure 10.4 Curves of capital outfit ratio of labor force, labor productivity, capital output ratio

fitting chart[6] of the regression curve of $Y = A K_4^\alpha L^\beta e^{\lambda t} u$ and the curve of the observed value of sample of Y.

Standard deviation of parameter estimate value and value F: the standard deviations of parameter estimate values of K, L, t, as explanatory variables in the four production functions are very small. This illustrates that these estimate values are statistically obvious. At the same time, value F in the four production functions is also large and shows the overall significance of the regression parameter.

Value DW: Value DW in the four production functions is between 0.95 and 0.96, which is rather low. This demonstrates that there exists a certain serial correlation in a stochastic component.

α and β: In the four production functions, since K takes K_1, K_2, K_3, K_4 respectively, the values of α and β are slightly different. While α is between 0.14 and 0.18, β is between 0.89 and 0.94; $\alpha + \beta$ is between 1.03 and 1.12 and slightly greater than 1.

As shown in Figure 10.1, the growth of Y is lower than that of K and greater than that of L during the 31 years from 1952 to 1982. Their average annual increase during this period are respectively Y – 10.79%, K_1 – 11.85%, K_2 – 11.78%, K_3 – 11.93%, K_4 – 11.87% and L – 6.63%. In this way, the input of K is more than that of L in every 1% increase in Y. Thus, capital elasticity α of output is smaller than labor force elasticity β. Actually, β is 4–5 times larger than α in the production functions (1) – (4).

As depicted in Figure 10.4, the capital outfit of the labor force (taking fixed assets original value per capita K_3 / L for example) rises quickly, labor productivity (Y / L) is upward and capital productivity (taking Y / K_3, for example) is downward from 1952 to 1982. This illustrates that capital utilization effectiveness is comparatively low. The fixed assets original value of publicly-owned industrial enterprises with independent accounting in China increased from 14.88 billion yuan to 43.75 billion yuan during 31 years, an increase of 28.4 times. Without doubt, it laid a solid material and technical foundation for the future growth of the economy and accomplishing socialist modernization in China. However, rather than pursuing a high level of investment, we should focus on tapping potentialities, innovation and reform of the old equipment and improving its economic efficiency in the future. In 1982, the State Council made "Decision on Systematically Carrying out Technical Renovation in Existing Enterprises", which clearly put forward

> we laid particular stress on constructing new enterprises for a long time and ignored the technological transformation of the existing enterprises. It was quite severe that equipment was aging, technology was obsolete, measurement and testing condition was poor and product was backward. This was adverse to realizing socialist modernization. It has become urgent to carry out technical renovation systematically in the existing enterprises for the development of economy in China.
>
> (*China Economic Yearbook (1983)*, 1983, p. 19)[7]

The value λ: λ is between 0.017 and 0.024 in the production functions (1) – (4), which is the overall efficiency coefficient of various other factors to output except for the inputted factors K and L. The "other factors" include the development of science and technology, the impact of economic policy and the improvement of management. Overall, output efficiency increased 1.7% to 2.4% annually during 31 years, which contributed to total output value growth by 15.75% to 22.24%. This contribution rate has reached up to 40% to 50% in some developed countries at present. There is a big gap between China and developed countries. It is very important to take effective measures and improve overall output efficiency so as to achieve socialist modernization.

2.   Analysis of taking the value for α and β under different conditions

Capital elasticity α and labor force elasticity β are the two important parameters based on the Cobb-Douglas aggregate production function for publicly-owned industrial enterprises with independent accounting in China. We have carried out a range of calculations in order to examine the variation of taking the value for α and β under different conditions.

(1)   Impact of removing the term eλt on α and β

In the aforesaid production function $Y = A K^{\alpha}L^{\beta}e^{\lambda t}u$, explanatory variables K, L and t are highly correlated. What will happen if we remove term $e^{\lambda t}$ in the production function to overcome the multicollinearity between K, L and t?

We adopt the production function $Y = AK^{\alpha}L^{\beta}u$ with K taking the value of K_1 - K_4, respectively. The estimate results are as follows:

$$\ln Y = -3.383 + 0.22\ln K_1 + 1.12\ln L \tag{5}$$
$$(0.278)\ (0.012)\ (0.031)$$

$$\ln Y = -3.495 + 0.19\ln K_2 + 1.17\ln L \tag{6}$$
$$(0.271)\ (0.011)\ (0.028)$$

$$\ln Y = -3.364 + 0.22\ln K_3 + 1.12\ln L \tag{7}$$
$$(0.228)\ (0.009)\ (0.024)$$

$$\ln Y = -3.493 + 0.19\ln K_4 + 1.18\ln L \tag{8}$$
$$(2.517)\ (0.008)\ (0.066)$$

formula (5): $R^2 = 0.989$ SE $= 0.097$ F $= 2681.22$ DW $= 0.91$
formula (6): $R^2 = 0.990$ SE $= 0.099$ F $= 2931.01$ DW $= 0.90$
formula (7): $R^2 = 0.989$ SE $= 0.096$ F $= 2685.90$ DW $= 0.92$
formula (8): $R^2 = 0.990$ SE $= 0.097$ F $= 2964.72$ DW $= 0.91$

As shown in the second set of production functions, the values of α and β all rise after removing term $e^{\lambda t}$. The value of α rises from 0.14–0.18 in the first group of production functions composed by the formulas (1) – (4) to 0.19–0.22 and β rises from 0.89–0.94 in the preceding first group of production functions to 1.12–1.18. The reason for the increase is that removing the term $e^{\lambda t}$ transfers the impact of term t to the coefficients of term K and L; namely, the impact is taken up by α and β, making their implications less clear.

At the same time, value DW in the second set of production functions falls from 0.95–0.96 in the first group of production functions to 0.90–0.92 because time t is an autocorrelation variable and its impact also transfers to the stochastic component and increases serial correlation after removing term $e^{\lambda t}$.

(2)   Impact of different function forms on α and β

We adopt production function $Y / L = A (K / L)^{\alpha} e^{\lambda t} u$ to make an estimation. The sample period was from 1952 to 1982. Y / L, as the absolute index is directly taken from *China Statistical Yearbook (1984)*, in which the sample values from 1958 to 1963 are smoothed through interpolation. K / L takes values of K_1 / L, K_2 / L, K_3 / L, K_4 / L, respectively, in which the samples from1958 to 1962 are smoothed. The calculation results are as follows:

$$\ln(Y / L) = 6.051 + 0.29\ln(K_1 / L) + 0.018t \qquad (9)$$
$$(0.876)\ (0.012)\ (0.00002)$$

$$\ln(Y / L) = 6.358 + 0.26\ln(K_2 / L) + 0.019t \qquad (10)$$
$$(0.654)\ (0.009)\ (0.00002)$$

$$\ln(Y / L) = 6.272 + 0.27\ln(K_3 / L) + 0.019t \qquad (11)$$
$$(0.663)\ (0.010)\ (0.00002)$$

$$\ln(Y / L) = 6.619 + 0.24\ln(K_4 / L) + 0.021t \qquad (12)$$
$$(0.436)\ (0.007)\ (0.00001)$$

formula (9): $R^2 = 0.91$ SE $= 0.090$ F $= 300.69$ DW $= 1.11$
formula (10): $R^2 = 0.91$ SE $= 0.090$ F $= 302.75$ DW $= 1.11$
formula (11): $R^2 = 0.91$ SE $= 0.089$ F $= 307.23$ DW $= 1.09$
formula (12): $R^2 = 0.92$ SE $= 0.088$ F $= 314.28$ DW $= 1.10$

Compared with the first group of production functions, we realize from the third set of production functions that the estimation value of λ has little change. Originally, it was between 0.017 and 0.024 and now it is between 0.018 and 0.021.The estimation value of α rises from 0.14–0.18 to 0.24–0.29. This demonstrates that α is internally influenced by L due to imposing the restriction of $\alpha + \beta = 1$ in the third set of production functions. At this time, the implication of α is not clear. R^2 reduces to 0.91–0.92 in the third set of production functions. This illustrates that the goodness-of-fit of the third set of functions is dissatisfactory. But value *DW* rises in the third set of production functions. This reveals that the serial correlation of stochastic component reduces.

We turn to apply this production function $y = a + \alpha k + \beta l + u$ to make an estimation. The variables y, k, l are, respectively, the annual growth rates of Y, K, L and are calculated according to the previous smoothed samples. The result is as follows:

$$y = 3.71 - 0.04k_1 + 1.02l \tag{13}$$
$$(22.836)\ (0.127)\ (0.114)$$

$$y = 4.03 - 0.07k_2 + 1.22l \tag{14}$$
$$(18.455)\ (0.101)\ (0.118)$$

$$y = 1.56 + 0.15k_3 + 1.18l \tag{15}$$
$$(22.007)\ (0.107)\ (0.110)$$

$$y = 2.05 + 0.12k_4 + 1.17l \tag{16}$$
$$(17.194)\ (0.078)\ (0.112)$$

formula (13): $R^2 = 0.33$ SE = 10.198 F = 13.53 DW = 1.60
formula (14): $R^2 = 0.33$ SE = 10.190 F = 13.60 DW = 1.60
formula (15): $R^2 = 0.33$ SE = 10.159 F = 13.85 DW = 1.61
formula (16): $R^2 = 0.33$ SE = 10.168 F = 13.78 DW = 1.61

We recognize that R^2 declines sharply after adopting the fourth group of production functions, which shows that the goodness-of-fit of this function form is quite dissatisfactory. Correspondingly, the overall standard deviation SE of the function and standard deviation of parameter estimate value all rise significantly. The value of α becomes negative in the production function formulas (13) and (14). Obviously, it is exceedingly inaccurate to estimate α and β with this production function form.

(3)   Impact of different data processing methods on α and β

The above four sets of production functions adopt the smoothed data from 1952 to 1982. Now we employ the original samples from 1952 to 1982 and add a dummy variable to the years from 1958 to 1960, namely D = 1 in these three years, D = 0 in other years. We re-estimate the first set of production functions $Y = A K^\alpha L^\beta e^{\lambda t} u$. The result is as follows:

$$\ln Y = 1.650 + 0.23\ln K_1 + 0.30\ln L + 0.054t + 0.365D \tag{17}$$
$$(1.343)\ (0.019)\ (0.043)\ (0.0002)\ (0.033)$$

$$\ln Y = 1.921 + 0.21\ln K_2 + 0.29\ln L + 0.058t + 0.370D \tag{18}$$
$$(1.310)\ (0.015)\ (0.044)\ (0.0002)\ (0.033)$$

$$\ln Y = 1.560 + 0.21\ln K_3 + 0.35\ln L + 0.054t + 0.347D \tag{19}$$
$$(1.385)\ (0.018)\ (0.039)\ (0.0002)\ (0.033)$$

$$\ln Y = 1.847 + 0.18\ln K_4 + 0.34\ln L + 0.059t + 0.349D \tag{20}$$
$$(1.330)\ (0.013)\ (0.040)\ (0.0002)\ (0.033)$$

formula (17): $R^2 = 0.986$ SE $= 0.118$ F $= 615.72$ DW $= 1.26$
formula (18): $R^2 = 0.985$ SE $= 0.117$ F $= 577.10$ DW $= 1.26$
formula (19): $R^2 = 0.985$ SE $= 0.118$ F $= 605.98$ DW $= 1.28$
formula (20): $R^2 = 0.985$ SE $= 0.118$ F $= 577.69$ DW $= 1.28$

Compared with the first group of production functions, we draw from the fifth set of production functions that the value of β declines sharply from the original 0.89–0.94 to the present 0.29–0.35. The value of α rises from the original 0.14–0.18 to the present 0.18–0.23. The value of λ rises from the original 0.017–0.024 to the present 0.054–0.059. The constant term $\ln A$ changes from negative to positive. How can these be explained? From Figure 10.1, L increases strongly from 1958 to 1960. The number of employees of publicly-owned industrial enterprises was 7.48 million at the end of 1957 and jumped to 23.16 million in 1958, an increase of 2.1 times. Although the amount declined slightly in 1959 and 1960, it still maintained at a high level of 19.93 million and 21.44 million. The growth and the level of L are much higher than that of K during these three years. The reaction of the Cobb-Douglas production function to the variation of sample data is so sensitive that the sharp increase of L during these three years affects the estimation of the entire sample period, making β decline greatly. The declining portion of β is transferred to and taken up by α, λ, $\ln A$.

We adopt the original sample from 1952 to 1982, add dummy variable $D = 1$ to the years from 1958 to 1960 and re-estimate the second set of production functions $Y = A K^\alpha L^\beta u$. The result is as follows:

$$\ln Y = -1.986 + 0.53\ln K_1 + 0.62\ln L - 0.016D \tag{21}$$
$$(0.503)\ (0.019)\ (0.051)\ (0.032)$$

$$\ln Y = -2.246 + 0.45\ln K_2 + 0.75\ln L - 0.141D \tag{22}$$
$$(0.568)\ (0.019)\ (0.052)\ (0.030)$$

$$\ln Y = -2.070 + 0.50\ln K_3 + 0.68\ln L - 0.027D \tag{23}$$
$$(0.467)\ (0.016)\ (0.044)\ (0.031)$$

$$\ln Y = -2.428 + 0.40\ln K_4 + 0.84\ln L - 0.182D \tag{24}$$
$$(0.517)\ (0.016)\ (0.043)\ (0.028)$$

formula (21): $R^2 = 0.977$ SE $= 0.141$ F $= 606.51$ DW $= 1.01$
formula (22): $R^2 = 0.975$ SE $= 0.149$ F $= 548.38$ DW $= 1.06$
formula (23): $R^2 = 0.977$ SE $= 0.141$ F $= 603.28$ DW $= 1.07$
formula (24): $R^2 = 0.974$ SE $= 0.151$ F $= 528.53$ DW $= 1.14$

Compared the second set of production functions, β in the sixth group of production functions plunges from the original 1.12–1.18 to the present 0.62–0.84 and α increases from the original 0.19–0.22 to the present 0.40–0.53.

We are now able to proceed to another data processing by eliminating 11 samples from 1952 to 1962 and estimating with 20 samples only from 1963 to 1982 by adopting the first group of production functions $Y = A K^\alpha L^\beta e^{\lambda t} u$. The result is as follows:

$$\ln Y = -0.555 - 0.24\ln K_1 + 0.99\ln L + 0.050t \tag{25}$$
$$(24.473)\ (0.696)\ (0.113)\ (0.004)$$

$$\ln Y = -0.687 - 0.27\ln K_2 + 1.03\ln L + 0.050t \tag{26}$$
$$(13.357)\ (0.506)\ (0.140)\ (0.002)$$

$$\ln Y = -3.769 + 0.26\ln K_3 + 0.96\ln L + 0.008t \tag{27}$$
$$(23.613)\ (0.364)\ (0.081)\ (0.003)$$

$$\ln Y = -3.211 + 0.21\ln K_4 + 0.94\ln L + 0.010t \tag{28}$$
$$(14.459)\ (0.240)\ (0.079)\ (0.002)$$

formula (25): $R^2 = 0.975$ SE $= 0.099$ F $= 337.97$ DW $= 1.35$
formula (26): $R^2 = 0.976$ SE $= 0.099$ F $= 339.26$ DW $= 1.35$
formula (27): $R^2 = 0.977$ SE $= 0.099$ F $= 340.35$ DW $= 1.31$
formula (28): $R^2 = 0.976$ SE $= 0.099$ F $= 340.13$ DW $= 1.32$

As a result of reducing the sample data quantity from 31 to 20, we find out from the seventh set of production functions that α turns to negative and the standard deviation of estimate value of α in the seventh set of production functions greatly increases.

From the calculation of the above 7 sets or 28 equations, we can subsequently understand how to apply the Cobb-Douglas aggregate production function to publicly-owned industrial enterprises with independent accounting in China.

First, it is appropriate to take K, L, t as explanatory variables. If we remove term t to overcome multicollinearity between K, L, t, the impact of overall output efficiency will be transferred to and taken up by α and β, making the implications of α and β not clear.

Second, when applying the production function $Y / L = A(K / L)^\alpha e^{\lambda t} u$, due to imposing the restriction of $\alpha + \beta = 1$, α is inherently influenced by L. This makes the implication of α unclear. The production function $y = a + \alpha k + \beta l + u$ is simple and inaccurate.

Last, as a result of the abnormal fluctuation of sample data, it is difficult to estimate the production function. However, we should make a careful choice in multiple calculations by adopting a large sample so as to process data properly.

A further study needs to be engaged in error term analysis and the analysis of K in different stages.

III Study of the agricultural aggregate production function in China

1. Brief account of agricultural development in China

In Figure 10.5, there are variation curves of agricultural net output, number of end-year agricultural laborers and total planting area of farm crops from 1952 to 1983 (all are converted to index in the figure). As depicted in Figure 10.5, the

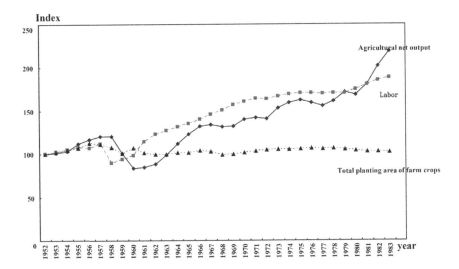

Figure 10.5 Variation curves of agricultural net output value, labor and total planting area of farm crops in China

development of agricultural net output was full of twists and turns during the 32 years and grew rapidly after 1978 since the Chinese government implemented a new rural policy. The average annual growth rate of agricultural net output was 2.06% during the 26 years from 1952 to 1977. It was 6.83% during the six years from 1978 to 1983.The growth rate of agricultural labor force during the 21 years from 1952 to 1954 and from 1960 to 1977 exceeded that of agricultural net output. It is not surprising that labor force elasticity coefficient of output will sometimes be negative in setting up the agricultural aggregate production function in China. This signifies that there is surplus in agricultural labor over a long period of time. There was no great change in total cultivated area of crops from 1952 to 1983.

2.   *Agricultural aggregate production function in China*

The study of the agricultural aggregate production function in China is not adequate because the relevant data is incomplete; especially, it is difficult to determine exactly the usage of agricultural production funds. We introduce the Cobb-Douglas production function ("Research and Practice", 1984)[8] with the total agricultural income as dependent variable established by Xigang Zhu from Institute of Agricultural Economy at Chinese Academy of Agricultural Science. The estimation result is as follows:

$$Y = 0.3252e^{0.0105t} X_1^{0.2315} X_2^{0.1647}$$
$$(-10.64)\ (2.71)\ (8.89)\ (7.93)$$

$X_3^{0.5314} X_4^{0.3788} e^{0.0708x5} \; e^{-0.0172x6}$
(29.18) (9.06) (2.48) (−0.21)

$R^2 = 0.993$

Samples come from 250 groups of statistical data of people's communes of 28 provinces, municipalities and autonomous regions (short of Tibet data) from 1972 to 1980.

The digit in parentheses below each parameter is the test value t of the parameter estimate; Y – total agricultural income (100 million yuan) of people's communes; X_1 – collective cultivated area (10,000 acres); X_2 – number of agricultural laborers (10,000 persons); X_3 – production cost (10,000 yuan); X_4 – dummy variable of cultivated land. The dummy variable is determined by regional factors such as geographic location, land quality, multiple crop index and output level, and its value is between 1.0 to 4.0; X_5 – dummy variable of policy; X_5 is 0 from 1972 to 1978, 0.5 in 1979 and 1 in 1980; X_6 – weather variable, which is represented by the proportion of damaged area due to inundation and drought in various regions accounting for the total planting area.

We draw from the above production function that the labor force elasticity coefficient of the total agricultural income is 0.1647 and less than the capital elasticity coefficient of 0.5314. The situation in industry is the converse. We realize that economic policies have a great impact on agriculture. The annual growth rate of total agricultural income is 7.08% due to the implementation of a new economic policy, while the agricultural overall efficiency represented by term t is low, which is only 1.05%. We should continue to carry out corrective rural economic policies on the one hand and vigorously promote agricultural science and technology and improve economic effect of agricultural production on the other hand. They are the key to accelerate agricultural development in China.

(Originally published in *Function of Econometrics Model in National Economic Management*, Economic Science Press, 1987)

Notes

1 As far as we know, the earliest article published on the production function in China was the thesis submitted at the first annual meeting of the Chinese Association of Quantitative Economics held in February, 1982, in Xian, Shaanxi Province. It was published afterwards in the book entitled *Quantitative economic theory, model and prediction*. (1983). Beijing: Energy Resources Press.
2 As far as we know, the earliest articles published on input-output analysis in China were in 1961 and 1962, for example Jiapei, Wu (1961, August 1). Discussion on Economic Mathematics. *The People's Daily*; Bingquan, Li. (1962). Economic Mathematical Model of Balance between Production and Distribution Sectors. *Chinese Science Bulletin*, 2; Jiapei, Wu. (1962). Issues on Inter-Sector balance sheet. *China Economic Studies*, 7–8; Jiapei, Wu, & Shouyi, Zhang. (1962). Study on balance sheet of Inter-Sector Production and Distribution. *Economic Research Journal*, 8.
3 The calculation in the second part of this article was taken charge of by Comrade Feihong Gong, associate researcher of the Institute of Quantitative & Technical Economics at Chinese Academy of Social Sciences, to whom I express my deep gratitude.

4 *China statistical yearbook, 1984*. (1984). Beijing: China Statistics Press.
5 In this article, the parameter estimation adopts the ordinary least square method (OLS). Tongsan Wang wrote an article entitled "Study on Parameter Estimation of 'Econometric Model of Production, Distribution and Final Use of National Income in China' " published in *The Journal of Quantitative & Technical Economics*, No.1, 1985, in which he respectively adopted ordinary least square method (OLS), two-stage least square method (2SLS), three-stage least square method (3SLS) and limited information maximum likelihood method (LIML) to estimate the industrial aggregate production function in China. He pointed out that there are no obvious impacts of multicollinearity between explanatory variables on the estimate value of OLS, 2SLS, 3SLS methods, but there is a severe impact on the estimate value of the LIML method. In view of this, this article only adopts the simple OLS method when making parameter estimation.
6 Author's new annotation: Figure 4 in the original article was relatively complicated and is omitted.
7 *China economic yearbook, 1983*. (1983). (Vol. 8, p.19). Beijing: Economic Management Magazine.
8 Xigang, Zhu. (1984). Research and Practice on Determination of Contribution of Agricultural Technical Advance in China. *Journal of Agricultural Economics*, 6.

11 On the Phillips curve in China

Two significant economic relationships – the rate of economic growth and price increase rate, the unemployment rate and price increase rate – are crucial for governments of various countries to carry out macroeconomic regulation, which involve the issue of the Phillips curve. This article aims to examine whether the relationship described in the basic Phillips curve applies to China (some in academic circles consider not) and if so, how the Phillips curve deforms in China and what the important policy implications are.

I   Three kinds of Phillips curves and deformations

Clarifying what the Phillips curve is and how it will deform are the prerequisites for clearly illustrating the above issues.

1.   The three kinds of Phillips curves and three pairs of economic variables

There are three expressions of the Phillips curve illustrating three pairs of economic variables. The first expression is called the "unemployment-wage" Phillips curve, demonstrating the relationship between the unemployment rate and change rate of money wage, which was first proposed in 1958 by the New Zealand economist A. Phillips, who had been undertaking research in the UK. It is a curve (see solid line in Figure 11.1) with a negative slope tilting from lower right to upper left in the graph, with the lateral axis expressing the unemployment rate and the longitudinal axis denoting the change rate of money wage. The curve represents the corresponding adverse relationship between the variation in the unemployment rate and change rate of money wage, namely a negative correlation. When the unemployment rate rises, the change rate of money wage declines, whereas when the unemployment rate declines, the change rate of money wage rises. In the rising period of short-term and typical economic cyclical fluctuation, the unemployment rate descends while the change rate of money wage increases. During the economic downward period, the unemployment rate rises while the change rate of money wage declines. Accordingly, this curve is represented as a circle moving from the lower right to the upper left and then from the upper left to the lower right

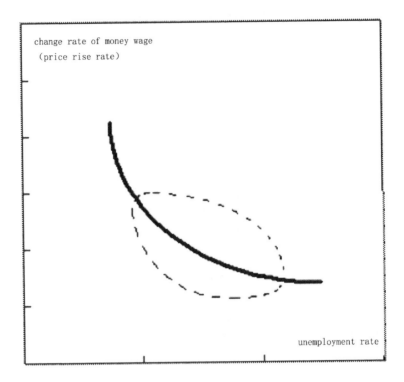

change rate of money wage
(price rise rate)

unemployment rate

Figure 11.1 First and second kinds of Phillips curve

(see dotted line in Figure 11.1) in the low position and flat shape slightly slanting to the upper left. This illustrates that variations in the unemployment rate and change rate of money wage are in an inverse relationship, with a low range of alteration in the change rate of money wage at a low level.

The second expression is called the "unemployment–price" Phillips curve, indicating the relationship between the unemployment rate and price rise rate, put forward by the American economists Samuelson and Solow in 1960. They substituted the price rise rate for the change rate of money wage in the original Phillips curve. This substitution is realized through the assumption that the formation of the production price adheres to the average labor cost with fixed value added, namely the unit price of a product is composed of the average labor cost and a fixed percentage of other costs and profit. In other words, price variation is only related to the variation in money wage. This expression is the same as the first expression, only differing in that the longitudinal axis alters with the price rise rate (see Figure 11.1). The curve demonstrates the corresponding converse relationship in the variation of the unemployment rate and the price rise rate. In the rising phase of short-term and typical economic cyclical fluctuation, the unemployment rate falls while the price rise rate increases. During the phase of economic reduction, the unemployment rate rises whilst the price rise rate declines. This is displayed as the curved circle in Figure 11.1.

The third expression we term is the "output-price" Phillips curve, showing the relationship between the economic growth rate and the price rise rate, which is commonly employed by many economists. This kind of Phillips curve substitutes the economic growth rate for the unemployment rate in the second expression effected through "Okun's law". The American economist Okun proposed in 1962 that the unemployment rate and the economic growth rate are in a corresponding inverse relationship in terms of variation. Thus, the variations in the economic growth rate and the price rise rate present a corresponding equidirectional relationship. In empirical research, the deviation of the actual economic growth rate from the potential economic growth rate ("deviation" for short) or deviation of the actual output level from the potential output level is applied rather than the indicator of economic growth rate directly. This deviation signifies the gap between total social supply and demand and pressure in terms of price increase over a certain period of time. The actual economic growth rate indicates the output increase determined by the total social demand within a definite period, while the potential economic growth rate demonstrates the total supply provided by social labor, material and financial resources at a certain technical level in a determinate time. There are two implications of the potential economic growth rate, one of which relates to the normal potential economic growth rate achieved by full and regular utilization of various resources, the other being the maximum economic growth rate achieved through making the maximal use of various resources. Thus, we adopt the first implication. This expression is a curve (see solid line in Figure 11.2) with a

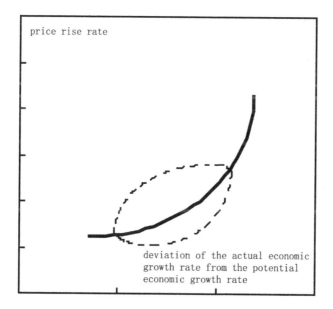

Figure 11.2 Third kind of Phillips curve

positive slope inclining from the lower left to the upper right in the graph with the lateral axis expressing the deviation and the longitudinal axis denoting rate of the price increase. The trend of the curve is just in the inverse direction of the first and second expressions, illustrating the corresponding equidirectional relationship in the variation of the deviation and price rise rate, namely a positive correlation. When the deviation rises, the price rise rate also increases; when the deviation declines, the price rise rate falls. In the rising period of typical, short-term economic cyclical fluctuation, the price rise rate climbs with the rise in deviation as demand expands. During a period of economic fall, the price rise rate descends with the decline in deviation as demand contracts. Thus, this curve is represented as a curve circle moving from the lower left to the upper right and then from the upper right to the lower left (see dotted line in Figure 11.2) in the low position and flat shape slightly slanting to the upper right. This signifies that the variations in the deviation and price rise rate are in an equidirectional relationship with a low range of alteration in price increase rate at a low level.

The above three shapes of the Phillips curve reflect the situations of some Western countries, such as the United States and the UK in the 1950s and 1960s, respectively displaying the corresponding converse relationship between the unemployment rate and the change rate of money wage, the corresponding inverse relationship between the unemployment rate and the price rise rate, and the corresponding equidirectional relationship between the economic growth rate and the price rise rate. We call the three shapes of the curves the "basic Phillips curve" and the two converse relationships and single equidirectional corresponding relationship "basic Phillips curve relationships".

2.   *Deformation of the Phillips curve*

In the practical economy, the basic Phillips curve often deforms due to various impacts. Taking the "output-price" Phillips curve, for example, there are two kinds of deformation.

The first deformation is that the basic Phillips curve relationship remains unchanged, namely the variations in deviation and the price rise rate maintain the basic equidirectional relationship. However, there is movement in the position of the curve circle A or a locality change in the shape of the curve circle B. For example, the whole curve circle moves upwards (in Figure 11.3, curve circle A is the basic Phillips curve and it moves up to B), illustrating that the overall price rise rate increases while the deviation remains at the original level. Curve circle B is called the "inflation expectations-augmented" Phillips curve, which adds the inflation anticipation factor to the basic Phillips curve. This is the revision of the short-term Phillips curve proposed by Friedman and Phelps of the monetarist school in the late 1960s. In the graph, with the proportion of the deviation of the actual output level from the potential output level as the lateral axis and the price rise rate as the longitudinal axis, the two curve circles showing the American situation from 1971 to 1976 and from 1976 to 1983 move in the upper left direction (similar to curve circle C in Figure 11.3, the vertical dotted line in the center representing the

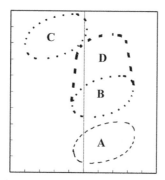

Figure 11.3 First deformation of the output-price Phillips curve

potential output level), signifying the Phillips curve under stagflation. On the one hand, curve circle C is on the left-hand side of the potential output level, demonstrating that the actual output level is lower than the potential output level and production is in stagnation. On the other hand, the circle is at a high position, illustrating that the price is rising. The monetarist school employed the inflation expectations-augmented Phillips curve to explain the deformation of the basic Phillips curve from the 1970s to the 1980s in Western countries like the United States and to interpret the phenomenon of stagflation. The locality change of the curve circle B displayed in Figure 11.3 shows that it rises upwards to a steep curve circle D owing to the impact of price rises, which we term a steep Phillips curve. We will encounter this shape of curve circle in the subsequent analysis of the deformation of the Phillips curve in China.

The second deformation is that a fundamental change has taken place in the shape of the curve circle and the basic Phillips curve relationship: the equidirectional variation in the deviation and the price rise rate no longer exists. In one case, the basic Phillips curve A in Figure 11.4 turns around and changes to curve circle E, slanting to the upper left and showing that the variations in the deviation and the price rise rate are no longer in an equidirectional relationship, but rather form a converse relationship. The price rise rate falls while the deviation rises, whereas the price rise rate increases while the deviation declines, caused by the related supply impact. We term this the "output-price" Phillips curve in the inverse direction; we will encounter this in the following analysis of the deformation of the Phillips curve in China. In the other case, the monetarist school proposes that, in the long term, the Phillips curve will deform into a vertical line located at the potential economic growth rate (see vertical dotted line F in Figure 11.4), demonstrating that the actual economic growth rate tends to be the potential economic growth rate in the long term and price variation is irrelevant. The rational anticipation school argues that even in the short term the actual price rise rate is identical to the average social inflation expectation and the actual economic growth rate is

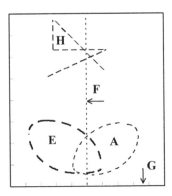

Figure 11.4 Second output-price Phillips curve

equal to the potential economic growth rate under the hypothesis of general equilibrium and rational anticipation. As a result, price variation is unrelated to the economic growth rate. Thus, the Phillips curve in the short term is also represented as a vertical line positioned at the potential economic growth rate. Certainly, the hypothesis is so strict that it does not coincide with economic reality. There is another case in which the price does not change or remains almost stable, although the deviation moves constantly when the government freezes the price. At this moment, the Phillips curve will deform into a horizontal line coinciding with the lateral axis, the line of the zero price rise rate (see lateral axis G in Figure 11.4). We call this the horizontal "output-price" curve. In the subsequent analysis of the deformation of the Phillips curve in China, we will find an almost horizontal curve circle. Sometimes during various years of economic cyclical fluctuation, the Phillips curve will deform into a very irregular shape (see curve H in Figure 11.4) owing to many irregular stochastic factors that affect variations in the economic growth rate and price rise rate. At this time, the relationship between the variation in the deviation and price rise rate is both equidirectional and inverse. It may be irrelevant and irregular.

II   "Output–Price" curve in China

This section focuses on the study of the "output-price" Phillips curve and the "unemployment–price" Phillips curve in China. In terms of the "output-price" curve in China's periodic economic fluctuation, there are five representative shapes, of which two are before the reform and three are after the reform (for more on China's periodic economic fluctuation, please see Liu Shucheng, 1996).

1.   *Description of status*

The first shape before the reform is the "output-price" Phillips curve in the inverse direction. In the original planned economic system in China, a representative shape

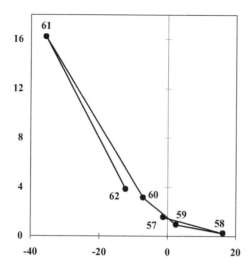

Figure 11.5 "Output-Price" curve from 1957 to 1962

of the "output-price" curve was the curve in the economic cycle from 1958 to 1962, starting from the trough of the economic growth rate in 1957 (see Figure 11.5). In Figure 11.5 (and later also in Figure 11.6), the lateral axis stands for the deviation of the actual economic growth rate from the potential economic growth rate. The actual economic growth rate is represented by the growth rate of constant national income. We take 5.7%, the average annual growth rate of constant national income from 1953 to 1977, as the potential economic growth rate in the planned economic system. The longitudinal axis is the price rise rate represented by the commodity retail price. The curve in Figure 11.5 starts from 1957, moves in the lower right direction in 1958, then flies far out to the upper left in 1959, 1960 and 1961 and turns back in the lower right direction in 1962, which is completely the converse of the basic "output-price" Phillips curve presenting the inverse relationship between the variation in the deviation and the price rise rate. When the deviation rises (line segment from 1957 to 1958 and from 1961 to 1962), the price rise rate falls. When the deviation declines (line segment from 1958 to 1961), the price rise rate climbs.

The second shape before the reform is the horizontal "output-price" curve. In the original planned economic system in China, a representative shape of the "output-price" curve was the curve in the two rounds of economic cycles from 1969 to 1972 and from 1973 to 1976, starting from the trough of the economic growth rate in 1968 (see Figure 11.6). During these periods, although the deviation moves hard left and right, the price rise rate varies little and only moves feebly up and down around the lateral axis (zero line of the price rise rate) at about 1% in each direction.

The first shape after the reform is the basic Phillips curve. After implementing the economic reform and opening-up policy, with the transition from the planned

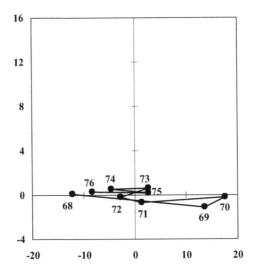

Figure 11.6 "Output-Price" curve from 1968 to 1976

economic system to a socialist market economy system, the relationship between the economic growth rate and price rising rate is characterized as the equidirectional variation of the basic Phillips curve.

Figure 11.7 is the curve in the economic cycle from 1982 to 1986, starting from the trough of the economic growth rate in 1981. In Figure 11.7 (and later the same in Figures 11.8 and 11.9), the lateral axis stands for the deviation of the actual economic growth rate from the potential economic growth rate. The actual economic growth rate is represented by the growth rate of GDP in constant prices. We take 9.1%, the average annual growth rate of GDP in constant prices from 1981 to 1990, as the potential economic growth rate of the same period and take 10%, the average annual growth rate of GDP in constant prices from 1981 to 1996, as the potential economic growth rate of the period from 1991 to 1996. The longitudinal axis is the rate of increase of the commodity retail price. In Figure 11.7, the curve starts from 1981 and the deviation gradually rises from left to right, with the price rise rate slightly declining at first and then increasing. From 1984 to 1986, the deviation gradually falls from right to left with the lagged increase of the price rise rate (line segment from 1984 to 1985) and its subsequent fall. On the whole, this curve circle inclines slightly to the upper right at a low position with a flat shape, more or less displaying the shape of the basic Phillips curve.

The second shape after the reform is the steep upper-left located Phillips curve. Figure 11.8 is the curve in the economic cycle from 1987 to 1990, starting from the trough of the economic growth rate in 1986. It moves to the upper left and is extremely steep in comparison with the last round of the cycle. From 1986 to 1987, the deviation rises, with the price rise rate also increasing.

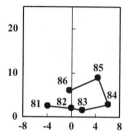

Figure 11.7 "Output-Price" curve from 1981 to 1986

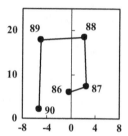

Figure 11.8 "Output-Price" curve from 1986 to 1990

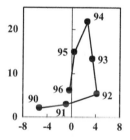

Figure 11.9 "Output-Price" curve from 1990 to 1996

From 1987 to 1990, the deviation declines from right to left, with the lagged and steep ascension of the price rise rate (line segment from 1987 to 1988) and its subsequent slow and steep fall (line segment from 1989 to 1990). The upper-left movement of the curve, respectively, illustrates that the price rise rate increases and the deviation greatly declines.

The third shape after the reform is the steep upper-right positioned Phillips curve. Figure 11.9 is the curve in the economic cycle from 1991 to 1996, starting from the trough of the economic growth rate in 1990. It again moves to the upper right and is still steep in comparison with the last round of the cycle. From 1990 to 1992, the deviation gradually rises from left to right, with the price rise rate increasing slowly. From 1992 to 1996, the deviation gradually declines from right to left, with the lagged and steep ascension of the price rise rate (line segment from 1992 to 1994) and its subsequent steep fall (line segment from 1994 to 1996). The upper-right movement of the curve, respectively, indicates that the price rise rate again climbs and the economy is in a high growth situation in this round of the economic cycle.

2.   *Analysis of causes*

Before the economic reform and opening-up policy, the "output-price" curve presents a completely different shape from the basic Phillips curve; in other words, the basic Phillips curve relationship no longer exists. This is closely related to the original planned economic system. Under the original system, there are two representative situations. In one case, the government implements rationing of many commodities so as to restrict demand due to material shortage. However, the price is not frozen and varies with supply owing to many restraints on demand.

When the economic growth rate rises with the improvement of supply, the price rise rate descends. The opposite is the case when the economic growth rate declines with the deterioration of supply and the aggravation of material shortage, the price rise rate then increases to a great extent. This forms the "output-price" Phillips curve in the inverse direction, as shown in Figure 11.5. In the other case, when the price is almost frozen, the fierce fluctuation of the economic growth rate does not reflect in the price variation. This forms the horizontal "output-price" curve in Figure 11.6.

After the economic reform and opening-up policy, the relationship between the economic growth rate and the price rise rate, on the whole, presents the equidirectional relationship in variation displayed by the basic Phillips curve because the market mechanism starts to play a role during the transition to the socialist market economy system, which reflects the essential characteristic of market economy that price varies with market demand and supply. However, under such circumstances, the Phillips curve again deforms precipitously. Especially during the two rounds of economic cycles from 1987 to 1990 and from 1991 to 1996, when the actual economic growth rate deviates from the potential economic growth rate, rises to a peak and then starts to fall, namely when the "output-price" curve moves rightwards, reaches the top and then turns around, the price rise rate lags behind in reaching the peak for one year or two years in a precipitous way. What are the causes of the lagged peak of the price rise rate in comparison with the peak of the actual economic growth rate? Why is the peak so steep? On the whole, this is the overall outcome of various factors co-acting to influence the price increase. The factors involve the following.

First, there is the deviation of the actual economic growth rate from the potential economic growth rate. The deviation increase inherently transmits to the rise in the commodity retail price through two mechanisms. The first is that, on the condition of strong demand expansion (represented in currency expansion and investment and consumption demand expansion), the actual economic growth rate exceeds the potential economic growth rate and drives the price of the means of production to increase with the gradual enhancement of bottleneck constraints in energy, transportation and main raw materials. The actual economic growth rate reaches its peak first and then falls to a small extent. At this time, the price rise rate of the means of production lags behind in reaching the peak and leads to the price increase of means of subsistence (means of consumption) through a cost-push effect of materials. The peak of the price rise rate of the means of subsistence appears later than that of the means of production, while the peaks of the rise rate of the commodity retail price and means of subsistence emerge simultaneously. This transmission process was very evident and typical from 1991 to 1996. There are four peaks in Figure 11.10. Peak 1 is the peak of the actual economic growth

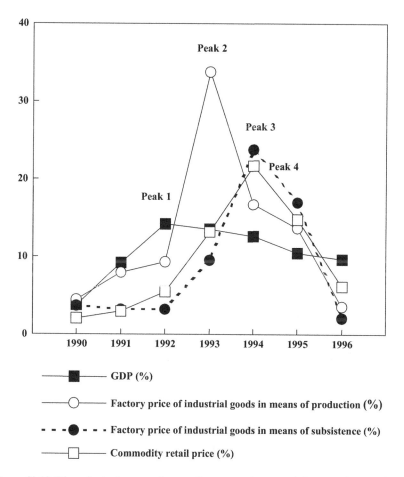

Figure 11.10 Rise of actual economic growth rate over its potential economic growth rate (1990–96)

rate (GDP growth rate) appearing in 1992. Peak 2 is the peak of the factory price rise rate of industrial goods in the means of production emerging in 1993. Peak 3 is the peak of the factory price rise rate of industrial goods in the means of subsistence developing in 1994. Peak 4 is the peak of the commodity retail price rise rate appearing simultaneously with Peak 3.

The second mechanism is that the increase in the actual economic growth rate drives an increase in staff wages, with the actual economic growth rate reaching its peak first and staff wages lagging behind. The rise in staff wages increases the labor cost of products for enterprises on the one hand and improves the workers' income causing an increment in consumption demand on the other hand, which transmits to the commodity retail price through a cost-push effect of labor force and demand-pull effect of consumption. This induces the peaks of the commodity retail price rise rate and the rise in staff wages to appear at the same time. Figure 11.11 illustrates the transmission process from 1981 to 1996, in which there are three peaks in the actual economic growth rate represented as A, B, C (1984, 1987, 1992), respectively, corresponding to the lagged peaks of the growth rate of total staff wages, A', B', C' (1985, 1988, 1994). This demonstrates that the demand-pull and cost-push effects are interwoven in the price increase in China.

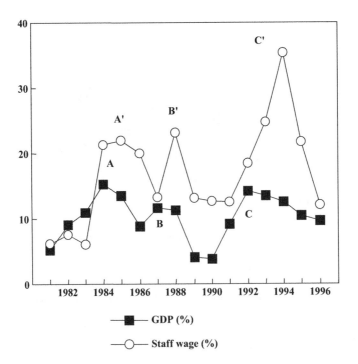

Figure 11.11 Driving force of rises in actual economic growth rate on staff wage increase (1981–96)

To undertake a quantitative analysis of the lagged relationship between the deviation and the price rise rate, we take samples from the three rounds of economic cycles, 1982 to 1986, 1987 to 1990, 1991 to 1996, and define the regression model (1):

$$p_t = 7.587 + 1.196(y_{t-1} - y^*) \qquad (1)$$

(1.537) (0.461)

(4.938) (2.594)

$R^2 = 0.34$(corrected value: 0.29), $F = 6.726$, $se_y = 5.706$, $df = 13$
Sample period: from 1982 to 1996

where the subscript t represents the year; p_t stands for the commodity retail price rise rate in year t; y_{t-1} is the actual economic growth rate in year $t-1$; y^* is the potential economic growth rate; $(y_{t-1} - y^*)$ represents the deviation of the actual economic growth rate from the potential economic growth rate in year $t-1$. In the data in parentheses below the estimate values of various parameters, the upper row is the standard deviation and the lower row is the estimate value of the t-statistic. R^2 stands for the determination coefficient, where the value in parentheses is the corrected value after considering the degree of freedom; F is the estimate value of the F-statistic; se_y represents the standard deviation of the estimate value of the price rise rate; df is the degree of freedom.

Various statistical tests of the model are significant. The goodness-of-fit -determination coefficient R^2 is 0.341 and accordingly, the correlation coefficient r equals 0.584. With the confidence level equal to 95% and the degree of freedom being (2, 13), the critical value (r^*) of the correlation coefficient arrived at by table lookups is 0.514. When $r > r^*$ signifies that the model is workable. According to the t-test, the parameter estimate values of $(y_{t-1} - y^*)$ and the intercept term are effective based on confidence levels of 97.5% and 99.5%, respectively. According to the F-test, the confidence level of the overall significance of regression is 95%.

The model passes the statistical test, verifying that the deviation and price rise rate are positively correlated with a lag. The deviation in year $t-1$ increases by 1%, the price rises 1.196% in year t. This model illustrates that there is a basic "output-price" Phillips curve relationship in China. However, owing to the low determination coefficient R^2, the explanatory ability of the model for the total variation between the actual value of the price rise rate and its average value is only 34%. Meanwhile, the standard deviation of the estimate value of the price rise rate (5.706%) is relatively large. This demonstrates that there are other factors that play a significant role in price increase in addition to the basic "output-price" Phillips curve relationship.

Second, there is the lagging inertia of the price increase. The price increase in the previous year inherently influences that of the next year with a lag, which can be comprehended in two aspects. As the deviation continuously rises, leading to the consecutive increase in the price rise rate, producers and consumers will generally anticipate inflation. Thus, inflation anticipation plays a significant role in promoting price increase. The peaks of the price rise rate in 1988 and 1994 corresponded to the previous price increases of consecutive years. If the new price increase factor in the previous year is strong, the carryover effect in the next year will also be strong (see Liu Shucheng, Zhou Fang, and Zhao Jingxing, 1996b). Hence, the price carryover effect plays a role. In view of the above, we add the commodity retail price rise rate (p_{t-1}) of year $t-1$ as a new explanatory variable, representing the lagging inertia of the price increase, to model (1) and arrive at model (2):

$$p_t = 3.948 + 1.139\,(y_{t-1} - y^*) + 0.436\,p_{t-1} \tag{2}$$

(2.084) (0.40) (0.191)

(1.895) (2.832) (2.277)

$R^2 = 0.54$ (corrected value: 0.46), $F = 7.038$, $se_y = 4.963$, $df = 12$
Sample period: from 1982 to 1996

Model (2) is better able to pass the various statistical tests. According to this model, with two explanatory variables, the deviation in year $t-1$ increases by 1%, the price rises 1.139% in year t; the price in year $t-1$ increases by 1%, the price rises 0.436% in year t. However, the determination coefficient R^2 is still low and the standard deviation of the estimate value of the price rise rate is high. This illustrates that there are still other important factors that work on the price increase.

Third, we consider the issuance of related reform measures. The above two factors explain why price increase lags behind economic growth. But why is the lagging so strong? It is due to the strong external impacts in the peak year of the price rise rate, in which the most significant is the issuance of price reform measures and other reform measures that influence the price increase. This can be termed a policy factor relevant to price reform. To analyze the function of the policy factor quantitatively, a common technique is to add a dummy variable in the regression model. We take D_t^1 to represent the policy factor of related price reforms that influence the price increase, given $D_t^1 = 1$ in 1988 and 1994, the two peak years of the price rise rate, and $D_t^1 = 0$ in other years. Considering that the government, for the purpose of curbing inflation, adopts other related measures to bring down the price rise rate obviously in some years in addition to taking measures of demand control and appropriate reduction of the economic growth rate, we take D_t^2 to stand for the related policy factor that restrains the price increase, given $D_t^2 = 1$ in 1990 and 1996, when the price rise rate declines distinctly, and $D_t^2 = 0$ in other years. In this way, we derive model (3):

$$p_t = 3.056 + 0.583\,(y_{t-1} - y^*) + 0.559\,p_{t-1} + 9.563\,D_t^1 - 6.758\,D_t^2 \tag{3}$$

(1.185)(0.261) (0.128) (2.221) (2.736)

(2.578) (2.237) (4.365) (4.305) (2.470)

$R^2 = 0.88$ (corrected value: 0.83), $F = 18.065$, $se_y = 2.794$, $df = 10$

Sample period: from 1982 to 1996

Model (3) is even better able to satisfy various statistical tests. According to this model, the policy factor term (D_t^1) of related price reforms works strongly, inducing a price increase of 9.563% in 1988 and 1994, the peak years of the price rise rate. The related policy term (D_t^2), which restrains inflation, also functions powerfully and is negative, inducing a price decline of −6.758% in 1990 and 1996, when the price rise rate is effectively controlled.

In China, the direct issuance of related price reform measures plays a significant role in the price increase, mainly represented in the purchase price increase of agricultural by-products. The variation in the purchase price of agricultural by-products to a large extent reflects the functions of the price reform measures. For this reason, we take the purchase price rise rate of agricultural by-products (represented by a_t) in the current year as an explanatory variable to substitute for the dummy variable of policy (D_t^1 and D_t^2) in model (3) and define model (4):

$$p_t = 2.064 + 0.258 \, (y_{t-1} - y^*) + 0.195p_{t-1} + 0.470 \, a_t \tag{4}$$

(1.188) (0.273) (0.114) (0.087)

(1.737) (0.945) (1.711) (5.402)

$R^2 = 0.88$ (corrected value: 0.84), $F = 25.561$, $se_y = 2.707$, $df = 11$

Sample period: from 1982 to 1996

The goodness-of-fit of model (4) – determination coefficient R^2 is the same as in model (3), which is equal to 0.88, signifying that the explanatory ability of both models is identical. This illustrates that the price reform measures influence the price variation mainly through the purchase price variation of agricultural by-products. We calculate and conclude that the correlation coefficient between the purchase price rise rate of agricultural by-products and the commodity retail price rise rate reaches 0.914. According to the *t*-test, the confidence level of the parameter estimate value of the purchase price rise rate (a_t) for agricultural by-products is as high as 99.5%. However the confidence level of the parameter estimate value of the intercept term and p_{t-1} drops to 90%. The parameter estimate value of $(y_{t-1} - y^*)$ is unable to pass the statistical significance test because the purchase price rise rate of agricultural by-products and the deviation of the previous year are linearly correlated (correlation coefficient of 0.578) and the purchase price rise rate of agricultural by-products and the lagging inertia of the price increase of the previous year are also linearly correlated (correlation coefficient of 0.356). Nevertheless, this illustrates that the purchase price increase of agricultural by-products is the intrinsic result of the demand-pull effect generated by the previous economic growth and the cost-push effect brought about by the previous commodity retail price increase, especially the price increase of agricultural production goods, although it is a price reform act. From the perspective of the econometric model, we believe model (3) is more feasible in terms of expressing the functions of the policies related to price reform.

Fourth, there are bumper or poor harvests of grain. In China, agricultural production, especially bumper or poor harvests of grain, plays an important role in price increase. The peak of the price rise rate corresponds to a grain reduction year. The price variation and bumper or poor harvests of grain represent a negative correlation. In view of this point, we add the grain yield growth rate as a new explanatory variable (represented by g_t) based on model (3) and arrive at model (5):

$$p_t = 3.774 + 0.463(y_{t-1} - y^*) + 0.596p_{t-1} + 8.185D_t^1 - 6.365D_t^2 - 0.273g_t \qquad (5)$$

(1.228) (0.261) (0.124) (2.310) (2.609) (0.188)

(3.074) (1.778) (4.802) (3.543) (2.439) (1.455)

$R^2 = 0.90$ (corrected value: 0.85), $F = 16.488$, $se_y = 2.650$, $df = 9$

Sample period: from 1982 to 1996

The goodness-of-fit of model (5) – determination coefficient R^2 rises to 0.90. The explanatory ability of the model for the total variation between the actual value of the price rise rate and its average value increases to 90%. According to the t-test, the confidence level of the various parameter estimate values is 99.5% for p_{t-1} and D_t^1, 99% for the intercept term, 97.5% for D_t^2 and 90% for the grain yield growth rate (g_t). This demonstrates that grain yield does not directly have a strong impact on the price increase. The correlation coefficient between the grain yield growth rate and the price rise rate is −0.487. With the confidence level equal to 95% and the degree of freedom being (2, 13), the critical value (r^*) of the correlation coefficient arrived at by table lookups is 0.514. Thus, $r < r^*$ signifies that the grain yield growth rate and the price rise rate are to some extent negatively and weakly correlated. The practice indicates that under the current circumstances, it is not the variation in the total grain yield that promotes price increase, but it is the difference in the grain variety structure and regional yield that works, which is hard to reflect in this model.

Fifth, we turn to arbitrary price rise due to the profit-push effect. During the current systematic transitional period in China, due to the disordered marketing operation, there is a phenomenon of arbitrary price rises and fees in some sectors, industries and enterprises brought about by the utilization of their special power and monopoly status. In general, the arbitrary price rise generated by profit-push effect needs to be achieved through demand-pull effect under rapid economic expansion. From the perspective of the econometric model, it is difficult to add an individual explanatory variable again, the function of which can be displayed through the random residual term of the model.

We employ model (5) to carry out comprehensive quantitative analysis of the two peak years (1988 and 1994) of price rise rate and two years (1990 and 1996) with distinct decline.

In 1988, the peak year of the price rise rate, the actual price rise rate was 18.5%, whereas the estimate value drawn from the model is 18.1%. They are very close, with a mere difference of 0.4%. Calculated from the model, the deviation $(y_{t-1} - y^*)$ in 1987 pushed the price to increase 1.2% in 1988, accounting for 6% of the overall price rise rate (estimate value, same hereinafter). The lagging inertia of the price increase (p_{t-1}) in 1987 promoted the price to increase 4.4% in 1988, comprising 24% of the overall price rise rate. The policy factor of the related price reform (D_t^1) in 1988 allowed a price increase of 8.2%, accounting for 45% of the overall price rise rate. Owing to the reduction in grain production in 1988, the grain yield growth rate (g_t) induced a price increase of 0.6%, comprising 3% of the overall price rise rate.

In 1994, the peak year of the price rise rate, the actual price rise rate was 21.7%, while the estimate value drawn from the model is 22.1%. These are again extremely close, with a mere difference of 0.4%. Drawn from the model, the deviation in 1993 pushed the price to increase 1.6% in 1994, accounting for 7% of the overall price rise rate. The lagging inertia of the price increase in 1993 prompted the price to increase 7.9% in 1994, comprising 36% of the overall price rise rate. The policy factor of the related price reform in 1994 allowed a price increase of 8.2%, accounting for 37% of the overall price rise rate. Owing to the reduction in grain production in 1994, the grain yield growth rate (g_t) induced a price increase of 0.7%, comprising 3% of the overall price rise rate.

The above quantitative analysis indicates that the direct and primary factor that promotes price increase in the peak years of the price rise rate in China is the related price reform and the secondary factor is the lagging inertia of the previous year, which originates from the strong demand expansion and consecutive increase in the deviation in previous years. These factors taken together constitute the significant causes of the basic "output-price" Phillips curve deforming precipitously at the peak, the turning point of economic cyclical fluctuation in China.

In 1990, when the price increase was effectively restrained, the actual price rise rate was 2.1%, whereas the estimate value obtained from the model is 3.1%, i.e. a 1% difference. Calculated from the model, the deviation in 1989 induced a price decline of −2.3% in 1990. The lagging inertia of the price increase in 1989 was quite strong, inducing a price rise of 10.6% in 1990. The policy that curbed inflation in 1990 brought down the price by −6.4%. Due to the bumper harvest of grain in 1990, the grain yield growth rate induced a price decline of −2.6%. The model illustrates that the lagging inertia of the price increase of the previous year together with the intercept term generates 14.4% of the price increase pressure in 1990. However, the policy that controlled inflation offset 44% of the price increase pressure, the decline in the deviation offset 16% and the bumper harvest of grain offset 18%.

In 1996, when the price increase was effectively controlled, the actual price rise rate was 6.1%, whereas the estimate value obtained from the model is 5.1%, i.e. a 1% difference. Drawn from the model, the deviation in 1995 induced a price increase of 0.2% in 1996. The lagging inertia of the price increase in 1995 was also quite strong, inducing a price rise of 8.8% in 1996. The policy that curbed inflation in 1996 brought down the price by −6.4%. The high grain yield induced a price decline of −1.4%. The model demonstrates that the resultant force (including the deviation and lagging inertia of the price increase of the previous year together with the intercept term) inducing the price increase was 12.8% in 1996. However, the policy that controlled inflation offset 50% of the composite force inducing the price increase and the high grain yield offset 11%.

Quantitative analysis illustrates that the policy that curbs inflation plays a significant role in the trough year of economic cyclical fluctuation in China. In the meantime, with the consecutive decline in the deviation, demand expansion is restrained, inducing the alleviation of bottleneck constraints in energy, transportation and main raw materials and the relief of price increase pressure. All the above factors co-act to typically bring down the price rise rate. This explains why the basic "output-price" Phillips curve declines precipitously in the trough year of economic cyclical fluctuation in China.

The steep deformation of the basic "output-price" Phillips curve reflects the characteristics of China as a developing country, especially as a country undertaking economic restructuring and transitioning to a socialist market economy.

3. Policy implications

Regarding the relationship between the variation in the economic growth rate and the price rise rate after economic reform and opening-up policy, based on the above analysis, we conclude that we should not simply ask whether there is the issue of the Phillips curve, but should admit its existence and understand its steep deformation in the current economic cyclical fluctuation in China. From the macro regulation point of view, realizing the existence of the Phillips curve, we should properly control total demand and the economic growth rate to prevent the aggravation of inflation in the economic rising stage and appropriately squeeze total demand and lower the economic growth rate to curb inflation in the economic falling phase. With the perception of the steep deformation, we should take relevant measures and carry out comprehensive prevention and management counter plans directed against the various factors that lead to price increase while properly regulating total demand and the economic growth rate.

Acknowledging the existence of the Phillips curve and recognizing the certain corresponding relationship between the variation in the economic growth rate and the price rise rate in economic cyclical fluctuation is not identical to approving the Keynesian point of view. The Keynesian approach secretly changes the corresponding relationship that objectively exists to a substitution of subjective and arbitrary policy and trades the promotion of inflation for temporary economic growth. The Keynesian policy of stimulating inflation is actually the misuse of the Phillips curve. It is detrimental to simply deny the existence of the Phillips curve with the recognition that the economic growth rate and the price rise rate are generally unrelated. This will bring about vulnerability by arbitrarily increasing the economic growth rate without taking into account inflation. In practice, with the related data, domestic and international researchers draw the conclusion that the economic growth rate and the price rise rate are irrelevant, but they neglect the fact that the data they have employed reveals the long-term relationship between the economic growth rate and the price rise rate, or the relationship between the two averages in the mid-term, rather than the short-term relationship in economic cyclical fluctuation (see U.S. Woos, Jung, Peyton, and J. Marshall, 1986; Han Wenxiu, 1996).

Each government expects to achieve rapid economic growth under low inflation. The key point lies in the fact that fast economic growth is unable to exceed its potential consecutively and excessively. To realize the vigorous growth of the economy with low inflation in China, from the aspect of demand, we should lay stress on the control of the economic growth peak and prevent continuous over-crossing of the line, namely the appropriate growth line determined by the economic increase potential (see Liu Guoguang and Liu Shucheng, 1997). From the perspective of supply, we should fundamentally get rid of the bottleneck constraints in agriculture, energy, transportation and main raw materials to enhance the economic growth potential. We should actively promote two radical transformations – in the economic system and the economic growth pattern – and technical progress, not purely pursuing an excessively high economic growth rate, and strive for the quality and benefit of growth and sustainable development.

III   "Unemployment–price" curve in China

Now we investigate the "unemployment–price" curve in economic cyclical fluctuation in China. Due to the lack of the data on unemployment before the reform and opening-up policy, we will only deal with data available afterwards.

1.   Description of status

Figures 11.12, 11.13 and 11.14, respectively, provide the "unemployment–price" curve in three rounds of economic fluctuations. In the figures, the lateral axis stands for the urban registered unemployment rate, which is currently unable to reflect the unemployment situation fully in China. We thus mainly obtain the overall variation trend. The longitudinal axis expresses the price rise rate. Figure 11.12 is the curve of the economic cycle from 1982 to 1986, starting from the trough of the economic growth rate in 1981. Figure 11.13 is the curve of the economic cycle

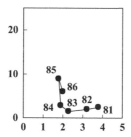

Figure 11.12 "Unemployment-Price" curve from 1981 to 1986

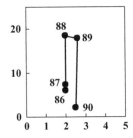

Figure 11.13 "Unemployment-Price" curve from 1986 to 1990

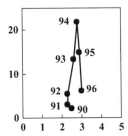

Figure 11.14 "Unemployment-Price" curve from 1990 to 1996

from 1987 to 1990, starting from the trough of the economic growth rate in 1986. Figure 11.14 is the curve of the economic cycle from 1991 to 1996, starting from the trough of the economic growth rate in 1990. As shown in the three figures, the "unemployment-price" curves in the latter two rounds of economic cycles present steep deformation, which are even steeper and more vertical than the deformations of the "output-price" curves in Figures 11.8 and 11.9.

As depicted in Figure 11.13, in the line segment from 1986 to 1988, which reflects the economic growth rate rising from the trough and staying at a high level, the unemployment rate should show a downward trend while the price rise rate increases, i.e. the segment ought to be inclined to the upper left, illustrating the inverse relationship between the variation in the unemployment rate and the price rise rate. However, the unemployment rate does not change by an iota and thus the segment presents a vertical line at an unemployment rate of 2%. This demonstrates that the urban unemployment rate does not decline and remains unchanged in the rising period of economic fluctuation in China and is irrelevant to the variations in the economic growth rate and price rise rate. After 1988, the price rise rate declines with the fall of the economic growth rate. The unemployment rate presents an upward trend with the curve moving to the right, signifying that the rising unemployment rate presents a converse relationship with the variation in the economic growth rate and the price rise rate in the falling period of economic fluctuation in China.

Figure 11.14 is characterized by the same features as Figure 11.13. In the line segment from 1990 to 1994, which reflects the economic growth rate rising from the trough and staying at a high level, the unemployment rate ought to exhibit a downward trend while the price rise rate increases. However, the unemployment rate does not change an iota and remains at the level of 2.3% in 1991 and 1992. From 1993, it rises all the way to 3% in 1996 and thus the curve moves to the right.

2.   Analysis of causes

The reasons why the urban unemployment rate does not decline in the rising period of economic fluctuation in China are as follows.

First, there is the labor supply impact. When the economy enters a rising period, it will lead to an increase in labor demand, which should make the urban unemployment rate decline. However, from the perspective of the labor supply, due to a large amount of surplus rural labor pouring into the cities, urban employment is severely affected. Meanwhile, at a time when the increase in the working-age of the population is at its peak in China, labor supply exceeds labor demand.

Second, there is the labor demand impact. From the perspective of labor demand, although labor demand and the quantity of employees are constantly increasing during economic growth, the increasing rate of employees presents a distinct downward trend. This is related to technical progress. Since the 1980s, industrialization in China has further developed. With the process of industrialization, technical progress and continuous improvement in technical production equipment and its organic constitution, the labor absorbed by the same amount of output will diminish. In the first half of the 1980s, the quantity of employees increased 3.3% annually in China, while it was merely 1.2% in the first half of the 1990s. The economic growth rate increasing by 1% drove an increase of 0.3% in the quantity of employees in the first half of the 1980s and an increase of 0.1% in the first half of the 1990s. Economic growth led to a decline of 67% in the growth elasticity of employees.

Third, there is the impact of the reform of state-owned enterprises and structural adjustment. The deepening reform of state-owned enterprises and structural adjustment of industry induce enterprises to reduce excess employees, leading to workers being made redundant.

The steep deformation of the "unemployment-price" Phillips curve reflects the characteristics of China as a developing country, especially as a populous country undertaking economic restructuring.

3.   Policy implications

The above analysis signifies that since the middle of the 1980s the urban unemployment rate has not fallen in rising periods of economic fluctuation in China, although the economic growth rate and the price rise rate increased. In the falling stage, the urban unemployment rate rises while the economic growth rate and price rise rate decline. This makes the urban unemployment issue increasingly severe. With the success of the "soft landing" of the current economic operation in China, the economy falls to the appropriate range of growth, with the price rise rate typically declining. Unemployment is becoming more prominent. It is not particularly effective to solve the issue of urban unemployment only by relying on stimulating aggregate demand and economic growth. In doing so, we may risk the strong rebounding of a price increase. Some international economists have already pointed out that governmental monetary policy may help deal with general inflation, but it has few effects in terms of coping with unemployment and will not work effectively at all in tackling massive unemployment. Different countermeasures and comprehensive treatment strategies aimed at different factors that cause unemployment should be taken accordingly to solve the urban unemployment issue in China, just like controlling inflation in recent years. Without doubt, it is much harder and takes a longer time to solve the issue of unemployment than that of inflation.

[Originally published in *Management World (GuanliShijie)*, No.6, 1997]

References

Han Wenxiu. (1996). Study of Relationship between Economic Growth and Inflation. *Management World*, 6.

Liu Guoguang, & Liu Shucheng. (1997, January 7). On Soft Landing. *The People's Daily*.

Liu Shucheng. (1996). New Stage of Economic Periodical Fluctuation in China. Shanghai: Shanghai Far East Publishing House.

Liu Shucheng, Zhou Fang, & Zhao Jingxing. (1996a). Analysis of Carryover Effect in Annual Link Price Index. *Economic Research Journal*, 4.

Liu Shucheng, Zhou Fang, & Zhao Jingxing. (1996b). Calculation and Analysis of Carryover Effect in Price Rise Rate. *The Journal of Quantitative & Technical Economics*, 6.

National Bureau of Statistics. China Statistical Yearbook, 1992 to 1996: China Statistical Abstract, 1997.

U.S. Woos, Jung, Peyton, & J. Marshall. (1986). Causal Relationship between Inflation and Economic Growth. *Reference of Cost and Price*, 17.

12 Further reforms of the distribution system in stimulating consumption

I   Current economic operational situation in China

It had been six years since the economic growth rate in China fell from the second half of 1993 to 1998. The decline trend reversed from the second half of 1998 to January and February 1999. However, in March and especially in April, new circumstances emerged that produced a fall of increased amplitude in the significant indicators of the national economy, such as industrial production, fixed assets investment, the total retail sales of social consumer goods and the introduction of foreign capital, a decline in prices and exports, an upsurge in residents' savings increase and a sharp rise in the balance of savings in excess of loans with banks. If the situation continues, the positive incipient economic resurgence momentum may be broken. It is time to take further effective measures because the longer the decline lasts, the more difficult the problems will be to resolve if the trend is unable to be reversed completely.

II   Foremost measures

Various comprehensive measures should be taken to prevent the economic growth rate from falling continuously. However, in the author's opinion, the most important point is to deepen the reform of the distribution system, raise residents' income and reduce their anticipated expenditures with the purpose of directly stimulating consumption; these measures are the leading ones to consider. The general train of thought is to carry out a reform of the distribution system with the aim of directly stimulating consumption and promoting economic development and social stabilization.

III   Shifting focus of positive fiscal policy to the direct stimulation of consumption

The positive fiscal policy adopted at the beginning of 1998 stressed infrastructure investment, which could avoid repeated construction under the circumstances of overcapacity in the processing industry, the widespread commodity supply exceeding the demand and a lack of investment projects with commercial benefit. It played a significant role in resisting the impact of the East Asian financial crisis and the subsequent spread of international financial turmoil and preventing the economic growth rate from following a probable extensive decline, and it effectively supported the economic growth in 1998. However, the stimulation of investment is merely indirect for final consumption that makes sense ultimately in promoting economic growth. With no final consumption built up and no vast market space, social investment is hard to achieve. As a result, it is difficult for the central government's financial investment to last for long, as it is fighting a battle on its own.

IV   Current situation of final consumption in China

We examine two crucial economic indicators. One indicator is the final consumption rate (namely the ratio of final consumption to the gross domestic product). This is the most fundamental and important ratio that determines whether the national economy is able to operate smoothly. According to the data on constant prices from the National Statistical Bureau or the World Bank, in recent years, the final consumption rate of China has fallen to its lowest level historically since the founding of new China and is actually very low in comparison with other countries. Correspondingly, the capital formation rate (total domestic investment rate) remains at a high level and is really very high compared with that of other countries. If we increase the investment rate and reduce the consumption rate further, this trend of economic decline will not be reversed and will become even more severe, not only at present but also at the beginning of the twenty-first century. The other indicator is the growth rate of residents' income. In rural areas, the average annual growth rate of rural households' net income per capita has been 7.9% for over 20 years. During the 14 years after 1985, the annual income increase rate was lower than the above average and fluctuated around 4% for all the years except for 1996. With such a low-income growth rate of rural residents, how can the rural market be stimulated effectively to support long-term economic growth? In urban areas, the average annual growth rate of urban households' disposable income per capita has been 6.1% for more than 20 years but also has been about 4% within the last four years. With such a low-income increase rate of urban residents and further deductions of the current and anticipated expenditures, such as housing, children's education, medical care, retirement, laying-off or unemployment, how can the urban market be stimulated efficiently to prop up economic growth in the long run? The reduction of urban residents' income directly damages the sales of agricultural products and township enterprises' products, further affecting the improvement of farmers' income. The decline in residents' income growth rate and the sluggish final consumption demand constitute the main reasons for the multiplier effect of financial investment on the whole national economy being reduced and shortened.

V   How to stimulate consumption directly

Stimulating consumption directly does not simply consist of issuing currency but involves combining the improvement of residents' income and the reduction of their expenditure anticipations with the deepening reform of the distribution system to integrate short-term demand stimulation with medium- and long-term systematic construction and to incorporate demand irritation with supply perfection. Raising urban residents' income specifically implies three different levels. The first one is the low-income group. It is essential to raise the income of the low-income group, including laid-off workers, retired employees and those below the minimum living standard with the purpose of better resolving the problem of social security and social stabilization. The second group is public employees. It is necessary to improve the wages of civil servants and staff in public institutions of scientific research, education, culture and health care to a great extent since their original wage level was very low. With the development of the socialist market economy, the distribution in the form of physical goods, welfare and unified allocation in the original system has become monetized, commercialized and market-oriented. The wage structure has not yet been changed fundamentally, with the reform of the wage distribution system lagging behind severely. At present, a small increase in wages not only cannot meet the need of socialist market economic development but also does not function to stimulate consumption. It is time to raise the wage level for public employees in the original system on a large scale to make the wage structure and salary determination mechanism adapt to the development of the socialist market economy. The third group consists of state-owned enterprises. In connection with an economic benefit, it is necessary to abandon control over the wages of state-owned enterprises to create a motivation mechanism for entrepreneurs and staff that is suitable for the socialist market economy as soon as possible. The improvement of urban residents' income will revitalize the township market and increase farmers' income. In terms of raising farmers' income, we should improve their income on the one hand and alleviate their burdens, like arbitrary apportioning and unjustifiable charges, on the other hand, with the aim of increasing their disposable income directly. In future, all the reform measures should not impair the vested interests of urban and rural people and should reduce the public expenditure anticipations for the related reform.

VI Direct stimulation of consumption will be advantageous to the integration of demand irritation and supply perfection

First, with the settlement of social security, it is easy for state-owned enterprises to dismiss unwanted staff and improve their efficiency, enabling them to accelerate the pace of eliminating poverty, invigorate enterprises and improve the supply. Second, economic recovery and growth should be based on micro foundations. The adjustment and upgrading of industrial and product structures will rely on enterprises. With the establishment of an incentive mechanism for entrepreneurs and staff, enterprises will be vigorous and enlivened; otherwise, they will lose their internal motivations. Moreover, the direct stimulation of consumption, which will activate the market and even the whole national economy, will create opportunities for social investment and increase new employment and financial revenue. This will be conducive to the economy entering into a good circle.

VII   Issues involved in the direct stimulation of consumption

Many details and new issues demand attention during the implementation of even an excellent policy, which should not be executed incorrectly. Raising residents' income must not be arbitrarily giving out money and should be connected with systematic construction. As for inflation, there was currently a negative gap of deflation, since the actual economic growth rate was lower than the potential one, providing a good opportunity to deepen the reform of the distribution system. Therefore, as long as the direct stimulation of consumption is appropriate, no severe inflation will be initiated. However, as time passes, we should prevent severe inflation from emerging when the economy recovers, especially at the time when economic fluctuation moves forward to its peak.

[Originally published in *Brief Report of Chinese Academy of Social Sciences (ZhongguoShehuiKexueyuanYaobao)*, No.52, June, 1999]

13 The "New Economy" in America

Deformation of the Phillips curve and its implications

The inflation rate, unemployment rate and economic growth rate are the three important monitoring indexes when a government carries out macro regulations. The Phillips curve illustrates the variable relationship between the inflation rate and the unemployment rate (or the economic growth rate), which has constituted the significant content of macro regulations in every country for half a century. The Phillips curve and its deformations have become one of the core issues of macroeconomic discussions and arguments. Since the 1990s, the American economy has produced its third constant growth tendency after the Second World War, which the American economists have referred to as entering the "New Economy" era. Under the "New Economy", new deformation of the Phillips curve has taken place with the coexistence of low inflation and low unemployment (or high growth), issuing a new challenge to the traditional macroeconomic theory and triggering extensive concern and heated debate in the academic sphere. This has provided some beneficial inspiration for macroeconomic regulation in China.

We proceed by investigating the evolutionary process of the Phillips curve in the United States since the 1960s.

The first period of long-term prosperity in the United States after the Second World War took place from February 1961 to December 1969, lasting for 106 months, during which the Phillips curve presented the standard or typical form within the economic expansion stage. The traditional Keynesianism took this opportunity and proposed a negative correlation between the inflation rate and the unemployment rate, namely the substitution relationship of the unemployment rate declining with a rising inflation rate or the inflation rate falling with an increasing unemployment rate.

Figure 13.1 depicts the Phillips curve[1] of the United States from 1961 to 1969, in which the longitudinal axis denotes the inflation rate and the lateral axis expresses the unemployment rate. The dots in the figure show the locations of the inflation rate and unemployment rate for each year. Connecting each dot from 1961 to 1969 derives the typical Phillips curve in the economic expansion stage, to which we apply a straight line A with an arrow symbol to signify it. As shown in Figure 13.1, with the sustainable growth of the American economy, the unemployment rate fell from 6.7% in 1961 to 3.5% in 1969, whereas the inflation rate increased from 1% to 5.5% within the same period, representing a concurrent situation of low unemployment and high inflation. This was the period during which Keynesianism flourished. The American government adopted the Keynesian policy of expanding the aggregate demand in its macroeconomic regulation, including expansionary fiscal and monetary policies. This resulted in long-term economic growth and a decline in the unemployment rate on the one hand and an increase in the inflation rate on the other hand.

Since the beginning of the 1970s, owing to the anticipation of overall social inflation generated by the long-term expanded aggregate demand in the 1960s together with the supply impacts of the two oil crises from 1973 to 1975 and from 1978 to 1981, the Phillips curve deformed from the combination of low unemployment and high inflation of the 1960s to that of high inflation and high unemployment of the 1970s. In other words, the original substitution relationship between low unemployment and high inflation deformed to the coexistence of high inflation and high unemployment, namely the vicious relationship of concurrent stagnation and inflation. As a result, Keynesianism was greatly challenged and subsequently withdrew from its leading position. As depicted in Figure 13.1, the inflation rate increased from 5.5% in 1969 to 13.5% in 1980, and the unemployment rate rose from 3.5% to 7.1% within the same period. We employ the straight line B with an arrow symbol in Figure 13.1 to illustrate the vicious deformation of the Phillips curve.

At the beginning of the 1980s, with the aim of curbing the constantly rising inflation, the American Federal Reserve Committee implemented a draconian retrenchment monetary policy, making the inflation rate fall and the unemployment rate rise. The Phillips curve reverted downwards to the negatively correlated substitution relationship. However, this time, the replacement relationship was between low inflation and high unemployment rather than between low unemployment and high inflation. As described in Figure 13.2, the inflation rate declined from 13.5% in 1980 to 3.2% in 1983, whereas the unemployment rate increased from 7.1% to 9.6% within the same period. We apply the straight line C with an arrow symbol in Figure 13.2 to demonstrate the standard Phillips curve in the economic contraction stage. From 1984 to 1989, the Phillips curve reverted upwards to the original substitution relationship, namely the standard form of straight line A. As displayed in Figure 13.2, the inflation rate increased from 3.2% in 1983 to 4.8% in 1989, whereas the unemployment rate declined from 9.6% to 5.3% in the same period. The second period of

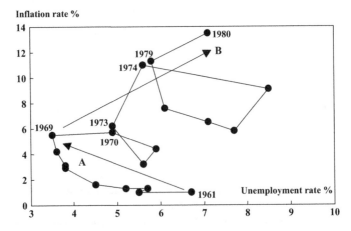

Figure 13.1 Phillips curve and its deformation in the United States (1960s and 1970s)

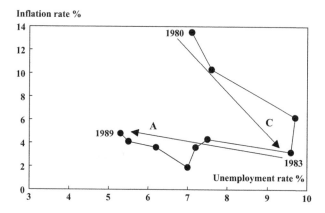

Figure 13.2 Phillips curve in the United States (the 1980s)

long-term prosperity in the United States after the Second World War occurred from November 1982 to July 1990, lasting for 92 months, during which the macroeco-nomic regulation policy that the American government adopted was a combination of an expansionary fiscal policy of the supply-side school, characterized by reducing tax and loosening government control to stimulate private investment and consump-tion, and a monetary policy, either tight or loose depending on situations.

At the beginning of the 1990s, with the purpose of restraining the recurrence of inflation, the American Federal Reserve Committee again employed a tight monetary policy. The Phillips curve was again represented in the substitution relationship by the standard straight line C, namely the combination of a declining inflation rate and a rising unemployment rate. As revealed in Figure 13.3, the inflation rate fell from 5.4% in 1990 to 3% in 1992, whereas the unemployment rate rose from 5.6% to 7.5% within the same period. Starting in 1993, the Clinton government applied a macro-economic regulation policy with a combination of a tight fiscal policy, characterized by a reducing fiscal deficit, and an adjustable monetary policy. On the one hand, cutting the fiscal deficit could reduce the Government's financing from the market to guarantee the money supply, which would be conducive to lowering the interest rate, stimulating private investment and consumption and maintaining economic growth. On the other hand, the American Federal Reserve Committee closely moni-tored the price trends, using the interest rate as the leverage to prevent inflation from rising. The policy of the supply-side school in the 1980s promoted the rapid develop-ment of high technology. The acceleration of economic globalization and the Asian financial crisis in 1997 reduced the world commodity price. With these integrative actions, the United States generated a new concurrent situation of low inflation and low unemployment; specifically, new virtuous deformation took place in the Phillips curve. The inflation rate further declined from 3% in 1992 to as low as 1.6% in 1998; simultaneously, the unemployment rate dropped from 7.5% to the low level of 4.5%, breaking the historical records of a "combination of low unemployment and high inflation", the "integration of high inflation and high unemployment" and a "coali-tion of low inflation and high unemployment" and achieving so-called economic

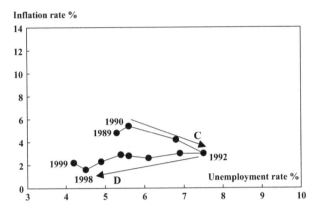

Figure 13.3 Phillips curve and its new deformation in the United States (the 1990s)

growth without inflation. We employ the straight line D with an arrow symbol in Figure 13.3 to signify the Phillips curve with virtuous deformation. The third period of long-term prosperity in the United States after the Second World War lasted from April 1991 to February 2000, lasting for 107 months, and became the longest economic expansion since 1854, when there were special periodical fluctuation records.

Currently, different views coexist in the international academic world regarding how long the economic growth trend in the United States can be sustained. In all events, the long-term growth of the American economy is able to provide some significant implications for macroeconomic regulation in China. Two points are worth mentioning. We should combine the expansion of the demand with the improvement of the supply (especially the promotion of the development of high technology). The appropriate low inflation is the outcome of the strict adoption of an "inflation control policy" rather than that of applying an "appropriate inflation policy". When the economy enters a growth stage, there is an inherent trend of inflation. To ensure sustained economic growth, it is necessary to follow an "inflation control policy" instead of an "appropriate inflation policy". We should clarify the causal relationship whereby the adoption of an "appropriate inflation policy" is just like pouring oil on the flames of the inherent trend of inflation in the economic expansion stage, leading to even more severe inflation. Just as Greenspan, the chairman of the American Federal Reserve Committee, pointed out, the uppermost factor in maintaining economic prosperity is a steady, low inflation rate. The vital task of the American Federal Reserve Committee is to control inflation.

[Originally published in *New Economy (XinJingji)*, No. 3–4, 2000]

Note

1   Date source of Figure 13.1 to Figure 13.3: the inflation rate is represented by the urban consumption price rise rate, American *Economic Report of President* (1999, p.395); unemployment rate, American *Economic Report of President* (1999, p.376). (1999).

14 On macroeconomic regulation and control in China

I   Reasons for macroeconomic regulation and control

From 1998 to 2001, the gross domestic product in China maintained growth at a level of 7.1% to 8% under circumstances in which it was countering the impact of the Asian financial crisis and the world's major countries, such as the United States, entering an economic recession simultaneously, and overcoming insufficient domestic demand. Based on the above, the growth rate of the gross domestic product recovered to 8.3% in 2002 and rose respectively to 9.3% in 2003 and 9.5% in 2004. China entered into a new round of economic cycle in 2002.

The Central Economic Working Conference, held in November 2003, employed the concept of economic cycle for the first time to analyze and estimate the economic trends in China and pointed out that "currently the economic development in China is in the ascending stage of the economic cycle." The utilization of the concept of economic cycle enables us to find out, at a stroke, the fluctuation tendencies of the current economic operations in China and its entire process.

In terms of quarters, economic growth in the first quarter of 2003 apparently accelerated and rose violently to 9.9%; it was maintained at 6.7% in the second quarter due to efforts to deal with SARS, and it consecutively remained at the high levels of 9.6% in the third quarter, 9.9% in the fourth quarter and 9.8% in the first quarter of 2004. At an important economists' symposium held in early April 2003, the economists held different views concerning whether the economy was overheated and whether it was necessary to carry out retrenchment macro regulation. Some economists believed that the economy was overheated all-around; some held that it was partially overheated, while some regarded the economic situation as excellent. The author put forward that we should closely observe and monitor the situation. After the third quarter of 2003, coal, electricity, oil and transportation were already in short supply; this was accompanied by information that there was a great reduction in the grain yield. The combination of high investment growth and a substantial reduction in grain predicted tremendous price increase pressure.

Under such circumstances, how should an economy running at a high growth rate of 9% be perceived? It has double implications. On the one hand, the economic growth rate in China has risen from 7%–8% several years ago to 9%, indicating that the economic operation has already been in the ascending stage of a new round of an economic cycle. Its economic impetus is the upgrading of the consumption structure, which is represented by housing and automobiles. This reflects continuous improvements in industrialization, urbanization, marketization and internationalization. However, on the other hand, an economic growth rate close to 10% is accompanied by some unstable and unhealthy factors that are worth mentioning in the economic operation. These factors can be logically summarized into 'Five excesses' in the acceleration of economic growth: (1) the rapid increase of some industrial investments induces excessively violent growth in overall fixed assets investment; (2) this factor leads to excessive tension in the supply-demand relations of coal, electricity, oil and transportation; (3) uncontrolled growth in investments drives an excessive supply of monetary credit; (4) due to massive reductions in cultivated land during rapid economic growth, grain yields decline excessively; and (5) all of the above will result in excessive price increases for food and production goods. If these problems are unable to be resolved by the prompt implementation of measures and are allowed to develop without restraint, a partial problem may evolve into a global issue; overheating in some industries may develop into overall violent economic ups-and-downs, and price increases for some products may grow into severe inflation.

Historical experiences and lessons have repeatedly reminded us that we must give significant attention to controlling excessively rapid increases in the rate of economic growth in the ascending stage of the economic cycle so as to avoid violent economic ups and the subsequent violent economic downs. Controlling the economic growth rate creates a dilemma. If the economic growth rate is as low as below 8%, it will be difficult to resolve the unemployment problem, and enterprises will have difficulties operating. Fiscal revenue will be reduced, leading to great difficulties in the development of various social undertakings. If the economic growth rate is as high as over 10%, bottleneck restrictions in the supply of resources such as energy, significant raw materials and transportation will become very serious. The whole operation of the economy will be in a tense situation, with an imbalance in the industrial structure and resulting severe inflation. Such rapid economic growth will be hard to maintain.

We can verify the above analysis based on the historical experiences since the reform and opening up (see Figure 14.1). After the crushing of the "Gang of Four" in October 1976, China's economy increased rapidly with a growth rate that reached as much as 11.7% in 1978. The Third Plenary Session of the 11th Central Committee of CPC, held in December 1978, proposed that the Party's work focus should shift from viewing the class struggle as its central task to concentrating on economic construction. It put forward a policy of reform and opening up to the outside world, and at the same time, the necessity of resolving the imbalance between major sectors of the national economy. It stressed that the infrastructure must be actively carried out in proper sequence, without a rush and in accordance with the economy's actual capability. Subsequently, the first retrenchment macro regulation was conducted for the whole economy in the beginning of the 1980s after the reform and opening up. This adjustment caused the economic growth rate to

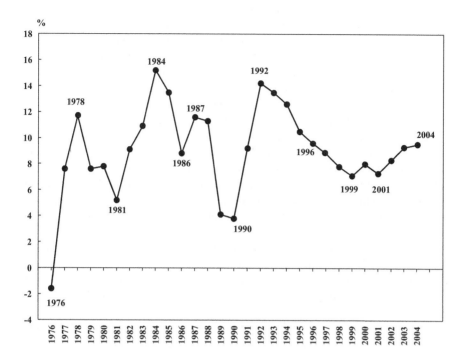

Figure 14.1 Fluctuation curve of the GDP growth rate in China

decline from 11.7% in 1978 to 5.2% in 1981, which formed the first cycle since the reform and opening up. Later in 1984, the economic growth rate increased rapidly to over 10% and subsequently reached up to 15.2%. The supply of coal, electricity, oil and significant raw material could not meet such a high rate of growth, leading to the second adjustment. The economic growth rate reversed to 8.8% in 1986, which formed the second cycle since the reform and opening up. In 1987, the economic growth rate again rose to 11.6%. Subsequently, an adjustment occurred, resulting in the decline of the economic growth rate to 3.8% in 1990 and forming the third cycle since the reform and opening up. The economic growth rate recovered to 9.2% in 1991, thereby entering the ascending stage in a new round of the economic cycle. Under the above-mentioned situations, Deng Xiaoping engaged in an inspection tour of south China at the beginning of 1992 and delivered an important speech. This opened up new prospects for the reform, opening up and modernization construction. However, since it was barely more than ten years after the reform and opening up in China, the original planned economic system had not been fundamentally transformed; therefore, problems like investment hunger, excessive anxiety for success and an overall mere pursuit of high speed had not been overcome. As a result, economic growth ascended to a peak of 14.2% very rapidly. Until 1996, the economic operation had successfully achieved "soft landings" due to macro regulation, and the economic growth rate steadily fell 1% annually, on average. Under circumstances in which China was countering the impact of the Asian financial crisis and dealing with the impact of the world's major countries, such as the United States, simultaneously entering an economic recession, and overcoming insufficient domestic demand, the economic growth rate continued at 7.1% to 8% until 2001, forming the fourth cycle since the reform and opening up. During 2002, 2003 and 2004, China's economy began the rising process in a new cycle, namely, the fifth cycle since the reform and opening up.

We should recognize that such a good situation is valuable. We should appreciate that the current economic growth recovered after the economic growth rate had been in the declining stage of the last cycle for nine consecutive years since 1993. Meanwhile, in view of the economic fluctuations since the reform and opening up, while China's economy is entering a new ascending stage, we must be prudent to avoid allowing the economic growth rate to again increase to 10%, thus inducing violent ups-and-downs. We must endeavor to extend the ascending stage and to avoid allowing it to end after one or two years. Based on such historical background, the Central Committee and the State Council, relying on the scientific development as a guideline, actively and resolutely adopted a series of macro regulation measures in the second half of 2003, and especially, in the first half of 2004.

It was not surprising that a wide debate arose in academic circles in 2003 to 2004 about whether the economy in China was overheated, because both the new round of the economic cycle and the macro regulation were the first that followed the preliminary establishment of the socialist market economic system in China. The debate, on the whole, can be summed up into ten representative views: (1) an overheated aggregate had already emerged; (2) a tendency toward overheating was appearing; (3) the economy was partly overheated. The macro regulation should be carried out through structural expansion and control; (4) on the whole, the economy was not overheated. We should not easily characterize the economy as being overheated; (5) the economy in China was not afraid of being heated, but it feared being cold. It was not a big problem for the current economy in China to be a bit heated; (6) the current economy was normally "heated". As long as there was market demand, it would not be regarded as "overheated", regardless of how heated the economy was; (7) it was impossible for an overheated economy to emerge, because supply and demand would automatically arrive at a balance through market price mechanisms; (8) the economy was cold, rather than overheated, as final consumption had not been stimulated; (9) consumption was cold, whereas investment was heated; and (10) the economy was not simply overheated or non-overheated, but was much more complicated in its practical operation.

Different judgments on the economic situation are implicit in different opinions on whether it is necessary to carry out macro regulation and how to conduct macro control. However, it is worth noting that it is apparently not in conformity with China's actual conditions to apply the Say's Law of Market by French economist Jean-Baptiste Say in the 19th century or Market Equilibrium Theory based on the modern market economies of developed countries in the 1970s to explain and solve the current macroeconomic issues in China, following its preliminary establishment of a socialist market economic system.

The historical experiences and lessons of violent economic ups-and-downs are actually being drawn from the original planned economic system and the transitional process, and are learnt from the Western market economic system. The market economy, especially before the Second World War, fluctuated drastically in the absence of governmental macro regulation. Considering the United States as an example, it experienced eight fluctuations with great amplitude in the first 40 years of the 20th century, of which the Great Crises or the Great Depression from 1929 to 1933 (see Figure 14.2) was the most severe. Immediately following the Great Crises, the Western market economies started to practice governmental macro regulation.

The American economy expanded at a high rate in 1901, but entered into a trough in 1904 with an economic growth rate of −1.2%; it rose to a peak in 1906, but fell in 1908 to a growth rate of −8.2%; it ascended again in 1909, but declined in 1914, with an economic growth rate that had descended to −4.4%. Subsequently, during the First World War, the American economy continued to expand until 1918, but fell in 1921 with a growth rate of −8.7%; it rose in 1922, but declined to −0.2% in 1924; in 1925, it ascended again, but dropped to −0.1% in 1927. Until 1929, it enjoyed a period of great prosperity. When the stock market crashed in October 1929, the Great Crises started, with the economic growth rate falling to −14.8% in

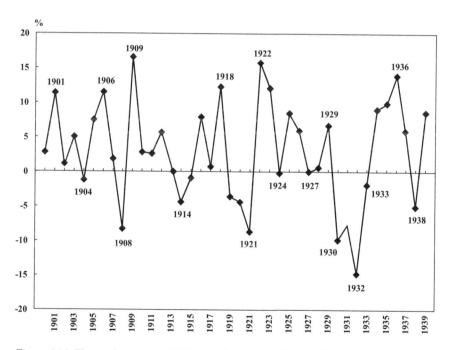

Figure 14.2 Fluctuation curve of GNP growth rate in the United States

1932. The negative economic growth lasted from 1930 until 1933. The American economy rose to a new peak in 1936 and declined to −5.1% in 1938.

In the 1920s, namely, before the Great Crises from 1929 to 1933, what was the situation in the American economy? The real estate construction industry and the automobile industry were the two pillars of American economic prosperity in the 1920s. However, subsequently, their decline became the prelude of the Great Depression from 1929 to 1933. This sheds light on our current situation. In terms of the American real estate construction industry, civil construction was greatly reduced during the First World War. The demand for the construction of new houses after the War was so great that new houses were being built almost everywhere. Nonetheless, the increasing demand still could not be met. The number of newly built urban and rural houses was 449,000 in 1921, and reached 937,000 in 1925, soaring by 100% and simultaneously inducing wild speculative activity in real estate. In terms of American automobile manufacturing in the 1920s, Calvin Coolidge, the 30th President of the United States, made a promise to the American people, asserting, when he came into power in 1923, that every American family would have a chicken in its pot and two cars in its garage. The annual production output of private cars was 1.468 million in 1921 and 4.455 million in 1929, increasing by two times during that time period. The annual production output of commercial vehicles was 148,000 in 1921 and 882,000 in 1929, growing in size by five times during that period. Based on the number of private cars owned, the total number was 8.13 million in 1920, with an average of one out of every 13 persons possessing a car. The total number increased to 23.12 million in 1929, with an average of one out of every 5.3 persons owning a car. The 1920s was a period in which American consumption credit experienced substantial development, which provided strong support for the development of housing and automobiles. Nevertheless, the advancing social purchasing power led to a tremendous amount of private debt. As consumer debt constantly increased, consumers' purchases of housing and automobiles started to decline. The housing construction industry began to decline after reaching a summit in 1925 and 1926, and the automobile industry drastically declined after 1927. Both declines were a prelude to the Great Depression from 1929 to 1933. The fictitious economy (stock market) rapidly increased, while the growth of the real economy, which was centered on automobiles and housing, began to fall. The stock market dived from a high platform, dropping swiftly and violently after reaching its peak in October 1929. The collapse of the stock market initiated the Great Depression throughout the whole economy.

In view of the drawbacks of spontaneous market adjustments, the Central Committee of CPC explicitly proposed that we should establish a socialist market economic system so as to enable the market to play a fundamental role in resource allocation under the state macro regulation when it set up the goals for economic system reform at the 14th Party Congress, held in October 1992, and formulated the "Decision of Central Committee of CPC on Several Issues of Establishing Socialist Market Economic System" at the Third Plenary Session of the 14th Central Committee of CPC, held in November 1993. Subsequently, the 15th and 16th Party Congresses repeatedly reaffirmed this goal. Therefore, market mechanisms and macro regulation are both organic parts of the socialist market economic system; they are complementary to each other and indispensable. Only by integrating market mechanisms and macro regulation are we able to bring the vitality of a market economy into play and maintain a steady economic operation. Macro regulation occurs throughout the whole process of the market economy, and it is not a matter that occurs on a single day. It has different policy orientations, operational procedures, strengths and implementation focuses at different stages of the economic cycle, in accordance with the constant variation in the economic situation. Currently, since the socialist market economic system has preliminarily been established in China, the economic operation bears both the characteristics of the original planned economic system that had existed before the transition, for example, the blind expansion impetus of some local governments, soft budget constraints with no liability for losses in the practice in some enterprises, and those of a market economy system, for example, the diversification of enterprise ownership and the marketization of enterprise behavior; further, it has the features of an immature market economy, for example, the non-legalization and irrationalization of enterprise behavior. Hence, continuous enhancement and improvement of macro regulation and control is even more necessary.

II   How to carry out macro regulation and control

After the failure of Keynesianism in the 1970s and 1980s, Western macro regulation continued to develop theoretically, and this caused the capitalist market economy to be continuously self-regulated as well. There is much in the macro regulation in China that is worthy of being summarized. The government instituted a series of macro regulation measures from the second half of 2003 to 2004. Let us look at the following schedule:

2003

- On July 18, the general office of the State Council issued an "Urgent Circular on Suspending the Approval of Various Development Zones".
- On July 30, the general office of the State Council sent out a "Notification Concerning Checks and Rectifications on Various Development Zones and the Enhancement of the Management of Construction Land".
- On Aug. 23, the People's Bank of China announced that it would raise the deposit-reserve ratio by 1% beginning on Sept. 21.
- On Nov. 3, the State Council dispatched an "Urgent Circular on Further Strengthening the Management and Readjustment of the Land Market Order".
- On Dec. 23, the general office of the State Council issued a "Circular on Transmitting and Issuing Several Opinions of the National Development and Reform Commission and Other Departments on Curbing Irrational Investment in the Steel, Electrolytic Aluminum and Cement Industries".

2004

- On Feb. 8, China Banking Regulatory Commission sent out a "Notice on Conducting a Special Inspection on the Loan Situation of Some Industries".
- On Mar. 24, the People's Bank of China announced that it would carry out a System of Differential Deposit Reserve Ratio and a System of Floating Interest Rates for Re-lending beginning on Apr.25.
- On Apr. 11, the People's Bank of China announced that it would increase the deposit-reserve ratio for 0.5% beginning on Apr. 25.
- On Apr. 26, the State Council dispatched a "Circular on Adjusting the Capital Ratios of Fixed Assets Investment Projects in Some Industries".
- On Apr. 27, the general office of the State Council issued a "Circular on Checking upon Fixed Assets Investment Projects". The emphasis in the checking-up was on projects involving steel, electrolytic aluminum, cement, office buildings of the Party and government organizations, as well as training centers, urban rapid railway transportation, golf courses, exhibition centers, logistics parks, large shopping malls and all newly started projects since 2004. Projects involving agriculture, forestry, water conservancy facilities (including six categories of small projects for rural areas, such as water saving irrigation, drinking water for humans and animals, rural biogas, rural hydropower, rural roads and grassland fences), ecological construction, education (excluding University towns), health and science (excluding Science and Technology Park Zones) were not included in the scope of the checking-up.
- On Apr. 28, an investigation was conducted into the allegation of violations in the construction of a steel project by Jiangsu Tieben Steel Co. Ltd.
- On Apr. 29, the general office of the State Council issued an "Urgent Circular on Deepening the Promotion of Land Market Administration and Rectification and Rigorous Land Management", and it decided to suspend the transition approval from agricultural land to non-agricultural construction land for half a year.
- On Apr. 30, the National Development and Reform Commission, the People's Bank of China and China Banking Regulatory Commission jointly enacted a "Notification Concerning Related Issues on Further Enhancing the Coordination and Cooperation of Industrial Policy and Credit Policy and Controlling Credit Risk" and a "Current Directory on Curbing Redundant Low-level Development of Some Industries".
- On July 19, the State Council printed and distributed a "Decision on Reform of the Investment Structure".
- On Oct. 21, the State Council printed and distributed a "Decision on Deepening the Reform and Intensifying Land Management".
- On Oct. 28, the People's Bank of China decided to increase the benchmark interest rates for deposits and loans of financial institutions beginning on Oct. 29.

We can perceive that several measures were taken and focused on in April 2004, which was the main time when the battles related to the macro regulation occurred.

We can ascertain the main features of the macro regulation using the above schedule.

First, in terms of the timing, this macro regulation is a precautionary, predictive and active adjustment. It is neither a "hard landing" nor a "soft landing". Instead, it continuously sustains sound economic development, steadily and rapidly, at an appropriate growth range through proper speed control.

Second, in terms of a breakthrough point, this macro regulation maintains strict control over the floodgates of land and credit to ensure the cultivation of land as a basis for increases in the grain yield and to curb blind investment in some over-heated industries.

Third, in terms of the pace, this macro regulation is a progressive way from taking preventive measures, such as observations, alerting, minor adjustment, to timely strengthening the effective measures on the definite issues.

Fourth, in terms of the implementation principles, this macro regulation is dis-criminatory in both assurance and control, without sudden brakes or rigid unifor-mity, rather than all-around retrenchment.

Fifth, in terms of the measures, this macro regulation comprehensively applies economic, legal and necessary administrative measures.

III Acquired achievements

This macro regulation has made remarkable achievements in preventing partial problems from growing into overall issues, avoiding violent economic ups-and-downs and excessive price increases, and maintaining steady and rapid economic growth, as well as social harmony and stability.

In terms of the steady and rapid economic growth momentum, this macro regu-lation has neither made the economic growth rate exceed 10%, resulting in an overall overheated economic situation, nor made it decline markedly, creating a "hard landing" situation; thus, it has avoided the contingent violent economic ups-and-downs and has extended the rising stage of the economic cycle.

Private enterprises have reacted strongly to the macro regulation. Some people believe that macro regulation is directed at private enterprises, but in fact, it is aimed at the whole economic operation issue, regardless of enterprise ownership. For example, the objects of macro regulation by the American Federal Reserve Committee were all private enterprises under a market economy. For this macro regulation, Nan Cunhui, the President of Chint Group Corporation, a private enter-prise in Zhejiang Province, pointed out that

> under the background of the nationwide economic expansion in the middle and late 1980s, some electric appliance enterprises in Wenzhou were obsessed with the desire for gain and sold shoddy goods as quality goods, leading to great quantities of counterfeit and inferior commodities. These enterprises closed down one after another afterwards. Due to the excellent quality, Chint stood out from others. The macro regulation made the private enterprises exhibit a good status.

It is thus evident that the macro regulation promoted the sound development of private enterprises.

Viewing the effects of this macro regulation from the perspective of price, the consumption prices of residents increased to 18.8% in 1988, along with the high level of economic growth. In the process of the overheated economy at the beginning of the 1990s, they rose from 3.4% in 1991 to 6.4% in 1992, 14.7% in 1993 and 24.1% in 1994, which was the peak of the price increases since the founding of the new China. Subsequently, the consumption prices of residents declined to 2.8% in 1997 during the economic "soft landing". Influenced by the Asian financial crisis and insufficient domestic demand, prices experienced mild deflation from 1998 to 2002. After being freed from the shadow of deflation, prices started to increase slightly in 2003 and 2004, during which the rise rates of the consumption prices of residents were 1.2% and 3.9%, respectively, which was the result of macro regulation. If there had been no timely macro control, prices would have increased much more.

Observing the results of this macro regulation from the perspective of grain, grain production experienced a significant turnaround in 2004, during which the annual total grain output reached 469.45 billion kg, with an annual increment of 38.75 billion kg, which was the highest since the founding of the new China. Macro regulation maintained strict control over the floodgates of land and credit. Why was land taken as an important measure in macro regulation? The grain sowing acreage in China had decreased from 1.702 billion mu in 1990 to 1.628 billion mu in 1994, along with high economic growth in the 1990s, but was restored to 1.707 billion mu in 1998. Subsequently, in recent years, the grain sowing acreage rapidly declined to 1.49 billion mu in 2003, but was restored to 1.52 billion mu during the macro regulation of 2004. The grain yield was 446.25 billion kg in 1990, and it reached the highest in history of 512.3 billion kg in 1998 and was maintained at above 500 billion kg in 1999. Then, it declined to 430.7 billion kg in 2003, in pace with the substantial reduction in the grain sowing area, inducing a short supply of grain. It was extremely difficult but the grain yield reached 469.45 billion kg in 2004 through the efforts of multiple parties.

IV   Existing problems

Currently, we should attach great importance to the following points: (1) maintaining steady and rapid economic development and avoiding violent fluctuations; (2) keeping price stability and preventing severe inflation; (3) doing well in the work concerning people's interests and maintaining social stability; (4) paying close attention to international finance and the fluctuation of oil prices, and protecting national economic security.

From a long-term and deep-seated perspective, the existing problems can be summarized as following issues: (1) the income gap and region disparities; (2) huge employment pressure; (3) difficult structural adjustments and the transformation of economic growth patterns; (4) the non-removal of systemic and functional obstacles that restrict steady and rapid economic growth and induce violent economic ups-and-downs.

V   What to do in the future

1   Macro regulation objectives. The macro regulation objectives for 2005 are as follows:
    (1) an increase in the gross domestic product to around 8%; (2) newly increased urban employment of 9 million and controlling the urban registered unemployment rate at 4.6%; (3) controlling the aggregate price increase of residents' consumption at 4%; (4) basic balance in international payments.
2   Policy orientations of macro regulation in the principle of 'dual prudence': (1) the expansionary and active fiscal policy implemented after the Asian financial crisis will be transformed to an appropriate and prudent fiscal policy whose main feature is the proper reduction of the fiscal deficit and appropriate decreases in the scale of the issuance of long-term treasury bonds for construction. The central budget deficit this year is 300 billion yuan, a year-on-year decrease of 19.8 billion yuan. The long-term treasury bonds for construction this year amount to 80 billion yuan, a year-on-year reduction of 30 billion. Meanwhile, an investment of 10 billion yuan in regular development projects is added in the central budget; and (2) prudent monetary policy will be continuously implemented. Rational control of the supply of money and credit should both support economic development and prevent inflation and financial risks.
3   Key point of macro regulation. We should control the fixed assets investment scale so as to prevent it from rebounding, and we should continuously control the floodgates of land approval and credit supply.
4   Macro regulation principles. We should better implement discriminatory principles with assurance and control.
5   Macro regulation measures. We should place additional stress on giving play to market mechanisms and applying economic and legal measures.
6   Macro regulation and enhancement of "three-dimensional rural issues concerning agriculture, countryside and farmers". We should accelerate the pace of reducing and exempting agricultural taxes in order to realize a wide range of substantial reductions of and exemptions from agricultural taxes in the country this year and effectuate a complete nationwide exemption from agricultural taxes next year. The original target of rescinding agricultural taxes in five years will be achieved within three years. There are 27 provinces, cities and autonomous regions that will implement the reduction of and exemption from agricultural taxes this year, and four regions – Heibei, Shandong, Yunnan and Guangxi – will implement it next year. The rural tax and fee reform is a profound transformation in the rural economic and social field. The complete exemption from agricultural taxes and the elimination of irrational burdens on farmers will terminate the practice of farmers paying

a grain tax to the government for working on the land, a practice that has persisted for as long as over two millennia.

7   Macro regulation and structural adjustment. We should press ahead to optimize and upgrade the industrial structure, adhere to the implementation of the new industrialization in carrying out macro regulation and promote economic restructuring based on advanced technology and focusing on improving the ability to engage in independent innovation. We should accelerate the development of new high-tech, which can greatly spur economic growth, and generic, key and matching technologies that can promote the upgrading of traditional industries. We must push forward the formulation of the targets and measures for key technological innovations in some significant fields and work hard to make new breakthroughs in this regards as soon as possible.

There are indications that Chinese enterprises and industries are facing severe challenges based on new techniques and intellectual property rights due to the current deficiency in self-innovation competence: (1) in the new high-tech industries, the intellectual property rights that foreign companies possess hold the advantage. According to statistics, the authorized patents that foreign companies have obtained amount to more than 60% to 90% in the communication, semiconductor, biology, medicine and computer industries; (2) China is less competitive in some industries with great processing and manufacturing capacities because of the insufficiency of self-dominated intellectual property rights. For example, the DVD production capacity of China is number one in the world. However, due to the absence of its own core technology, DVD exports are restricted by the intellectual property rights of foreign enterprises and the levies of high patent fees, thus weakening the advantage of cheap labor; (3) the dependency on foreign technical equipment is high. The more advanced the technical equipment, the more we rely on imports. The imports of manufacturing equipment products to China were around US$110 billion in 2001, occupying about 48% of the nationwide total imports; 95% of the integrated circuit chip manufacturing equipment and 70% of manufacturing equipment for cars, numerical control machines, textile machinery and offset printing relied on imports. Therefore, we must make breakthroughs in some significant and key fields and technical aspects through independent innovation, along with its introduction and adaptation, so as to promote structural adjustment.

8   Macro regulation and the construction of a harmonious society. In implementing macro regulation, we should promote the establishment of a harmonious society in which the basic features are democracy and legality, fairness and justice, honesty and friendship, vigor and security, the maintenance of social order and the harmony between humans and nature.

9   Systemic foundation of macro regulation. We must constantly eliminate the systemic and functional obstacles that restrict steady and rapid economic growth and induce violent economic ups-and-downs through deepening reform. This implies the following three aspects: (1) first, we must accelerate the

government's self-reformation and promote the transformation of governmental functions by firmly establishing a scientific view on development and correct views on past achievements in order to avoid the blind pursuit and one-sided competition for growth speed and place stress on improvements in the quality and efficiency of economic growth. The government must not meddle in what is not its business, but instead, should turn it over to enterprises, social organizations and intermediary institutions, and it must always attend to its affairs. In particular, the government should not monopolize the investment decisions and promotion of enterprises, or directly intervene in their production and operation activities. The establishment of a system for responsibility in the investments of government and state-owned enterprises will fundamentally resolve the issue of blind investment and investment decision-making failure with no one bearing the responsibility, thus enabling government at all levels not to become the root cause of an overheated economy; (2) we should establish policy rules and enhance legal construction to promote the standardization, institutionalization and legalization of macro regulation through deepening reform. In detail, we should build and perfect unambiguous policy rules in terms of the transformation of the direction, reinforcement and corresponding measures of macro regulation, the standardization of market access and the intensification of market supervision, so as to increase the transparency of macro regulation and enable correct anticipation and good effects in various social aspects; (3) we must deepen the reform of state-owned enterprises and promote the sound development of private enterprises, with the aim of laying a good micro-foundation for macro regulation carried out by the government's application of economic and legal measures. Only by continuously raising the market operation levels, the legal consciousness and the response capacity of micro entities to macro regulation can the government apply more economic and legal measures to improve macro regulation.

[Originally published in *Research on Economics and Management (Jingji Yu GuanliYanjiu)*, No.4, 2005]

15 On sound and fast development

On the eve of the Central Economic Working Conference, on 30 November 2006, the Political Bureau of the Central Committee of the CPC convened a meeting to analyze the current economic situation and discuss the economic work for the following year. For the first time, the meeting put forward the suggestion that efforts should be made to achieve sound and fast development of the national economy, which attracted the public's attention (2006)[1]

At the Central Economic Working Conference held in December 2006, it was further pointed out that sound and fast development was the essential requirement for the overall implementation of the scientific view of development while emphasizing the target of achieving the sound and fast development of the national economy (2006)[2]

The Government Work Report of the Fifth Meeting of the Tenth National People's Congress held on 5 March 2007 implemented the scientific view of development in an all-inclusive way and repeatedly emphasized the need to achieve sound and fast economic development.

In comparison with the well-known formulations of "More, Faster, Better and More Economical" and "Fast and Sound" which have been applied during more than half a century since the founding of new China, "Sound and Fast" changes the wording and for the first time "Sound" is put before "Fast". It seems simple but is actually not. This is a great transformation of historical significance, which records the exploration and the disturbances and frustrations experienced during the socialist modernization journey, fully demonstrating the remarkable achievements in China's economic development over more than half a century, especially since the reform and opening up, and distinctively embodying the essential requirement of the scientific view of development and great change in economic development concepts.

I More, faster, better and more economical: the strenuous exploration in the early years of new China

"More, Faster, Better and More Economical" was the concise and representative summarization of the general line of socialist construction that the Party put forward in 1958. The gestation, formation and practice process of this general line reflected the early strenuous exploration to find the socialism construction road applicable to China's national conditions after the founding of new China against the special international and domestic backgrounds of the time, namely the external military threats, the economic blockage of imperialism and the internal state of "poverty and blankness" left over from the old society.

Through three years' recovery of the national economy after the founding of new China, massive industrialization and socialist transformation of the agriculture, handicraft and capitalist industries and commerce started in 1953. In October 1955, Mao Zedong advocated the need to "run more good cooperatives fast" (Mao Zedong, 1977: 206) at the Sixth Plenary Session of the Seventh CPC Central Committee in the upsurge of promoting agricultural cooperation. This was the earliest prototype of the formulation "More, Faster, Better and More Economical".

Then, in 1956, the *People's Daily* published an editorial for the New Year entitled "Striving for Overall Outperforming Five-Year Plan Ahead of Time" and for the first time integrally proposed the principle of "More, Faster, Better and More Economical", extending it from guiding the agricultural cooperation movement to supervising various works. The editorial explained "More, Faster, Better and More Economical" in detail:

> more and faster development can catch up with the country and people's needs; sound development with a quality guarantee is against poor, shoddy and out-of-specification products; more economical means to spend less money to achieve more so as to make all that should be done and can be done well done with accumulated financial resources.

Although the editorial pointed out that the four elements in "More, Faster, Better and More Economical" were combined with each other and inseparable, the emphasized keynote was to fight for a greater development speed. Influenced by the editorial, there was a tendency for rash advancement and over-anxiety for success in the Party's practical work in 1956. To prevent this unhealthy trend, "opposition to rash advancement" was carried out in the Party's work. However, Mao Zedong sternly criticized the "opposition to rash advancement" in October 1957, considering it to be wiping out "More, Faster, Better and More Economical", and requested the restoration of the slogan (Mao Zedong, 1977: 474). Subsequently, on 12 December 1957, the People's Daily published an editorial entitled "Persistence in Construction Principle of More, Faster, Better and More Economical" and reiterated the slogan.

The *People's Daily* published an editorial for the New Year in 1958 entitled "Brave Winds and Waves", repeated the reiteration of the principle of "More, Faster, Better and More Economical" and proposed the slogan "Go All Out, Aim High". Mao Zedong put forward the idea that "we move forward in a wavy way under the general line of 'More, Faster, Better and More Economical' and 'Go All Out, Aim High'" (Mao Zedong, 1999: 372) at the Working Conference of the Central Committee of the CPC, namely the Chengdu Conference, held in March 1958, which gradually formed the general line of socialist construction with a preliminary expression. In May 1958, according to Mao Zedong's proposal, the Second Plenary of the Eighth National Congress of the CPC formally stated the general line of "To go all out, strive for the best and build socialism with greater, faster, better and more economical results".

On 21 June 1958, the *People's Daily* published an editorial entitled "Strive for High Speed", illuminating the general line in detail, and pointed out that "Faster is the key link of 'More, Faster, Better and More Economical'" and "Speed is the soul of the general line". The editorial proposed the magnificent target that

> after the basic accomplishment of socialist revolution, the most urgent demand of the people in China is to transfer the national economy to the modernized production track and rapidly and thoroughly shake off the poverty and backwardness left over by history, constructing China into a powerful socialist country with a highly developed economy and culture.

The editorial emphasized that "only by achieving this grant target with the highest speed and within the shortest possible time can we ultimately consolidate the socialist system both domestically and internationally".

Consequently, the original combined and inseparable slogan "More, Faster, Better and More Economical" gradually changed to the general line with a focus on "Faster" and high speed as the soul. In practice, this led to the "Great Leap Forward" movement, with the main contents of "Nationwide Steel-Smelting" and "Surpassing Great Britain and Catching up with the United States", which were characterized by high indicators, blind guidance and proneness to boasting and exaggeration.

During the "Great Leap Forward", the variation of the schedule in "Surpassing Great Britain and Catching up with the United States" mostly reflected the outstanding "Faster" and "High Speed". It was first proposed in November 1957 that China would catch up with and surpass Great Britain within 15 years. By January 1958, this formulation had adjusted to "spending 15 years or more in catching up with and surpassing Great Britain". However, two months later, in March 1958, it was revised to "spending 10 years or a little more on catching up with Great Britain and 20 years or a little more on catching up with the United States" at Chengdu Conference. In this way, the schedule for catching up with and surpassing Great Britain changed from "15 years or more" to "10 years or a little more". One month later, in April 1958, this formulation was amended to "there is a possibility of catching up with Great Britain within 10 years and the United States in another 10 years". Another month later, in May 1958, the government's interior formulation was to spend 7 years and 15 years on catching up with Great Britain and the United States, respectively. On16 June 1958, the formulation was rectified to "spending 5 years in surpassing Great Britain and 10 years in catching up with the United States". One day later, on 17 June 1958, the final formulation was "spending 2 years on surpassing Great Britain". In just a few months, the schedule for "surpassing Great Britain" had changed from "15 years or more" to 10 years, 7 years, 5 years and finally merely 2 years; the timetable for "catching up with the

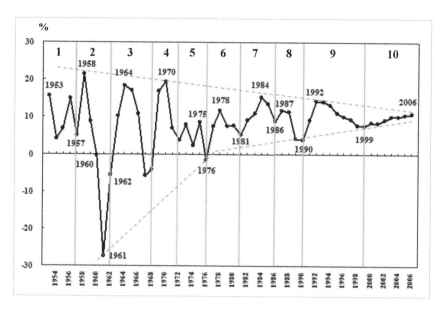

Figure 15.1 Fluctuation curve of the economic growth rate in China (1953–2006)

United States" had adjusted from "20 years or more" to 15 years and 10 years (Pang Xianzhi and Jin Chongji, 2003: 761–824).

The "Great Leap Forward" focusing on "Faster" in 1958 made the GDP growth rate increase to a peak of 21.3% at a stroke (see the second cycle in Figure 15.1). The overheated economic growth at ultra-high speed damaged the whole economy and disorganized the normal order of economic operation, leading to severe imbalance between major sectors of the national economy. Thus, the supply promptly encountered three bottleneck restrictions: (1) short supply in production goods, including coal, electricity, oil, transportation, steel and other raw materials; (2) short supply in industrial consumables; and (3) short supply in grain together with a serious natural disaster. It was difficult to sustain the high-speed growth due to the overall shortage induced. Subsequently, the economic growth rate dropped greatly in 1960, 1961 and 1962 and became negative, the greatest decline being −27.3% in 1961. Accordingly, the peak-trough gap of the economic growth rate was almost 50% (48.6%) from the summit of 21.3% in 1958 to the deepest valley of −27.3% in 1961. This was the cycle with the greatest fluctuation amplitude among the ten economic cycles since the founding of new China, a typical "violent up and down".

The "Resolution on Several Historical Issues of CPC since the Foundation of PRC" approved at the Sixth Plenary Session of the Eleventh Central Committee of the CPC in June 1981 made the following analysis of the general line of "More, Faster, Better and More Economical"(CCCPC Party Literature Research Office, 1982a: 754): the general line of socialist construction approved at the Second

Plenary of the Eighth National Congress of the CPC in 1958 and its basic point properly reflected the universal desire of the broad masses of the people for the urgent transformation of the backward economic and cultural situation in China and neglected the objective economic law. Around the time of the conference, all the party members and people of different races exhibited their great socialist enthusiasm and creative spirit in production and construction and made certain achievements. However, due to a lack of experience in socialist construction and cognition of economic development law and the basic economic situation in China together with over-anxiety for success and exaggeration of subjective will and efforts, the government rashly launched the "Great Leap Forward" and People's Commune Movement after the proposal of the general line without serious investigation, research and experiment, leading to a severe inundation of Leftism, which was symbolized by high indicators, blind guidance, proneness to boasting and exaggeration and absolute egalitarianism.

As a result, "More, Faster, Better and More Economical", the wording bearing the imprint of the times of the "Great Leap Forward" in the 1950s, is no longer used. From the founding of new China to 1976, although the socialist construction experienced severe frustrations, on the whole, great achievements were attained with the primary establishment of an independent and integral industrial system and a national economic system and the fundamental solution of "developing from nothing" during the industrialization process (Compilation Group of Outline of Modern and Contemporary History of China, 2007). In particular, Mao Zedong's famous works "On the Ten Major Relationships" (April 1956) and "The Question about Correctly Processing the Contradictions among the People" (February 1957) are significant and precious theoretical achievements obtained during the initial exploration of the socialist modernization in China.

II   Fast and sound: great development of world interest

In December 1978, the Third Plenary Session of the Eleventh Central Committee of the CPC brought order out of chaos and terminated the history of "taking the class struggle as the central task", shifting the Party's work focus to socialist modernization, thus commencing a new historical period of reform and opening up to the outside world and socialist modernization construction in China. It pointed out that

> in order to greet the great task of socialist modernization, the conference reviewed the experiences and lessons of economic construction since the foundation of China . . . Practice has proved that the national economy will develop steadily at a high speed with the maintenance of necessary social and political stability and the appreciation of the objective economic law. Contrarily, the economy will slow down or even stagnate and fall back.

The phrase "high speed" was still used at that time, but the emphasis was laid on "steady" development. It was proposed that "the infrastructure must be actively carried out in proper sequence according to the actual capability" (CCCPC Party Literature Research Office, 1982a: 5–6).

In the exploration of the 1980s, "speed" and "benefit" were gradually connected. At the end of 1981, the Government Work Report at the Fourth Meeting of the Fifth National People's Congress first proposed the issue of "economic benefit" and regarded it as the economic construction principle, pointing out that "we should establish a realistic pace and effective approach to economic development, which will truly benefit Chinese people based on the Chinese reality". In September 1982, the CPC's Twelfth National Congress added "raising economic benefit" to the general goal of economic construction for the first time and asserted that "within twenty years from 1981 to the end of the century, our general goal of economic construction is to strive to quadruple the annual gross output value of industry and agriculture nationwide under the premise of constantly increasing economic benefit." In October 1987, the CPC's Thirteenth National Congress further included "benefit" in the economic development strategy and put forward the idea that

> we must firmly implement the strategy of emphasizing benefit, improving quality, coordinating development and stabilizing growth, of which the basic requirements are to make efforts to improve product quality, strive to make readily marketable products, reduce material and labour consumption, realize rational allocation of production factors and raise fund utilization benefit and efficiency of resource consumption. After all, we must gradually transform the main extensive operation to the major intensive operation.

At the beginning of 1992, Deng Xiaoping emphasized in his South Talks,

> At present, the economic development of the surrounding countries and regions is faster than ours. If we do not develop or develop too slowly, there will be problems if common people make comparisons . . . It is necessary and possible to have several stages of fast development speed and good benefit in the future long process of modernization construction with well-prepared domestic conditions and a favorable international environment together with exertion of the advantage of socialist system-pooling resources to undertake major national activities.
>
> (Deng Xiaoping, 1993: 375–377)

The formulation of "fast development speed and good benefit" raised the issue of "Fast and Sound" development for the first time. Subsequently, in October 1992, the CPC's Fourteenth National Congress proposed to "find out a development approach of the national economy with high speed and good benefit" while establishing the reform objective of setting up a socialist market economic system.

Deng Xiaoping's South Talks and the CPC's Fourteenth National Congress instigated a new prospect for the reform, opening up and modernization. However, since it was just more than ten years after the reform and opening up in China, the original planned economic system has not been transformed fundamentally; the drawbacks, like investment hunger, over-anxiety for success and mere pursuit of high speed, have not been overcome. As a result, the economic growth ascended to a peak of 14.2% (see the ninth cycle in Figure 15.1) very quickly, leading to an overheated economy. Regarding this issue, the *People's Daily* published an article written by a commentator on 29 January 1993 entitled "Promoting Fast and Sound Economic Development", which reminded us that "in the excellent situation, we must remain sober-minded, seriously deal with and actively solve the problems existing in the rapid development and work hard to avoid the emergence of an overheated economy and strive for fast and sound economic development in the new year." Concerning the control of the overheated economy, the Party Central Committee repeatedly emphasized that

> we should better combine emancipation of mind with seeking truth from the facts and further implement the lines, principles, policies, goals and tasks determined by the CPC's Fourteenth National Congress to ensure fast and sound economic construction . . . We should fully stimulate, protect and bring the enthusiasm of the masses into play so as to promote fast and sound economic development.
>
> (Jiang Zemin, 2006: 295, 366)

Under the ideological guidance of "Fast and Sound", the national economic operation successfully achieved a "soft landing" from the second half of 1993 to 1996, both greatly reducing the price increase and maintaining appropriate fast economic growth (Liu Guoguang and Liu Shucheng, 1997).

In September 1997, the CPC's Fifteenth National Congress reaffirmed the formulation of "fast development speed and good benefit" and further put forward the suggestion that "we should find out a coordinated economic development approach with fast speed, good benefit and constant improvement of overall quality". The requirement for "constant improvement of overall quality" was further included.

In November 2002, the CPC's Sixteenth National Congress asserted that we must build a better-off society that benefits billions of the population in an all-encompassing way in the first 20 years of the twenty-first century and strive to quadruple the gross domestic product in 2020 compared with 2000 on the basis of optimizing the structure and improving the benefit. It was proposed that we should take the path of new industrialization, namely "practice new industrialization with high technological content, good economic benefit, low resource consumption, less environmental pollution and full exertion of human resource superiority." The protection of resources and the environment became more prominent in the acceleration of industrialization and the overall construction of a well-off society.

In October 2003, the Third Plenary Session of the Sixteenth Central Committee of the CPC formed and proposed a scientific view of development at a higher level with more abundant connotations and pointed out that "we should persist in people-oriented concept and establish a view of overall coordinated and sustainable development to promote an all-round economic, social and human development."

In October 2005, the Fifth Plenary Session of the Sixteenth Central Committee of the CPC approved the "Suggestion of Central Committee of CPC on Formulating the Eleventh Five-Year Plan of National Economy and Social Development". The suggestion emphasized that "development should be at a fast speed and more stress should be laid on improving growth quality and benefit" while proposing the "prevention of violent economic ups and downs and realization of fast and sound development". Here, "improving growth quality and benefit" was highlighted, implying sound and fast development, in which "sound" was put first and was beginning to gain currency.

Since the reform and opening up, the economic development of China has attracted the world's attention and has realized Deng Xiaoping's prediction of great foresight that it is necessary and possible to have several stages of "fast development speed and good benefit" in the long process of modernization construction.

III   Basic conditions of sound and fast development

At present, the reason why "sound and fast development" is put forward is that, on the one hand, we are provided with the basic conditions, and on the other hand, we urgently need to solve further the current prominent contradictions and problems in the economic development. In other words, "sound and fast development" is both realistically possible and urgently necessary.

Since the reform and opening up, great changes have taken place in China's economic life, which constitute the basic conditions for advancing to the new historical starting point of "sound and fast development". The basic conditions can be summarized as six great historical changes: (1) the economic system has transformed from a highly centralized planned economic system into a socialist market economic system; (2) the relationship between supply and demand has shifted from long-term shortage to certain relative surplus; (3) the economic operation has transformed from violent ups and downs into rapid and steady performance; (4) the GDP world ranking has risen from number 10 at the beginning of the reform and moving up to number 4; (5) the ranking of the value of foreign trade in the world has increased from number 27 at the beginning of the reform and moving up to number 3; and (6) people's lives have changed from solving the problem of adequate food and clothing to realizing the objective of a well-off society and further advancing to a well-off society all-round, with the GDP per capita increasing from below US$300 at the beginning of the reform and rising to nearly US$2000. These six great historical changes had provided for "sound and fast development" – a significant systematic basic condition, a necessary market pattern of supply and demand, a good economic operational environment, a solid material foundation, a favorable international economic condition and motivation for new development.

With regard to the economic system and the relationship between supply and demand, the most distinctive feature of the new era is the reformation and opening up to the outside world, in which the socialist market economic system of China has preliminarily been established and has entered a new stage of constant perfection. The established socialist market economic system aims to enable the market to play a fundamental role in resource allocation under the state macro regulation. The introduction of the market mechanism has vitalized the economic development under the socialist system. Constant enhancement and improvement of macro regulation will help to overcome the drawback of spontaneous market adjustment and maintain sound economic development. Promoted by the reform and opening up and the socialist market economic system, historic fundamental changes have taken place in the market pattern of supply and demand. Since the founding of new China, the long-standing shortage has basically been changed and a buyer market has preliminarily been formed, generating a certain relative surplus. It is difficult to realize "sound and fast" development along with the strong investment hunger and expansion impetus that existed under the original highly centralized planned economic system and severe short supply of commodities under the long-term shortage economy. The establishment and constant perfection of the socialist market economic system and the basic change of the commodity shortage provided a significant systematic basic condition and necessary market pattern of supply and demand for "sound and fast development". If there are no reform and opening up, the introduction of the market mechanism, the enhancement of macro regulation and the historical change of the market pattern of supply and demand, it would be hard for the economic development in China to follow a sound and fast track.

Concerning the economic operation, as displayed in the previous Figure 15.1, up to now the economic growth rate has experienced a total of ten fluctuating cycles since the founding of new China, five of which were from 1953 to 1976 when the "Cultural Revolution" ended. Among the five cycles, there were three "violent ups and downs", with the peak of the economic growth rate moving around 20%, specifically 21.3% in 1958, 18.3% in 1964 and 19.4% in 1970. The peak-trough gap from the highest point to the lowest point of the economic growth rate was largest in the second cycle, reaching as high as 48.6%, while the smallest one was 9.9% (see Table 15.1). Another five cycles occurred after 1976 when the "Cultural Revolution" ended and since the reform and opening up in 1978, in which the peak of the economic growth rate was more than 11% to 15% in the four existing cycles: in detail, 11.7% in 1978, 15.2% in 1984, 11.6% in 1987 and 14.2% in 1992. The peak-trough gap of the four existing cycles all declined to around 6% or 7%, which was still rather large. With an economic growth rate of 7.6%, 1999 was the trough year of the ninth economic cycle. The economic growth rate respectably recovered to 8.4% in 2000 and 8.3% in 2001, thus entering a new economic cycle. It was, respectively, 9.1% in 2002, 10% in 2003, 10.1% in 2004, 10.4% in 2005 and 10.7% in 2006. This displayed a prominent feature of the economic growth in China in recent years, namely that China's economy had been operated steadily and rapidly within the appropriate growth range of around 8%–10% for seven consecutive years from 2000 to 2006, in which four consecutive years, from 2003 to 2006,were around 10% or slightly higher. As indicated in the previous Figure 15.1, the new track of steady economic operation at a high

Table 15.1 Peak-trough gap of the economic growth rate of various cycles

Serial No. of Cycle	Starting and Ending Year	Peak—Trough Gap (%)
1	1953–57	9.9
2	1958–62	48.6
3	1963–68	24.0
4	1969–72	15.6
5	1973–76	10.3
6	1977–81	6.5
7	1982–86	6.4
8	1987–90	7.8
9	1991–99	6.6
10	2000–06	(In progress)

Table 15.2 High economic growth situation of four consecutive years and more in China

Year	GDP Growth Rate (%)	Price Rise Rate (%)
1963	10.2	−5.9
1964	18.3	−3.7
1965	17.0	−2.7
1966	10.7	−0.3
1992	14.2	6.4
1993	14.0	14.7
1994	13.1	24.1
1995	10.9	14.8
1996	10.0	6.1
2003	10.0	1.2
2004	10.1	3.9
2005	10.4	1.8
2006	10.7	1.5

level has never appeared in the history of economic development since the founding of new China.

In the history of economic development of new China for more than half a century, the economic growth rate exceeded 10% for four consecutive years three times altogether (see Figure 15.1 and Table 15.2). The first time was from 1963 to 1966, with the economic growth rate being 10.2% in 1963, 18.3% in 1964, 17% in 1965 and 10.7% in 1966, respectively. Apparently, although the economic growth of these four years was very high, it was very unsteady, presenting a steep peak. The second time was from 1992 to 1996, with the economic growth rate being 14.2% in 1992, 14% in 1993, 13.1% in 1994, 10.9% in 1995 and 10% in

1996, respectively. Obviously, the economic growth rate of these five years declined year by year and was in the downward range of economic fluctuation, appearing as a downhill trend. The third time was from 2003 to 2006, with rapid and steady economic growth, producing a high and stable situation. Meanwhile, the corresponding price situations of these three periods of high economic growth in consecutive years were different. In the first period from 1963 to 1966, the increasing rate of the commodity retail price was negative, respectively being −5.9% in 1963, −3.7% in 1964, −2.7% in 1965 and −0.3% in 1966, during which price control and a low price policy were implemented. In the second period, from 1992 to 1996, the rate of increase of residents' consumption price was, respectively, 6.4% in 1992, 14.7% in 1993, 24.1% in 1994, 14.8% in 1995 and 6.1% in 1996. In other words, this period corresponded to severe inflation as high as 14% to 24%. In the third period, from 2003 to 2006, the increasing rate of residents' consumption price was, respectively, 1.2% in 2003, 3.9% in 2004, 1.8% in 2005 and 1.5% in 2006, demonstrating that the price was in a good situation with a low and steadily increasing rate.

From the perspective of the overall tendency of the fluctuation curve of the economic growth rate in China, as shown in Figure 15.1, the economic growth and fluctuation presented a new trend since the reform and opening up – a rational decline from the peak, a distinctive rise from the trough and a reduced amplitude, namely generating a stabilization tendency of economic cyclical fluctuation changing from acuteness to smoothness (Liu Shucheng, 2006). It is difficult to achieve sound and fast development while the economic operation is frequently experiencing "violent ups and downs". Currently, the rapid and steady economic growth tendency has provided a good economic operational environment for sound and fast development.

With respect to the GDP and the value of foreign trade, the GDP in China has been constantly increasing (see Figure 15.2) since the reform and opening up. The GDP was RMB362.4 billion yuan in 1978, at the beginning of the reform and opening up. It rose to 1000 billion yuan in 1986 through eight years of efforts, during which an average of more than 80 billion yuan was incremented annually. It increased to 2000 billion yuan in 1991 as a result of five years' endeavors, during which an average of over 220 billion yuan was incremented annually. Within 15 years, from 1992 to 2006, the GDP in China increased on average by more than 1100 billion yuan annually. In 2006, it broke 20,000 billion yuan (20,940.7 billion yuan). The GDP of 2006 was 13.3 times that of 1978 in real terms and increased annually by 9.7% on average over 28 years. The GDP ranking of China in the world rose from number 10 in 1978 to number 6 in 2000 after the United States, Japan, Germany, Great Britain and France. From 2000 to 2004, it ranked steadily at no. 6, rose to no. 4 in 2005, surpassing Great Britain and France, and is estimated to remain in the fourth position in 2006. It will hopefully surpass Germany and rise to no. 3 in 2007. Meanwhile, the total amount of imports and exports of China was merely US$20.6 billion in 1978, at the beginning of the reform and opening up, and rose to US$1760.7 billion (see Figure 15.3) in 2006. The ranking of the total amount of imports and exports of

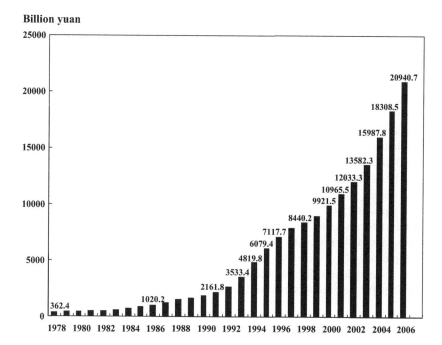

Figure 15.2 GDP of China (1978–2006)

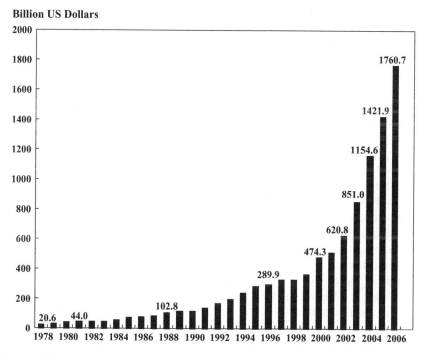

Figure 15.3 Total amount of imports and exports of China (1978–2006)

China in the world was no. 27 in 1978; it rose to no. 16 in 1990, no. 8 in 2000, no.6 in 2001 (the top five were the United States, Germany, Japan, France and Great Britain), number 5 in 2002 and number 4 in 2003. In 2004, it surpassed Japan, becoming the world's third-largest trading nation. The great improvements in comprehensive national strength and international competitiveness have laid a solid material foundation and provided favorable international conditions for sound and fast development.

Regarding the level of China's GDP per capita, it remained below US$300 throughout the period from 1981 to 1987, the early stage of the reform and opening up, and rose to the level of US$300-US$400 from 1988 to 1994. After the middle of the 1990s, it constantly increased and broke US$800 in 1998 and US$1000 in 2001, reaching nearly US$2000 in 2006. The improvement of the income level per capita promotes the upgrading of the consumption structure from food, clothing and daily necessities to housing and transportation, from the general level of food, clothing and daily necessities to these of a high level, stirring up sound and fast development.

The above analysis illustrates that China has prepared many favorable, mature conditions for supporting sound and fast economic development.

IV   Urgent need for sound and fast development

The fast economic growth in China has attracted attention throughout the world but accumulated many contradictions and problems worthy of great consideration. It will be difficult to maintain the fast economic growth if we fail to solve these contradictions and problems properly. This requires us to work hard not only on the word "fast" but also on the word "sound". At present, the prominent contradictions and problems that need further attention in the economic development of China involve the following four aspects:

1   Unstable factors of economic growth still exist. Since the reform and opening up, especially in the recent years, the stability of the economic growth in China has been constantly enhanced, but some influential factors are still apparent, mainly displayed in the massive scale of investment in total fixed assets, the excessively fast investment growth and the overheating investment tendency, which often occur in investment. Although the investment increase is restrained to some extent by each macro regulation, the systematic issue that induces excessively fast investment growth has not been solved fundamentally. The investment expansion impulse in some regions is still strong, thus, investment rebound and the induced risk of great economic fluctuation still exist. Together with some important related promoting factors in the recent years, such as the change in the party and government leaders at all levels in 2007, the Olympic Games held in China in 2008 and the celebration of the sixtieth anniversary of the founding of new China in 2009, all these factors may promote overheated investment and economic growth. In the meantime, we should be aware that the rapid expansion of

fixed assets investment for many consecutive years will lead to a production capacity surplus in some industries, which may cause a great decline in the future investment increase. It will be detrimental to the whole economic development organ if the economy fluctuates greatly, thus significantly influencing the overall economic and social development. Avoiding violent ups and downs in the rapid economic growth to maintain steadiness of economic operation remains a significant issue.

2   The extensive economic growth pattern has not changed fundamentally. Although the economic growth in China has been fast since the reform and opening up, the extensive economic growth pattern, with high input, high energy consumption, high material consumption, high pollution and more land occupation, remains essentially the same. The price that we pay for the economic growth is quite high. In particular, China is currently in the acceleration development period of industrialization and urbanization, which is a period of high consumption of energy and various resources and heavy polluting emissions. The contradiction between economic development and resource environment is becoming increasingly prominent. The approach of maintaining rapid economic growth by relying on high resource consumption and sacrificing environment is no longer workable. The Eleventh Five-Year Plan proposed an objective of a 20% reduction in energy consumption per unit of GDP and a 10% decrease in the main pollutant emission within five years and set them as obligatory targets. In 2006, various regions and sectors nationwide strengthened in this regard and attained positive progress, making the energy consumption per unit of GDP transform from a rise in the previous three years to a decline (of 1.2%) and the increase in the main pollutant emission slow down (the chemical oxygen demand and sulfur dioxide emission fell from increasing by 5.6% and 13.1%, respectively, in 2015 to increasing by 1.2% and 1.8%, respectively, in 2006). However, the target to achieve about a 4% reduction in energy consumption per unit of GDP and a 2% decrease in the main pollutant emission determined at the beginning of 2006 was not realized nationwide. It was very serious to propose the above two obligatory targets in the Eleventh Five-Year Plan, which should not be altered and should be firmly accomplished and achieved by all means possible.

Among various resources, land is a resource of special significance, which involves agriculture and especially the grain issue. It is the problem of feeding a population of 1.3 billion, which has always been of major importance and should not be neglected throughout the economic and social development in China. The cultivation land has been shrinking constantly during the process of the acceleration of industrialization and urbanization in China. Until 31 October 2005, the cultivated land area in mainland China was 1.831 billion mu and that per capita 1.4 mu, merely 40% of the world's average level. According to the latest statistics, until 31 October 2006, the cultivated land area in mainland China reduced to 1.827 billion mu and that per capita to 1.39 mu. In terms of the important national situation, China is a country with a great population and less land. Furthermore, effectively irrigated farmland only occupies 46% of the total cultivated land area and high-quality cultivated land (referring to cultivated land with abundant water resources and adequate heat) merely accounted for one-third, distributed across the south-eastern regions of rapid economic development and more construction land. According to the Eleventh Five-Year Plan, the preserved cultivation land will be 1.8 billion mu by the end of 2010, which is the bottom line that directly concerns the problem of feeding of 1.3 billion Chinese people. Therefore, the particular emphasis on strict control over land utilization in the macro regulation in recent years in China has been rooted in the grain issue or the feeding problem. Land saving and intensive utilization not only concern the current economic and social development but also matter to the state's long-term interests and national existential foundation. Uncorrectable historical mistakes should never be made with regard to the land issue, which will harm future generations.

To transform the economic growth pattern and follow a new industrialization approach, we must overcome the constraint of the technology bottleneck to alleviate the pressure on energy resources and the environment. The promotion of technical progress and the improvement of the ability to carry out independent innovation, which on the whole are not strong in China, should be accelerated urgently, since the gap in some fields compared with developed countries is still widening. In the long run, China will still face pressure from the developed countries' dominance in the economy, science and technology. The international scientific and technological progress and modernization in China all necessitate the stepping up of the construction of an innovation-oriented country.

3   The economic structural contradictions are relatively prominent. China has accumulated many structural contradictions in the rapid economic growth in recent years. The relatively prominent ones are the following: discordance between investment and consumption, an oversized investment scale, relative insufficiency of consumption demand, especially weak consumption capacity due to the low-income level of farmers and the urban low-income group; an uncoordinated proportion between primary, secondary and tertiary industries with a large proportion in industry, especially in heavy industry, a small proportion in the service industry, an unchanged weak agricultural base and difficulties in steadily increasing grain production and keeping farmers' incomes growing; development discordance between urban and rural areas and between different regions; a large trade surplus; and outstanding contradiction of the imbalance in international payments. With the constantly wider opening of China to the outside world, especially under the circumstances of further development of the economic globalization trend and continuous acceleration of international industrial transference, the international balance situation will increasingly influence the steady development of the domestic economy.

4   The economic growth lacks harmony. Since the reform and opening up, the social structure in China has changed profoundly and deep adjustments

have been made to the interest pattern. On the whole, people's income level and living standard are constantly improving. However, there are still many low-income groups living with financial difficulties. The income gap between different social members is enlarging. In the meantime, since the development of social undertakings is backward, some issues that involve people's vital interests, such as education, health, housing, employment and social security, have not been properly resolved. The masses have strong complaints about the above issues. While the economy increases, China faces the serious question of how it can build a harmonious socialist society and simultaneously accelerate the development of various social undertakings to let people share the fruit of development. With the aim of realizing social harmony, we must insist on regarding economic construction as the central work and vigorously develop productivity to create the necessary material foundation for a harmonious society. Nevertheless, economic development and an increase in the aggregate social wealth will not automatically effectuate social harmony. The contradiction of the imbalance between economic and social developments will be aggravated if we simply focus on economic development and neglect social and human developments. Finally, economic development is difficult to carry out smoothly.

The above analysis indicates that fast growth is in a sense no longer so difficult. However, the biggest issue that China is facing concerns enabling the economy to develop more soundly and further solving the above contradictions and problems in the economic development.

V   How to realize sound and fast development

Realizing sound and fast development entails working hard to solve the conflicts and problems in the above four aspects, giving the priority to "sound". Solving the contradictions and problems in the above four aspects constitutes the contents of "sound" in four respects. In other words, they make up four key points in achieving sound and fast development, namely constantly improving the stability of the economic growth trend, increasing the sustainability of the economic growth pattern, enhancing the coordination of the economic growth structure and raising the harmoniousness of the economic growth benefits. This is what is often called constantly improving the economic growth quality and benefit.[3]

1   Constantly improving the stability of the economic growth trend. This requires us to give full play to the fundamental role of the market mechanism in resource allocation and simultaneously to enhance and improve macro regulation. This is applied throughout the whole process of socialist market economic development and is not a matter of a single day's work. However, according to the constant development and variation of the economic situation, resulting in new situations and issues emerging in economic operation,

macro regulation will adopt different policy orientations, operational procedures, strengths and implementation focuses. Currently, we should continuously implement prudent fiscal and monetary policies, maintain the
sustainability and stability of the macroeconomic policy and constantly
perfect these policies and measures. In macro regulation, we must persist
with the principle with assurance and control and without rigid uniformity,
apply more economic and legal measures to guide and standardize economic
behavior and handle the central-local relationship correctly to encourage the
full enthusiasm of both.

2   Continuously increasing the sustainability of the economic growth pattern.
    This necessitates the promotion and acceleration of the transformation of
    the economic growth pattern. At present, we should take energy saving and
    low consumption, environmental protection and land saving and intensive
    utilization as the breakthrough and key to the transformation of the economic
    growth pattern. We should always bear in mind our responsibility to the
    people and our future generations, enhance the consciousness of anxiety and
    the sense of crisis and accelerate the construction of a resource-efficient and
    environment-friendly society, while the whole society energetically advocates
    economizing, environment-friendly and civilized production and consump-
    tion modes. In the meantime, we should expedite the construction of an
    innovation-oriented country and the establishment of a technology innovation
    system centering on enterprises and market orientation with the combination
    of industry–university–research, perfect the incentive mechanism of inde-
    pendent innovation and implement the fiscal and taxation policy, financial
    policy and government procurement system to encourage and support inde-
    pendent innovation.

3   Unceasingly enhancing the coordination of the economic growth structure.
    To achieve this, it is necessary to deal appropriately with the significant
    proportional relationships between major sectors of the national economy
    and constantly adjust and optimize the economic structure. The relationship
    between investment and consumption is a basic and significant proportional
    relationship that guarantees normal economic operation. Currently, for the
    purpose of adjusting the relationship between investment and consumption,
    we must persist with the principle of expanding the domestic demand with
    the focus on adopting various measures to increase urban residents' income,
    especially that of the medium- and low-income groups, perfecting the
    consumption policy and striving to cultivate new hot consumption spots to
    encourage residents to increase their consumption demand. Meanwhile, we
    should maintain strict control over the floodgates of land and credit to
    regulate the scales of fixed assets investment and credit and maintain
    appropriate growth of fixed assets investment. In terms of the adjustment
    and optimization of the industrial structure, we must first speed up the
    development of modern agriculture and persistently and practically promote
    socialism's new rural reconstruction. We should vigorously develop the
    service industry, especially modern service industries like logistics, finance,

information, consultancy, tourism and community service. We need to expedite the development of the high-tech industry to revitalize equipment manufacturing and reconstruct and upgrade the traditional industry by applying modern technology extensively. With regard to regional development, we must persist in overall planning and all-round consideration, rational planning, taking advantage, implementing policies and promoting regional coordinated development. In relation to opening up to the outside world, we need to transform the foreign trade growth pattern, optimize the import and export structure and attempt to reduce the foreign trade surplus; simultaneously, we should stress improving the quality of foreign capital introduction, optimizing the structure and importing more advanced technology, management experience and high-quality talents.

4   Constantly increasing the harmoniousness of the economic growth benefits. The economic growth benefits include the economic benefits and social returns. The economic benefits mainly consist of product quality, fund usability and resource utilization efficiency. The social returns extensively involve the promotion of social undertakings, humanism, the improvement of people's livelihood and sharing the fruit of economic growth among all the people. At present, we should place emphasis not only on improving the economic benefits but also on increasing the social returns. In other words, we should make the economic growth contribute to realizing social harmony. Specifically, we need to insist on humanism, maintain social fairness and justice and pay more attention to the development of various social undertakings, like education, health and culture. At the same time, we must properly handle the relationship between economic growth and income distribution, constantly perfect the social security and income distribution system through a persistent, positive employment policy and emphasize better provision of basic public services for rural and urban low-income groups, thus actively improving people's livelihood and resolving the most direct and practical issues that concern most people. During the process, we should deal appropriately with the relationship between the satisfaction of people's needs and the possibility of government financial resources, make efforts to give proper play to the government's functions of serving the public and distribute more public resources to those people who directly benefit and act within our capability to avoid the possibility of over-the-top expectations and divorce from reality, finally forming a harmonious situation in which each tries his best and will be paid on the basis of his ability and achievement in terms of economic development.

With the view of performing well in the above four respects and realizing sound and fast economic development, we must still firmly and actively promote various reforms, such as reforms of the economic system, political system, cultural system and social system, to meet the demands of economic and social development on the basis of adhering to the reform of the socialist market economy, and to accelerate the construction of a system guaranteeing the implementation of the scientific viewpoint of development, building of a harmonious socialist society and achieving sound and fast economic development.

"Sound and Fast" development is an inseparable organic unity. Putting the word "sound" at the front does not imply by any means that we have no intention to demand "fast". Instead, we seek "fast" on the basis of "sound", making "fast" last longer, because six great significant historical changes have taken place in China's economic life since the reform and opening up, as we have previously mentioned. However, we should not forget that a major and basic country condition has not changed, that is, China is still and will be in the long term in the primary stage of socialism, which is identical to the undeveloped period. Currently, although the aggregate economic scale of China is comparatively large, ranking number 4 in the world, the income level per capita is still very low. According to the latest data from the International Monetary Fund, the GDP per capita of China in 2005 was merely US$1716, ranking number 108 in the world and falling into the lower–middle income countries, only equivalent to one twenty-fifth of that of the United States, one twentieth of Japan and one quarter of the world's average level and equal to that of Samoa, Ukraine, Congo and Morocco. To continue the improvement of people's income level and living standard and alleviate the employment pressure during the acceleration of industrialization and urbanization, we need to maintain a certain fast speed of economic growth to narrow the urban-rural gap and regional disparity gradually and increase the state financial resources with the aim of accelerating the development of various social undertakings and providing more public services.

In conclusion, advocating "Sound and Fast" development involves conscientiously implementing the scientific viewpoint of development and speeding up the construction of a harmonious socialist society, shifting the work focus to the overall improvement of economic growth quality and benefits and preventing one-sided pursuit of and blind competition for growth speed, to enable us finally to march on towards the magnificent target of the overall construction of a well-off society.

[Originally published in *Economic Research Journal (JingjiYanjiu)*, No.6, 2007]

Notes

1 Refer to the relevant report in (2006, December 1). *The People's Daily*, p.1.
2 Refer to the relevant report in (2006, December 8). *The People's Daily*, p.1.
3 The content of "sound" implies the economic growth quality and benefits that the theoretical circles once discussed and summarized (Liang Yamin, 2002

References

CCCPC Party Literature Research Office. (1982a). *Collection of Important Literature since the Third Plenary Session, Part One*. Beijing: People's Publishing House.
CCCPC Party Literature Research Office. (1982b). *Collection of Important Literature since the Third Plenary Session, Part Two*. Beijing: People's Publishing House.

Compilation Group of Outline of Modern and Contemporary History of China. (2007). *Outline of Modern and Contemporary History of China*. Beijing: Higher Education Press.

Deng Xiaoping. (1993). *Selected Works of Deng Xiaoping* (Vol.2). Beijing: People's Publishing House.

Jiang Zemin. (2006). *Selected Works of Jiang Zemin* (Vol.1). Beijing: People's Publishing House.

Liang Yamin. (2002, April). Overview of Research on Quality Issue of Economic Growth. *Journal of Lanzhou Commercial College*, 18, 2.

Liu Guoguang, & Liu Shucheng. (1997, January 7). On Soft Landing. *The People's Daily*, p.9.

Liu Shucheng (Ed.). (2006). *Research Report on Economic Cycle in China*. Beijing: Social Sciences Academic Press.

Mao Zedong. (1977). *Selected Works of Mao Zedong* (Vol.5). Beijing: People's Publishing House.

Mao Zedong. (1999). *Mao Zedong Collected Works* (Vol.7). Beijing: People's Publishing House.

Pang Xianzhi, & Jin Chongji (Eds.). (2003). *Mao Zedong Biography (1949–1976), Part One*. Beijing: The Central Literature Publishing House.

Index

Note: Page numbers in *italic* indicate a figure or table

For Product Safety Concerns and Information please contact our EU
representative GPSR@taylorandfrancis.com Taylor & Francis Verlag GmbH,
Kaufingerstraße 24, 80331 München, Germany

Printed and bound by CPI Group (UK) Ltd, Croydon, CR0 4YY

01/05/2025

01858444-0001